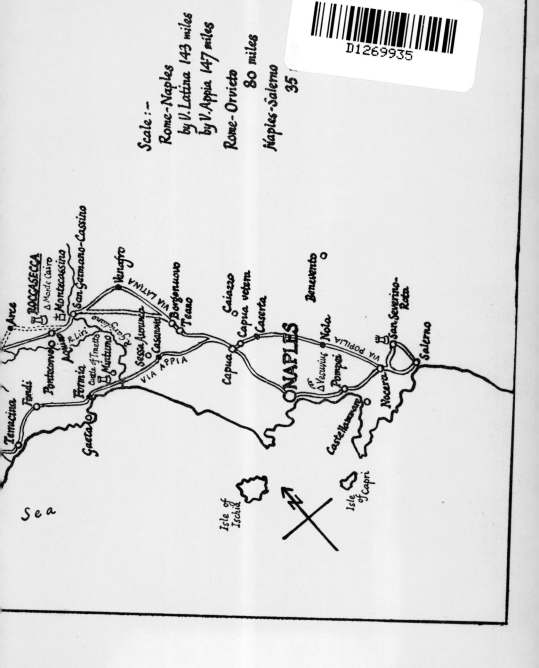

Scale :-

Rome–Naples
by V. Latina 143 miles
by V. Appia 147 miles

Rome–Orvieto
80 miles

Naples–Salerno
35

Saint Thomas Aquinas

THE "TRIONFO" OF SAINT THOMAS
(Pisa, St. Catherine's)

by Francesco Traini

(Florentine School, mid-fourteenth century)

Saint Thomas Aquinas

A Biographical Study

BY

FATHER ANGELUS WALZ, O.P.

*Lecturer in Church History
at the Angelicum, Rome*

English Translation by
FATHER SEBASTIAN BULLOUGH, O.P.

THE NEWMAN PRESS
Westminster, Maryland
1951

NIHIL OBSTAT: Fr. Gualterus Gumbley, O.P.
Fr. Gervasius Mathew, O.P., S.T.L.

IMPRIMI POTEST: Fr. Hilarius Carpenter, O.P., S.T.L.
Prior Provincialis Provinciae Angliae

LONDINI
die 6 Octobris 1948

NIHIL OBSTAT: Edwardus A. Cerny, S.S., D.D.
Censor Librorum

IMPRIMATUR: Franciscus P. Keough, D.D.
Archiepiscopus Baltimorensis

die 11 Maii 1951

Author's Preface

TWENTY years ago, on the occasion of the sixth centenary of the canonization of St. Thomas, the desire was expressed by Fr. Sadoc Szabó, who at the time was Regent of the Angelicum, the Pontifical College of the Dominicans in Rome, for the publication, in addition to the *Xenia thomistica,* of a scientific study of the writings of the Holy Doctor, and of another treating of his life. The first task was carried out by Fr. Ambrose Bacic, with his *Introductio compendiosa in opera S. Thomae Aquinatis,* which first appeared in the pages of the review *Angelicum,* and was then published separately in Rome in 1925. The second task was accomplished by the *Delineatio vitae S. Thomae de Aquino,* which appeared in the same review in 1926, and was then also published separately in Rome during the following year.

Since that time there have been new researches into the life of the Prince of Theologians; sources have been newly edited—such as the completion of the *Fontes vitae S. Thomae Aquinatis,* and events have occurred which have further glorified the Angelic Doctor—for example, Pius XI has insisted so strongly, in the apostolic constitution *Deus scientiarum* of May 24, 1931, on the teaching of Aquinas, and on December 16 of the same year, the same Holy Father declared Albert the Great, Thomas' master, a Saint and Doctor of the Church. These things have called for a revision and re-casting of the biographical material contained in the *Delineatio.*

The present work includes the substance of the *Delineatio* with suitable additions and corrections.

Three short chapters on the character of St. Thomas, his

writings, and the honor paid to him by the Church, have been added to the strictly biographical part of the book. The bibliography provides a list of the sources for the life of St. Thomas, mentions the principal works written about him, and gives the titles of various books which provide a background to his life and work. Finally, there is a chronological table of his life and his writings.

This book has a different approach from those of Sertillanges, Grabmann, Puccetti, Diaccini, or Chesterton, and differs also from that of Castagnoli or the recent works of Taurisano and Toso.

A word about the illustrations. As there exists no authentic portrait of St. Thomas, pictures have been chosen which reflect the Master's authority in the style of different periods. Traini's "Trionfo" expresses the medieval outlook, while Zurbaran portrays St. Thomas amid the glory of the four Latin Doctors, representing the enthusiasm for the Angelic Doctor that was found in Spain during the "second period" of scholasticism. The stately fresco of Seitz in the Galleria dei Candelabri at the Vatican expresses eloquently and delicately the homage of a later era, the "third period" of scholasticism which begins in the time of Leo XIII.

These fruits of recent researches will, we feel sure, have some appeal either to those who are studying St. Thomas, or simply to those who love him.

Angelicum, Rome,
November 15, 1943.

Translator's Note

THIS book is a translation of *San Tommaso d'Aquino, Studi biografici sul Dottore Angelico*, published in Rome in 1945. Fr. Angelus Walz is a member of the South-German province of the Dominican Order, but he chose to write in Italian, the general language of Rome, where he has been teaching for so many years. It is according to the desire of the Master-General of the Order that the present work is being translated into the principal European languages, for it incorporates all the latest researches on the life of St. Thomas, and is indeed at the moment the most exhaustive critical and synthetic presentation of the whole life of the Master that has appeared during the last 40 years.

The author has made over 160 additions and corrections for this edition: mostly details and references to works and editions that have appeared since he wrote.

The translator has added references to English translations of works referred to, and has ventured to supply a brief note on the organization of the Dominican Order, a matter that may be unfamiliar to many English and American readers, but which is important for the understanding of certain biographical facts. He has also drawn a map to illustrate St. Thomas' journeys in Italy.

Contents

List of Illustrations

Chapter One

D'Aquino of Roccasecca

1225–1231

HIS HOME-LAND — HIS FATHER'S NOBLE LINEAGE —
HIS MOTHER, BROTHERS, AND SISTERS — THE YEAR AND
PLACE OF HIS BIRTH — VISIT TO NAPLES WITH HIS
MOTHER — THE CASTLE OF ROCCASECCA STRUCK BY
LIGHTNING — CHILDHOOD IMPRESSIONS: LIFE IN THE
MEDIEVAL CASTLE

IT was under the blue sky of Italy, in that part of the kingdom of the Two Sicilies [1] known as *Terra di Lavoro*,[2] which touches the edge of the Roman Campania [3] and from time immemorial had owed allegiance to the Holy See,[4] that Thomas was born in his family home, the castle of Roccasecca,[5] in the county and diocese [6] of Aquino. He inherited a distinguished name, but he was to make it far more distinguished still. His family was renowned alike for valor, virtue, and nobility.

The Aquinati were originally Lombards,[7] and their first forbear that we can trace with any historical certainty is one Rodipert,[8] who received from Adenulf, Count, and later Prince, of Capua, the post of *Gastaldus* [9] of Aquino in the year 887. *Gastaldi* and Counts, as Pocchettino explains, were originally stewards of a prince, and were therefore officials, not vassals. These *Gastaldi* and Counts had duties of a military, police, and judicial nature, but between the ninth and tenth centuries most of them had become simply independent lords with a rather vague relation of allegiance to their respective princes.

1

As the family grew in importance, we find, about 949, that the princes conferred on the *Gastaldus* Adenulf II the title, and the rights that went with it, of Count of Aquino. After this, mention is made of several branches of the family of the Counts of Aquino.[10] Adenulf III, nicknamed Summucula, " great-grandfather of those who are now (*i.e.*, after 1100) known as the Counts of Aquino," in 996 took possession of the castle of Roccasecca, which had been built by Abbot Manson of Montecassino on the slopes of Monte Comarino, a spur of Monte Cairo.[11] The castle, called Roccasecca, or " the dry rock-citadel," from the scarcity of water on the site, had been built in 994,[12] and the lords of Aquino acquired it by violent and fraudulent means. Adenulf in 999 claimed both the title and rank of Count.[13] With Lando IV, however, who died after 1137, the title of Count of Aquino disappears,[14] and one of his sons, Pandulf, called himself " Lord of Aquino " and began a new branch of the family. This is the second house of Aquino, that of the Counts of Acerra, which was later to have so strong a protagonist of Frederick II in Count Thomas I, and which reached its highest splendor in Thomas II, who married Margaret, the illegitimate daughter of Frederick.[15] Frederick's biographer observes that he had a special preference for the house of Aquino.[16] The younger son of Lando IV, Ronald I, " Lord of Roccasecca," by an exchange of territory with Pope Adrian IV, got possession of Montesangiovanni in the Papal States, in addition to owning one-third of the county of Aquino.[17]

Aquino, a small town which during the Roman Republic enjoyed the rights of a *municipium*,[18] was, together with the surrounding country along the River Liri, a fief divided after the manner of Lombard law among several members of the same family.[19] It is recorded by the chroniclers of the late twelfth century that Richard, son of Ronald of Aquino, became Count of Acerra in 1171 and most devoted to the cause of the Norman dynasty, but had later to submit to the Emperor Henry VI, who had come in 1194 to claim by force of arms the hereditary rights of his wife Constance. When, however, the Emperor returned to Germany, Richard rebelled. For this he was not only deprived of the title of Count of Acerra, but was condemned to death. After this his nephews, grandsons of Ronald I, who were called Ronald II and Landulf, fortified themselves in the castle of Roccasecca, but nevertheless suffered much at the hands of the adherents of Henry VI.[20] Eventually, however, they evaded the danger, and later, in 1210, Landulf and others of the family allied themselves with Innocent III and the young Frederick II, and took up arms against Diopold, Count of Acerra.[21] Ten years later, in 1220, Landulf was appointed by the Emperor and King of Sicily to be *justiciarius* of the *terra laboris*.[22] His colleague in office was a relative of his own, Thomas I, of the branch of Pandulf, who had by then been nominated Count of Acerra.[23] So it happened that this Landulf (the same who had defended Roccasecca, and was still alive in 1243)[24] took the side of the Emperor and remained faithful to him. At the same time he sought every advancement for his own family and had great hopes that his sons would bring it still greater glory. " Thomas' father did not have the title of Count, but only that of *miles*, or knight, which he bears also in the *Necrologium*," i.e., the register of deaths at Cassino.[25] But we also find the phrase " vir nobilis domus Landulfus de Aquino."[26] " Thomas' father, Landulf, was indeed a happy father; he was a valiant warrior and also a diplomat like his ancestors, but above all he was the father of a fine race."[27]

His wife was a noblewoman of Naples,[28] called Theodora,[29] of Norman origin;[30] it is said that she came from Theate, that she was greatly praised for her piety, and that she lived probably at least until 1255.[31]

Apparently they had many children.[32] It will be simplest and most useful to give here the complete list, although it is difficult to arrive at the exact genealogy, because so many members of the family bore the same name.

The following were certainly sons of Landulf, Lord of

Roccasecca, and of Lady Theodora: *Aimo,* who, owing to his devotion to the Holy See, had for a time to go into exile from the territory of Naples, but reappears later, restored to honor; he died between 1266 and 1269; [33] *Ronald,* at first an adherent of Frederick II, later sided with the Pope and died for his "fidelity to the Church"; [34] *Landulf* (or perhaps *Adenulf*), of whom nothing is known except that after his death St. Thomas wished to know what had happened to him, and learned by revelation that he was in Purgatory; [35] *Thomas,* the subject of our study. Further names [36] are attributed to elder brothers of St. Thomas: Adenulf,[37] James,[38] and Philip; [39] but it may well be that they were sons of another Landulf d'Aquino,[40] a contemporary of St. Thomas' father.

Landulf and Theodora had apparently four or five daughters: the first being *Marotta,* who became Abbess of St. Mary's Convent at Capua, and died, no longer in office, round 1259.[41] The second was *Theodora,* who married Roger, Count of San Severino and later of Marsico, and who died after 1294.[42] Roger and Theodora had a son, Thomas, Count of San Severino, who took part in 1319 in the preparation of the cause for the canonization of his holy uncle, and assisted at the solemn ceremony in 1323, when he was proclaimed a Saint of the Church. The third daughter was *Mary:* she married William, the eldest son of the house of San Severino, who lived at the castle of Marano in the Abruzzi. She died after 1284. They had a daughter called Gaitegrima or Catherine of San Severino.[43] Of the fourth daughter we do not know the name, but only that she was killed by lightning while a child.[44] There is mention also of a fifth, *Adelasia,* but—according to Pelster—it is not certain whether she was really the sister of St. Thomas. Scandone, however, speaks of her as such.[45] She married Roger dell'Aquila, Count of Traetto (now Minturno).

The precise year of Thomas' birth is uncertain; efforts have been made to determine it by means of various calculations. Since William da Tocco [46] states (apparently on good authority) that Thomas died at the age of forty-nine, the most important historians hold that he was born in 1225,[47] though the dates 1226 [48] and 1227 [49] cannot be excluded. Denifle, De Groot, Mandonnet, Castagnoli, and (at least to some extent) Scandone are in favor of the first date; the second is held by De Rubeis, Prümmer, and Pelster; while the third is advocated by Quétif-Echard and Berthier. Abate proposes 1220.

There is no doubt about the place of birth of St. Thomas, for it is certain that the last son of Landulf and Theodora was born in the castle of Roccasecca.[50] The house, still standing, in which Thomas most probably first saw the light, is situated within the lower walls of the castle of Roccasecca, and is easily distinguishable by some gothic windows.

There are, however, two other places that claim to be the birthplace of the Saint. These are the towns of Aquino and Belcastro in Calabria. But both of these are quite out of the question, not merely because the historical sources do not mention them, but because the claims rest upon documents patently forged for literary or diplomatic purposes. Anyway, after the studies of Scandone [51] on the true birthplace and his exclusion of any place other than Roccasecca, it is not worth pursuing the argument.

The youngest son of Landulf and Theodora d'Aquino received the name of Thomas at Baptism.[52] The Pope at the time was Honorius III (1216–1227). The name of the Bishop of Aquino at the time is uncertain, since the list of bishops is incomplete between the years 1206 and 1251.[53] The Emperor in Germany and Italy was Frederick II, who was also King of the Sicilian realm. B. Jordan of Saxony was Master-General of the Order of Preachers.

Although very little has been handed down about the early years of St. Thomas, and that little is further clothed with legend, we must at least mention what there is.

Once upon a time Theodora went to Naples, leaving Landulf at home to defend Roccasecca against the papal troops,[54] and taking the baby Thomas with her. While they were at Naples, Theodora went with some other ladies to the baths, and the baby was brought too, carried by a nurse. While his mother was disrobing before entering the bath, he stretched out his hand and picked up off the ground a bit of paper, which he clutched firmly in his fist. His mother wanted to take it away from him, but he began to cry and would not stop until he was allowed to keep it. Then his mother, looking to see what was written on it, saw the words *Ave Maria*. He had to be given his bath with that bit of paper in his hand, otherwise he could not have been kept quiet.[55] It is further related that he put the bit of paper into his mouth.

In this episode the old biographers [56] saw a presage not only of his devotion to Our Lady, but also of his passion for books and the meditation of the Scriptures, upon which he was later engaged with so much profit to himself and others.

Another event was considered by the authors [57] to be a sign of divine protection over his earthly life. At the castle of Roccasecca, as in most medieval castles, there was a tower that stood much higher than the walls or the other towers. On the various floors of this tower were the servants' quarters, and at the bottom a stable for the horses. One room belonged to a woman who often looked after the younger children of the master of the house. At this particular moment Thomas was there, together with the little sister whose name we do not know. Suddenly there was a terrible thunderstorm and the tower was struck by lightning. The little girl was killed, and also the horses in the stable down below. The mother in a state of panic rushed to the scene, but found Thomas quite safe and sound, and still fast asleep next to the nurse.

Thomas' first impressions came from the solicitous care of his pious mother, and of the nurse who must have been an excellent person, and into whose care the child was placed by his mother. "From the cradle the child Thomas breathed in an atmosphere of unrelenting battle, felt the flame of the struggle for newly-found liberty, daily heard the rattle of arms and the ironclad footfall, watched the pageantry of tourneys, weddings, and princely cavalcades, and listened to the music and song of the troubadours in the graceful *volgare* or newly-grown Italian tongue which was being fostered by the mighty lords of the medieval castles." [58]

These early impressions at home were heightened by the view from the castle over his native land. These things were deeply engraved on his child's mind. For the castle, high upon the hill of Roccasecca which is joined by a mountainous range to Monte Asprano,[59] dominates the territory subject to the lords of Aquino, to the south and to the west.

This was the background of family and nature on which he laid the foundations of his education and his first aquaintance with life. And surely he must some time have gone with the grown-ups to the town of Aquino, and to the palace there [60] that belonged to the chief branch of the family, the Counts of Acerra. Surely he also visited the church there, built in 1127 and called S. Maria " della Libera." [61]

Although St. Thomas had no immediate connexion with the neighboring town of Aquino, nevertheless he can legitimately be called *de Aquino,* or as the later neo-classical Latin had it, *Aquinas,* for he was descended from the noble and powerful family of the d'Aquino, who owe their origin to the town of that name.

Chapter Two

Montecassino

1231–1239

HE GOES TO MONTECASSINO AT THE AGE OF ABOUT
FIVE YEARS — BENEDICTINE " OBLATES " — MONASTIC
EDUCATION — EARLY STUDIES — HIS LOVE OF DIVINE
THINGS — FAREWELL TO THE ABBEY

IT was a common practice in the Middle Ages for a noble
family to destine their youngest son for the ecclesiastical state.
So it happened that Landulf d'Aquino, in 1217, succeeded in
having one of his sons, by name James and then about twenty
years old, appointed to the office of Abbot of the canons'
Church of St. Peter, at Canneto. The election was, however,
declared null and void, for it had been made in contravention
of the rights of the Holy See.[1] After this failure, Landulf (if
it is really Landulf, the father of James and St. Thomas)[2]
awaited another opportunity. This came in the person of his
youngest son, Thomas, in connection with another ecclesiastical position, that of Superior of the Church of Canneto.

In that part of the Campania Romana that is near to Montecassino, young boys were often dedicated to God at the famous
abbey of St. Benedict. "The parents (of Thomas) also willingly dedicated to God their child of five" and "they sent
him, suitably accompanied by his nurse, to the aforesaid Abbey
of Montecassino."[3] Thus Thomas d'Aquino found himself in
the company of sons of noble families, who were "there re-

8

ceiving education in good manners according to the custom of the district." [4] In connexion with the above quotations we may well ask what exactly was the status of the boys whom Thomas joined: were they those dedicated to God in the abbey to become monks, or those who were merely there for purposes of education and instruction? At any rate, in the early Middle Ages it was possible for boys to come to the monasteries to receive the first rudiments of letters, and then be free to return to the world.[5] It appears that such boys did indeed become " oblates," [6] but it is not certain that they wore the monastic habit.[7]

The problem about the position of Thomas in the Abbey of Montecassino, that is to say, whether he was a mere oblate, or actually a monk, has been studied and skilfully solved by Dom Thomas Leccisotti. After an examination of the older authors, such as Serry, Gattola, De Vera, and Tosti, and of recent writers like Roeder, Renaudin, Berlière, Mandonnet, Scandone, Deroux, and Riepenhoff, Leccisotti once more investigates the sources and is able to arrive at a sure and balanced opinion.[8]

What is certain is that Thomas was offered to the monastery for a good and spiritual purpose, that is, " therein to be instructed in holy manners and to prepare himself for God's illumination." [9] But to this purpose was perhaps added another: it may be that his parents were hoping that if he should reach some high position in the abbey, they would have some share in the monastic revenues. Bartholomew of Capua, who was *protonotarius* and *logotheta* (a sort of chancellor) of the Kingdom of Naples, expressly says " that the father made the young Thomas into a monk, with the object of placing him at the head of the Cassinese Abbey." [10] Now, since in the ordinary way abbots could not very well be outsiders, one must conclude that Thomas was a real oblate,[11] and that if God had not arranged otherwise, he would have gone on to make monastic profession. A remark appears, in fact, in the

Necrologium of Montecassino, on St. Thomas Aquinas: " primo casinensis monachus factus." [12]

Leccisotti explains the motives of Landulf d'Aquino as follows: " The Abbey of Montecassino was a feudal lordship of prime importance. Thus it attracted the gaze of one who was at once a fond father and a local lord. It would give so much personal satisfaction to his fatherly heart to see one day one of his own sons on the abbatial chair of St. Benedict; but it would also bring to him certainty that if the future hoped-for abbot faithfully discharged his duty as custodian of the vast property committed to his care, his parents at any rate would never be molested, or have their designs on any other objectives interfered with. The Emperor himself could not possibly disapprove of such a step, which would place the son of one of his faithful vassals in a position of such importance, which moreover was usually a very citadel of the opposing camp."

When, therefore, the alternating fortunes of war permitted, Landulf set about realizing his dream. His youngest son, born to him in the very castle of Roccasecca founded by a Cassinese abbot, the boy Thomas who had already given no uncertain signs of an inclination toward heavenly things, was dedicated to God on the summit of Montecassino: a proof of his father's piety and a pledge of political alliance.

" It is now admitted beyond dispute that Thomas was a real oblate at Montecassino. His parents sought to make him into a monk both for a certain motive of piety, but above all in the hope ' perveniendi ad magnos eius (monasterii scilicet casinensis) sumptus.' Now since to realize an object one must make use of the proper means, they doubtless tried everything that would further their plan. The means that lay so obviously to hand, and also had every chance of success, was to be used. Thomas was offered ' Domino nutriendus ' (as St. Gregory says) according to the Rule of St. Benedict." [13]

The precise age at which boys could be brought to the monastery is not laid down. The Rule of St. Benedict admits even *impuberes* as oblates.[14] From the biographer William da Tocco we learn that Thomas was brought to Montecassino at the age of five.[15] If he was born in 1225 or 1226, his entry to the monastery would be around 1230 or 1231, which was in a fairly happy period in the fortunes of abbey, and after its wanderings were over. The boy Thomas, son of the Lord of Aquino, was received by a relative of the d'Aquino, Landulf Sinibaldo, who was abbot at the time (1227–1236) [16] of the arch-abbey of the Benedictine monks. He had gone to Rome in 1228 to be ordained priest and had immediately been sent by Gregory IX as ambassador to Frederick II, who had just returned from the attempted crusade. This mission of Abbot Landulf did not, however, prove very successful.[17] And further, some of the house of Aquino took up arms on behalf of Frederick II and reoccupied much of the district round Montecassino.[18] And then, when the pontifical troops entered the territory of Naples, the abbey was compelled to take sides with Frederick, for the imperial troops were encamped at the foot of the hill. The abbey itself was fortified under the direction of the abbot.[19] This, however, did not prevent attack, and in 1229 the monastery was occupied by the papal legate,[20] Pelagius Galvani, Cardinal Archbishop of Albano. After this occupation a treaty was signed in the Church of San Germano on July 23, 1230, between the Pope (whose ambassador was the Blessed Guala, O.P.) and the Emperor. Thus began a period of relative peace.[21]

This moment of peace and tranquillity seemed to Landulf d'Aquino to be a most opportune time to present his little son [22] to the abbey, in the hope of renewing happy relations with his family, and of promoting the honor and general good of his house.

Before a boy was accepted as an oblate, a formal request had to be made by his parents,[23] but the actual presentation of the boy was not necessarily made by the parents in person, for it could be made by someone else on their behalf. This was apparently the case with Thomas, for after the request had been made by the parents and accepted by the abbey, he was brought to the monastery "suitably accompanied by his nurse." [24]

With regard to the acceptance of oblates from among the nobility, St. Benedict writes in chapter 59 of the Rule: "If . . . they should wish to give an alms to the monastery for their own gain, let them make such a gift as suiteth them, and, if they will, reserve the fruits thereof for themselves." This recommendation of the Patriarch of the Monks of the West seems to have been observed in the case of Thomas, if we are thus to understand the gift of a mill from Landulf to the Abbot of Montecassino. The deed of this gift, dated May 3, 1231,[25] supposes already a former gift of twenty pounds in gold made to the abbey.[26] But we cannot say definitely that these gifts were always made in the case of the presentation of an oblate in the true sense, since there is ample evidence to show that gifts of the kind were sometimes made in return merely for the education and instruction in letters that the children received in the monastic schools.[27]

The wonderful fame and splendor achieved by the Abbey of Montecassino under Abbot Desiderius (1058–1086), who afterwards became Pope Victor III (1086–1087), vanished, as it were, overnight. But prestige remained even during the dark and sometimes sad period that followed. And Stephen Marsicano, abbot from 1215 to 1227, was called by Richard of San Germano "vir non minus studii quam honestatis amator." He was the immediate predecessor of Landulf, under whose rule the young Thomas came to Montecassino.[28] The years round 1220–1230 and 1240–1260 were bad periods, both spiritually and temporally, and it was Abbot Bernard Ayglier (1263–1282) who set about repairing the damage with so much zeal and happy result.[29] When Thomas arrived at Montecassino, the decadence had already begun, but he neither saw it at its worst, nor did he feel its effects, having been called by Providence to a higher destiny.

Having decided the matter of whether or no Thomas was a

true oblate, we must turn to some observations on the place itself where he lived, and on the education he received there together with the other oblates. " The oblates were formed in the calm succession of days that were one like another, except when events in the outside world disturbed them. They took part in the daily monastic routine, with certain modifications on account of their age. A skilled master watched over them, guided their spiritual progress, schooled them in discipline, and so formed them gradually but deeply, assisted by frequent reading and instruction, and above all by the atmosphere of the place itself.

" There is no doubt that they lived in the abbey itself. The relatively recent theory that the little oblates lived in the neighboring monastery of Albaneta, in the hills to the north-west of the abbey, is based upon one of those only too frequent errors by which people attribute to a past age the outlook and circumstances of their own. . . . No, in the thirteenth century S. Maria dell'Albaneta was still a real monastery, and in any case it would have been highly imprudent to make it a residence exclusively for boys, while Saracens and other soldiery were constantly warring in the neighborhood." [30]

If, then, Thomas' education was, as it seems, that of an oblate, we must think of him as under the direction of an elderly Father, who looked after the boys and acted as their spiritual guide.[31] The fact that we have no information about any other oblates who would have been his companions is either to be explained by the mere absence of record, or by the very educational system itself in which each oblate came under the care of a special master.[32] Reading and writing was learned *pari passu* with the main moral and religious principles. Reading was practiced in the liturgical books, and so in the Sacred Scriptures themselves.[33]

Doubtless the lines of Alfanus to Theodinus could be applied to the oblates of this period:

Lectio psalmorum, numerus, modulatio cantus,
Ius tibi secreti cum praece iuncta dabant.

" In fact, the psalter was the reading-book of the young oblates, and the psalms, learnt by heart, were the fundamental note of that life which was led in an atmosphere permeated by liturgy and chant."

Of the cultivation of the arts we find confirmation in the life of Aquinas himself. " During the years of intense scientific work, that began with him so early in life, when his mind was so intent on the highest philosophical and theological speculation, he cannot have had time or opportunity for exercising himself in writing verse. Yet we find he has such a wonderful mastery of the art. It is more than probable that he acquired this skill in his earliest years, during his literary schooling at Montecassino." [34]

The Rule of St. Benedict was placed in the hands of the oblates not only as a reading-exercise, but also so that its precepts should sink deep into their youthful minds. And indeed we find in the writings of Aquinas phrases, as it were, reminiscences, from the Holy Rule.[35]

The art of writing, or calligraphy,[36] although like everything else at the abbey it had in the thirteenth century become decadent, was still cultivated. The rules of language and style were taught together with grammar. Thus the way was open to the great treasures of literature and to the whole output of the world of letters. During these studies Thomas learned the elements of culture and science as they had been taught for centuries, and which he was to pass on to a later age in a manner much more liberal than that in which he had received them.

Ptolemy of Lucca asserts that at Montecassino St. Thomas made progress " in logicalibus et naturalibus," which phrase is known to indicate a fairly advanced stage of studies.[37] In addition to Latin and various scientific subjects, the *volgare* (*i.e.*, the Italian language) was also taught.

According to the thirteenth century *Consuetudines* of Montecassino, a daily conference in Italian was given to the whole community in the chapter-room. To know the *volgare* well, it was necessary not only to study the language itself, but also its early literature, which is almost entirely in verse. At the time the Sicilian school was at the height of its fame. But also locally there were important literary productions: for instance, the celebrated *Placiti* of the tenth century; the *Ritmo,* perhaps of the twelfth; and certainly in the twelfth century the *Dramma della Passione,* in which Our Lady's lament was sung in the *volgare.* Surely the little oblates assisted at some of these performances.[38]

It was also at Montecassino that St. Thomas, while growing in human wisdom, grew in the wisdom of divine grace. Here probably he made his First Communion.

A curious fact appears in the writings and actions of so many illustrious men: and this is the profound influence that the presence of mountains has upon the thoughts and religious aspirations of mankind.[39] The position of Montecassino upon its hill can only have fostered in a wonderful way St. Thomas' own growing spiritual desires.

There are many holy mountains in the East: the West has the mountain of Cassino. It towers majestically above the Campania Romana and dominates the valleys of the Liri and the Garigliano which meet near Cassino. There is an immense prospect over the highlands of the Abruzzi and the hilly district that lies along the Tyrrhenian Sea. Only to the north is Montecassino overshadowed by the bare peak of Monte Cairo or Cario, not far away along a chain of hills. It was at Montecassino that the Cross of Christ threw down the pagan symbols; here amid the gigantic walls still standing St. Benedict's abbey was built; here for so many centuries the praises of God have been sung; and here the ferocity of invading hordes has been arrested and transformed by the gentleness and peace of Christ's saints.

At Montecassino it might have been said with the Psalmist of St. Thomas: "In his heart he hath disposed to ascend . . . going from virtue to virtue." [40] Before him he had the world of nature and the world of culture: these became to him a reflection of the world of supernature, and led him to the contemplation of the Lord and Maker of all.[41] The mountain, the solitude, and the monastic silence all helped him toward that contemplation. He learned how to rise from the simplest things to the highest, and so " to discern more readily than other men the very presence of God." [42] And under the discipline and careful instruction of a master, of the monk appointed to be his teacher and his guide, he felt " as if impelled by a divine instinct to grow in wisdom." [43] He loved the *beata solitudo,* the monastic peace and silence; he avoided childish amusements; and sometimes he withdrew from the company of others, " holding in his hand a paper whereon were written notes of his elementary studies." We know that the reports sent to the family on his conduct and progress were a source of much joy and consolation, especially to his mother.[44]

" Among the events to be recorded at Montecassino during the young d'Aquino's sojourn there, is the earthquake of July 1, 1231, which was repeated at intervals during that month. Great was the damage in the district, and great the fear of the inhabitants, who were moved to make a penitential pilgrimage to Montecassino. In the same year, at the request of the Holy See, a Franciscan house was opened at San Germano. In 1234 the young oblate perhaps had occasion to behold the Emperor Frederick himself when he visited San Germano. Two years later, in 1236, occurred the struggle between the abbey and Philip d'Aquino, and the boy who had passed on his way to the abbey through so many ruins of war and amid sinister soldiery, was now witnessing the efforts of the imperial agents (in whose number were his own family and his godfather) to obtain military possession of the stronghold." [45]

These were difficult times for Montecassino; and although arms were for the moment laid down, it happened that when the clash of arms and the voices of discord arose once more, Thomas left the abbey on the advice of those who represented to him the will and authority of God. The motto *Pax* was obliterated by the turmoil.

According to William da Tocco and Bernard Gui, the abbot, having in view the brilliant intellectual capacities of the young Thomas, recommended Landulf, Lord of Roccasecca, to place his son somewhere where he would have better opportunities for study.[46]

Thomas left the Benedictine abbey, according to De Rubeis, in 1235 or 1236; according to Tosti, "at the age of twelve"; or, according to De Groot, in the year 1237.[47] The biographers are either deliberately silent, or else had no care, about the immediate causes of his departure. But it is plain that the reasons were the political calamities of the time, the general unrest, and the expectation of a still worse period in store both for the abbey and for the whole district. The abbot's recommendation was quite easy of acceptance, for of course an oblate was not committed for good to the monastic life, and in any case retained the right and indeed the duty to decide his future for himself. St. Thomas himself in the *Summa Theologiae*[48] was to maintain that it is quite legitimate to pass from one Order into another 1) from a desire for greater perfection, 2) owing to the collapse of observance, 3) for reasons of health.

After the death of Abbot Landulf in 1236, the government of the abbey was entrusted to an administrator, until in February, 1239, the double consent, papal and imperial, was obtained to the election of Stephen of Corvaria,[49] who took office in that same month of February. But Gregory IX's excommunication of Frederick in March was only the signal for the struggle to break out afresh. In April the abbey was occupied by imperial troops and turned into a fortress, some of the monks being expelled. In June an edict of Frederick banished from the kingdom all religious born outside its territory.[50] Eight monks remained, and the abbot took refuge in the dependent monastery of San Liberatore alla Maiella. For about twenty years the abbey was to be but a den of thieves.

It is obvious that in such circumstances there was no more room for boys at Montecassino. It is most probable (as Mandonnet has observed) that Landulf d'Aquino, fully acquainted in advance with the imperial plans, took care to place his son in safety before the storm broke.

The boy, by now a growing youth, was free from his obligations as an oblate. His father's desire had brought him back to the world, probably not without sorrow, most likely not earlier than April, 1239. It does not seem possible to maintain that his departure took place before then. " Later events show that his parents had not given up hope, and it would not have been advisable or useful to remove him too young, and send him to Naples. They were clearly compelled to this decision by the sheer force of circumstances." [51]

And if this was indeed the occasion of Thomas' removal from the abbey, Landulf d'Aquino certainly had to postpone until better times his scheme of making his youngest son the future abbot of Montecassino.

But meanwhile Thomas had received during his sojourn there the seeds of an interior life which remained with him a permanent possession.

Chapter Three

Undergraduate at Naples

1239–1243

FREDERICK II, FOUNDER OF THE UNIVERSITY OF
NAPLES — THOMAS' UNIVERSITY STUDIES — LECTUR-
ERS AND STUDENTS IN THE FACULTY OF PHILOSOPHY
— THOMAS' DOMINICAN VOCATION

THE Emperor Frederick II, King of Jerusalem and of Sicily,
with the object of promoting higher education in his kingdom
of Sicily,[1] founded a University in 1224 at Naples. This was not
only to provide his subjects with a convenient opportunity for
instruction at home, but it was also to prevent them from going
to the various centres of study abroad and was to form a bond
between himself and the intelligentsia of the country.

For a long time past the Kingdom of Sicily had had its schools
of grammar and of medicine at Salerno. But owing to the
" shortage or absence of learned men," and to the fact that the
university methods of teaching were there unknown, Salerno
seemed an unsuitable place for an institute of higher studies.[2]
" This seat of learning and of general culture," as the University
of Naples was styled in the Act of its foundation,[3] was not
restricted to students from Frederick's kingdom. It was the
king's confessed intention that the new university should draw
students away from that of Bologna, and foreign students were
therefore welcome at Naples.[4] The subjects taught were the
arts, ecclesiastical and civil law, medicine (the faculty was

19

transferred from Salerno),[5] and theology. This last was expressly mentioned among the other subjects in 1234,[6] and the instruction was confided to the mendicant friars, probably the Dominicans, until their expulsion from Frederick's kingdom in 1239.[7] From 1229 to 1235 lectures were suspended, because the Puglie had been invaded by the pontifical troops.[8] Another temporary interruption took place in 1239, when Frederick was so annoyed at being excommunicated a second time by the Pope that, although he was himself the founder, he seriously thought of abolishing the university altogether. But the professors besought him, and his anger abated. On November 14, 1239, courses started again and continued with renewed vigor until the middle of the century.[9] In 1252 King Conrad moved the university to Salerno, but in 1258 Manfred put it back to Naples.[10] Yet it was only under the influence of Charles I of Anjou in 1266 that the *alma mater parthenopaea* really revived once more.[11] It was in this renewed university that Aquinas lectured for a time in theology.[12]

After Montecassino, Thomas was sent to study at Naples, probably in 1239. He had been to Naples before as a small child, when his mother took him to the baths. Now he returned there " at the desire of both his parents," [13] a boy with a keen mind and healthy body. The advice of the Abbot of Montecassino had had something to do with this decision.

" If indeed this move was made on the recommendation of the abbot, it is most probable that he lived, at least for a time, at the small monastery of St. Demetrius, which was a Cassinese foundation and the usual residence for monks who visited Naples. Such a course would be the obvious one for the parents to adopt, since they had not given up hope of his being a monk, and of course would not wish to leave the boy on his own in the big city." [14]

We have supposed that Thomas was impressed at Montecassino by the mountains and the silent hills: here at Naples he must have felt the contrast: the busy city, the gentle curve of the famous bay, and the restless sea beyond.

Before being entered for special studies, Thomas would have had to do a course in the Faculty of Arts. For beginners this course provided the basis for all later studies; for more advanced students it formed an introduction to the problems of philosophy.[15]

The elementary part of this faculty was concerned with the trivium and quadrivium of the monastic schools, with the addition of natural philosophy.[16] Thomas had already been through the rudiments at Montecassino, so that he would now pass on to literary studies in the Faculty of Arts. These were principally concerned with instruction and exercise in the art of *cursus,* or skill in correct speech and writing.[17] The *cursus* was a rhythmic prose whose words were disposed according to certain rules of a special kind of harmony. The basis of the *cursus* was the word-accent, not metric quantity. This sort of highly artificial prose is well known to us through papal documents from the fourth to the seventh centuries, after which a certain decadence set in, remedied, however, by the monks of Montecassino in the eleventh century. The period of perfection was reached in the thirteenth century, with, for instance, the famous *Ars Dictaminis* of Thomas of Capua (✝ 1243).[18]

These literary studies were the continuation and completion of various subjects. In the Faculty of Arts after the trivium and quadrivium came logic and natural philosophy.[19] Frederick II, who gave much encouragement to these studies, ordered that they should be based on the writings of Aristotle and his commentators.[20] Kantorowicz gives a list of the lecturers at Naples at the time.[21] Since 1231 there had been in existence a translation of Aristotle made by Michael Scotus under the aegis of the emperor.[22] This Aristotelian trend in the studies at Naples should be specially noted in view of Aquinas' own Aristotelian outlook. From the very beginning of his philosophical studies he had lived surrounded by followers of Aristotle; from his youth he had heard propounded Aristotelian principles; and as time passed, he learned to penetrate them ever more deeply, and ever more skillfully to apply them. Even if Frederick's encouragement of peripatetic philosophy did not exactly open the way to the greatest philosopher and theologian of the Catholic world, at any rate the road was thereby rendered more easy. It seemed to be part of God's provident design that St. Thomas should be born at the very time when Aristotelianism was making its appearance in the schools of the West, even though so much of its interpretation was false. It was, however, this Aristotelianism which St. Thomas' mental acuteness was to bring to such perfection and turn to such service to Christian philosophy.

William da Tocco[23] has preserved for us the names of two masters under whom Thomas probably studied at Naples: Master Martin who taught grammar and logic, and Peter of Ireland who taught natural philosophy. That the latter was definitely an Aristotelian has been shown by the recent researches of Professor Klemens Baeumker,[24] Msgr. Pelzer,[25] and Msgr. Grabmann.[26]

To these two masters could be added others mentioned in Kantorowicz's list, among whom was Erasmus, a monk of Montecassino, who taught theology at Naples from 1240, and, in the opinion of many, may already have had an influence on Thomas during his period at the abbey.[27]

Thomas was an apt student,[28] and the seeds of philosophical science planted by the aforesaid masters could not but promise a rich harvest of excellent speculative work. His keen and receptive mind soon showed itself by his firm grasp of principles and the exactitude of his answers.

Before long he was called upon to do some coaching of other students, and it was immediately apparent that he exceeded some of the lecturers in sheer brilliance as well as in sureness of knowledge and skill in conclusions.[29] Whoever is disposed to doubt this exceptional and precocious intelligence of Thomas should bear in mind that especially in the lands of the South there have from time to time appeared boys thus remarkably gifted in their early youth. We have an example in a period not so far removed from our own in St. Alphonsus Maria de' Liguori, who became a Doctor of Law at Naples at sixteen years of age.

But amid all these studies of the arts and sciences Thomas was not forgetting the ultimate goal of the mind and heart,[30] the honor, contemplation, and love of God. At Montecassino he had sought God, the Creator of all things; here he was seeking before all knowledge, God "the lord of all knowledge."[31] Amid the bustle of the city and the business of the university, he preserved his own religious spirit. Perhaps he kept away from students whose pursuits were too profane. Kantorowicz[32] has traced the names of a few of his fellow-students.

He put himself under spiritual direction. The guides that he chose were to give him an ideal of life that differed somewhat from the outlook that had hitherto been traditional. After leaving Montecassino with a loving gratitude towards the Order of St. Benedict, he met in Naples the Dominicans whose ideals and guidance appealed to him. The Friars Preachers had sprung up at the same time as the proud new towns and cities of the thirteenth century, and had contributed in no small measure to their constitution.[33] They were ardent spiritual leaders, showing new spiritual paths, and profoundly influencing the university centres, both in teaching and the spiritual direction of the students.[34] The old monastic Orders, from their retreats among the hills and dales of the open country, wholly dedicated to the praise of God and the salvation of their own souls, were watching the new movement. The new Orders established themselves at the centers of progressive thought, seeking by their apostolate to turn the busy lives of men toward their highest destiny. They preached, they taught, they held up before men the example of the Christian life. They lived in poverty, relying on the charity of those to whom they preached and ministered. Thus the monastic ideal of the Church was enlarged to include the mode of life of the mendicants.

Thomas felt attracted to the mendicant orders, and in particular to the Friars Preachers, to whom he was probably led precisely by his veneration for the Benedictine life; for they more than any of the mendicants have preserved monastic observance and the Benedictine spirit as a principal means of preparation for the apostolate.

Leccisotti [35] sums up the three reasons which led Thomas to decide not to abandon religious life, but rather to re-embrace it in the mendicant form: "First of all, the boy had always, by God's grace, longed for the peace of religious life in which to occupy himself with the things of God ' ac talentum naturalis ingenii sibi commissum augmentare.' Now it had happened that the mystical vine which the patriarch Benedict had planted had somehow been wrecked, and at the time it seemed beyond repair. No one could possibly have foreseen the restoration that was to come.

" Secondly, Thomas was no longer a child. He may well have become aware of his father's plans for his future. His increasingly spiritual outlook would have made them repellent to him, to be resisted at all costs. In fact, we cannot help noticing in the life of the holy Doctor a sort of constant horror of all dignities, a horror which he kept to the end of his days. So deeply was this feeling implanted in his nature that we cannot help thinking that it dates from these early years, when he came to realize the ignoble efforts being made by his parents, which would have brought him to disaster.

" Thirdly, there was the ideal of the Friars Preachers . . . the boy thirsting for knowledge, meditative, monastically trained, was naturally attracted."

After all, what could have attracted Thomas more than the *studium veritatis* put forward by St. Dominic to the world of his time, and by his sons through the centuries [36] right down to the present day? What could have attracted him more than the idea of the apostolic priesthood which brings to yearning souls the infinite fruits of Christ's Passion?

St. Dominic's ideal was so beautiful that the other mendi-

cant orders which arose about the same time (though without
so clear and precise an aim) gradually adopted the practice
of preaching as a means of saving souls, becoming thus likened
to the Friars Preachers.[37] So it can be said that St. Dominic
has in reality a much larger number of followers than the
mere number of religious of his Order.

The shining figure of St. Dominic is most happily described
in the ancient liturgical antiphon:

> O lumen ecclesiae, doctor veritatis,
> Rosa patientiae, ebur castitatis,
> Aquam sapientiae propinasti gratis,
> Praedicator gratiae, nos iunge beatis.[38]

The saintly figure of Dominic and his brilliant foundation
attracted d'Aquino, the well-born undergraduate. The splendid
work of the Order was carried on with enthusiasm and success
by Blessed Jordan, who followed St. Dominic as head of the
Order.[39] Jordan often preached before university audiences.
He could also be called the first University Chaplain, for in
Paris he used to give special afternoon conferences for the
students.[40] He won them by his lovable nature, his perfect
life, his gentleness, his radiant words. Not infrequently, when
he was telling them how to lead a good life, how to get to
know and love Our Lord, or how to understand the truths of
the Faith, many found themselves so overcome with admiration for the manner of life which produced such marvelous
preachers that without further ado they presented themselves
as candidates for the Order of Preachers. Sometimes he addressed undergraduate gatherings with the precise object of
getting vocations. In France he did this in Paris,[41] in Lombardy
at Bologna,[42] Padua (where he got Albert, the German),[43]
Modena,[44] and Vercelli,[45] and in various parts of Germany.[46]
In England he preached the University Sermon at Oxford.[47]
His last sermons before he left to visit the houses of the Order
in the Holy Land were those he preached in 1236 to the stu-

dents of Naples,[48] or anyway he intended to stop at Naples on his return from Syria; but his ship was wrecked and he and all the crew and passengers perished.[49] He was buried at Acre.[50]

In any case, his spirit, his memory, and his care for the Neapolitan students were continued through the labors of Father John of San Giuliano.[51] At least it was he who looked after the young student d'Aquino, and "finding him of the most suitable disposition, had him decide to enter the said Order, so that what God had deigned to foretell of him should indeed be brought about."[52] The story is in fact told that Thomas' mother, shortly before he was born, heard from the hermit Bonus (a holy man who lived near Roccasecca) a prophecy about the future greatness of her child, and that his parents were going to destine him for the Benedictine life, but God for the Dominican.[53] One thing is, however, certain, that this John of San Giuliano, who was known to William da Tocco[54] and to the *logotheta* Bartholomew of Capua,[55] took much trouble over St. Thomas' Dominican vocation. Thomas would also have known Father Thomas Agni, of Lentini. This illustrious son of St. Dominic was the first prior of the Dominican house at Naples, founded in 1231. In 1234 the priory was dedicated to St. Dominic, the holy founder who had by then been canonized.[56] Father Thomas of Lentini had a distinguished subsequent career: first he became Bishop of Bethlehem, and then Archbishop of Cosenza; finally he was made Patriarch of Jerusalem and died in the Holy Land in 1277.[57] According to a reliable source,[58] it was he who had the honor of giving the religious habit to the young Thomas Aquinas.

It would be impossible to have a true idea of what was going on in the mind of the youthful Thomas, if one failed to take into account what he wrote when already advanced in years and at the height of his fame, about the mode of life which he had desired "for so long, and with all his heart."[59] For what he then desired with all his youthful ardor, and embraced with all the understanding, enthusiasm, and generosity of youth, he afterwards described in the mature terms of the *Summa Theologiae.*[60]

Thomas Aquinas found his heart's desire in that form of religious life which had been instituted for the salvation of souls by means of preaching and teaching: the apostolic Order of Preachers, founded by St. Dominic.

Chapter Four

The Young Dominican

1243–1245/8

THE CEREMONY OF CLOTHING AMONG THE FRIARS PREACHERS — THE NOVITIATE — DISPLEASURE OF THE FAMILY — THE YOUNG FRIAR IS APPREHENDED — HIS DETENTION AT MONTESANGIOVANNI CAMPANO AND AT ROCCASECCA — HE REGAINS HIS FREEDOM

TRANSLATOR'S NOTE ON THE ORGANIZATION OF THE DOMINICAN ORDER: Readers who are unfamiliar with the Order of Preachers may well be puzzled by the use of certain terms in the next and following chapters. The present sketch is intended to explain such terms. Numbers in brackets refer to the paragraph in the *Constitutions* of the Order, and for historical facts reference is made to Fr. ANGELUS WALZ'S *Compendium Historiae Ordinis Praedicatorum*, Rome 1930 (2nd ed., 1948).

The normal unit is the single house or *priory*, at the head of which is the *prior*. Priors are elected by their community for a period nowadays limited to 3 years [418]. The various priories in a given geographical area (usually a political unit) are grouped into a *province*. This is governed by a *provincial*. The provincial holds office for a period nowadays of 4 years [418], and is elected by the *provincial chapter*, which is a representative gathering of the province, composed of the various *priors*, each accompanied by a *socius*, also elected by the community (to represent the subjects) [386 sqq.], and certain other privileged members of the province, such as STMs and PGs (*cf. infra*) [361]. The provincial chapter nowadays meets every 4 years [506]. All the provinces are

28

subject to the head of the whole Order, who is called the *master-general*. He nowadays holds office for 12 years [418, 471], and is elected by the *general chapter*, which is a representative gathering of the whole Order, composed of the *provincials* and two *diffinitors* from each province, previously elected at their own provincial chapter, and also certain privileged persons in the Order [514]. During the period of office of a master-general there should be two intermediate general chapters, one being a gathering of the *provincials* and the other of the *diffinitors*, while an elective chapter includes both [515]. In earlier years both general and provincial chapters were held annually (Walz, 79, 86; 2nd ed., 99, 106), but this had to be altered in the sixteenth and seventeenth centuries, when the known world had become so greatly enlarged (cf. Walz, 294; 2nd ed., 353). Apart from elections, the *provincial chapter* legislates and makes appointments for the province, and the *general chapter* for the whole Order. (It is important to understand the working of these chapters for the following of St. Thomas in Italy: ch. VIII.) The limit of offices to a stated period is relatively modern legislation: prior and provincial in 1627 [Walz, 296; 2nd ed., 356], and master-general in 1862 [Walz, 451; 2nd ed., 541].

A man who joins the Order is *clothed* and thus becomes a *novice* (nowadays for one year, *cf. infra* p. 33), after which he *makes profession, i.e.,* takes vows. If he is a candidate for the priesthood, he then begins his course of studies (usually of 7 years), towards the end of which he is ordained. If he is destined for more intense study or for teaching in a study-house of the Order, he concludes his course with the degree of *Lector in Sacred Theology* (STL). This degree may in turn lead to the examination "ad gradus" after at least 7 years' teaching, and so to the degree of *Master in Sacred Theology* (STM), for which a further 6 years' teaching is required [704–709]. These degrees are purely Dominican institutions, and that of *Master* is one of the greatest honors in the Order. The regulations governing these degrees are relatively modern. being undetermined until 1596 (Walz, 322; 2nd ed., 431–2). The privileges of Masters date from 1303 (Walz, 130; 2nd ed., 217). Another special title of honor in the Order is that of *Preacher-general* (PG), which is conferred on a distinguished preacher, nowadays with at least 15 years' experience [763]. The privileges attached to this office date from the earliest days of the Order (Walz,

155; 2nd ed., 253), though the precise conditions for receiving it were only fixed in 1518 and 1589 (Walz, 346; 2nd ed., 466).

St. Thomas was both a Master in Sacred Theology and a Preacher-general.

THE older religious Orders all have a distinctive habit to show even by this exterior mark that these are people who have left the world and have taken a new outlook on life, although admittedly in the Middle Ages the difference between the dress of religious and of lay people was not so great as it is today. There is a special ceremony, full of spiritual significance, that accompanies the act of clothing a person in the religious habit.

Among the Friars Preachers the clothing ceremony is as follows: The postulant (or candidate) is brought by the master of novices into the middle of the chapter-room (unless the clothing is done in church), and there, "lying prostrate with his arms spread in the form of a cross, he receives the formal question: What do you ask? and he answers: God's mercy and yours. Then the prior bids him rise and begins to explain to him the austerities of the Order." First of all there are the three vows of poverty, chastity, and obedience which cannot be altered; and then there are the constitutions, which a superior can have reason to adapt to varying circumstances. Finally the prior asks the postulant if he still wishes to persevere. If he answers in the affirmative, the prior adds: May the Lord complete what He has begun. The community answers: Amen. Then the novice-master leads the postulant up to the prior and bids him kneel down. Meanwhile the brother vestiarian has brought the habit which he offers to the prior. The prior then proceeds with the help of the novice-master to clothe the postulant in the white habit and black cappa of the Friars Preachers. The moment that the actual clothing begins the community kneels down and the cantor intones the *Veni Creator Spiritus*, which is followed by other prayers. After the clothing, the novice prostrates himself again, but at the termination of the prayers he is once more bidden to rise, and the novice-master leads him to the altar-steps, where the prior gives him the brotherly kiss of peace. The novice then goes to each of the community in turn and receives the embrace that is a sign of peace and brotherly love. Meanwhile the *Te Deum* is sung. Finally the prior formally hands over the newly-clothed novice to the novice-master and declares that the year of probation has begun. " If during this year," he adds, " you find that you like our life, and we find that we approve of your conduct, you will be able to make your profession; if not, both sides will be free. Try therefore willingly to bear this yoke for the love of God, and try to obey your novice-master in everything as you would me." [1]

The clothing of Thomas d'Aquino with the Dominicans of Naples, who belonged to the Roman Province,[2] took place according to Prümmer in 1240 or 1241, according to De Rubeis, Mandonnet, and Pelster [3] in the course of 1243 or the beginning of 1244. From 1243 to 1244, or even 1245, the head of this province was Father Humbert de Romans,[4] who was later to become master-general of the Order. Bernard Gui states that the prior who clothed Thomas was Father Thomas Agni of Lentini.[5] Doubtless Thomas had reached the age required by law for entry into religion,[6] but since both the clothing ceremony and the year of novitiate do not come at fixed times, it is not possible to draw any definite conclusions from this fact.[7]

Thomas had chosen the religious state in order to find peace of mind, and to be with God. And indeed God blessed him with a peace which the world cannot give, a peace which he was able to preserve throughout the battles waged against his choice and his desires, battles which were so soon to begin and which never entirely ceased during his whole lifetime.

Mandonnet is of the opinion that Thomas would have entered the Order of Preachers earlier than in point of fact he did, but that his spiritual director, Father John of San Giuliano, who well knew the attitude of the aristocracy toward the mendicant orders, considered that undue haste would be

imprudent. This experienced priest would have had two reasons for counseling delay: in the first place, Thomas would
probably spend the vacations with his family and would have
an opportunity of sounding the family's feelings on the matter
of his Dominican vocation. Secondly, he could not but remember the recent occurrence of 1235, when this very priory of
Naples, the church, the house, and the Fathers themselves,
had been attacked by an armed band in the employ of a certain noble family, who had thus manifested their displeasure
at one of the family's having become a Dominican.[8]

He had quietly entered the Order with the single ardent
desire for eternal things. But the event caused the greatest
commotion. No one objected to his interior motives; but the
stir was caused by the apparent dashing of the hope of a distinguished university career which was so evidently promised
by his well-known brilliance in studies. The news quickly
spread among the great families, the students, and the professors of Naples, that d'Aquino, who, though so young, had
already won fame in the university [9] and the admiration alike
of masters and pupils, had thrown away all ambition and gone
to hide himself among the mendicants.[10] His companions had
always liked him: but now it was different. He had been a lad
so full of energy, so handsome and charming, so good and so
clever: now they were turning against him and against the
institute which he had joined.

Of course the news caused much trouble at Roccasecca, but
we shall see more of this presently.

Throughout the history of the Order the novitiate has been
a period of testing. But it was different in the thirteenth century from what it is now. At that time the novitiate was
looked upon as an immediate trial of the full normal life of
the Order. The object of the novitiate was not so much a sort
of long retreat with regular instructions and only a partial
share in the work of the Order; it was rather a trial of the
life that the friar would lead for the rest of the time until his
death. The work of the novice-master, who was simply ap-

pointed by the prior of that house, was therefore to teach his charges to follow the life of the community into which they had been received at clothing. There was no sort of *clausura* that separated the novices from the others. The novitiate was a time when one simply learned to live the Dominican life, learned to follow the rules and customs of the Order and the spiritual and material obligations of the Constitutions, shared in the worship, community-life, and penance, and received direct formation in the particular work of preaching. A most important element in this was study, and the novice-master was specially directed to see that the novices applied themselves day and night to their studies, and that wherever they were they should never waste time but always be occupied with reading or meditation.[11]

The period of the novitiate, when the novice was under the care of the novice-master, lasted at that time for at least six months; according to the decree of Pope Innocent IV on June 17, 1244, it was extended to one year. But in the case of Brother Thomas, the novitiate had hardly begun when it was rudely interrupted by action from outside.

As soon as the news that Thomas had entered the Dominican Order arrived, his mother, Theodora d'Aquino, together with a small company, hastened to Naples to make him go back on his decision and so preserve him for the family. But his superiors had foreseen that his entry into a mendicant order might provoke such an attack, and they were unwilling that the Order should lose so precious a subject. Accordingly they had already sent him off to Rome with some of the brethren. From there he was to have gone on to Paris for purposes of study. The friars traveled through Terracina along the Via Appia, proceeded through Anagni along the Via Latina, and so reached Rome, where they stayed at Santa Sabina.[12] (This route, which is that given by Tocco, is criticised by Mandonnet, who claims that it would have been unwise to take the Via Latina, which passes close to Aquino.) The Church of Santa Sabina had been given to the Order of Preachers [13] on

June 5, 1222, by Honorius III, who also gave them the adjacent convent as a residence for those who looked after the church.[14] It was at Santa Sabina that St. Dominic had worked for the sanctification of souls and his own, and here many of his successors, as masters-general of the Order, fixed their residence when in Rome on business of the Order. Such were Blessed Jordan of Saxony, St. Raymond de Peñafort, and the Venerable John of Wildeshausen, usually known as The Teutonic. It was John who was there at Santa Sabina (according to P. Mandonnet) when the novice from Naples arrived in Rome.[15] As it happened, John was about to leave for Bologna to attend the general chapter of 1244, and Thomas Aquinas set off northwards in his company.[16] Perhaps they felt that even Rome was not safe for him. It was probably the fact of this journey that led Thomas of Cantimpré to suppose that Aquinas entered the Order at Bologna.[17]

The *Vitae Fratrum* gives the pursuit of theological studies in Paris as the reason for this journey: Parisius ad proficiendum.[18] The author does not mention the interrupted novitiate, though in itself this is not a grave omission. In any case, the continuation of both novitiate and studies of the young friar were perforce postponed by the fierce opposition of his family to the choice he had made.

His mother Theodora pursued him to Rome, but found him already gone. Her zeal, however, went after him, and she called upon her sons, as William da Tocco puts it, " to lay hands upon him and bring back her son Thomas to her, under strong escort, their brother whom the Friars Preachers had clothed in their habit and taken away out of the kingdom." [19] These other sons of Theodora were at the time near Acquapendente in Tuscany, as soldiers and knights in the imperial army.[20] Frederick II had come in August, 1243, to make war on the papal cities of Tuscany. The brothers, in obedience to their mother's command, immediately devised a plan which they submitted to the emperor. Then, fortified by his permission and approval, they sent out bodies of soldiers about the

roads and lanes of southern Tuscany. Thomas was found " resting near a fountain, in the company of four brethren of the
Order." The *Vitae Fratrum* and Ptolemy of Lucca state that
the master-general was there when the young friar was captured.[21] Tocco does not mention the fact. The brothers at once
started to try to turn Thomas from his purpose of remaining
in the Order. They tried to strip him of his habit, but Thomas'
strength was too much for them, and they failed. Eventually
they let the other friars go, and Thomas, dressed as a Dominican, they brought back to his mother. It was more a case of
arresting him than merely bringing him home. All this happened probably during the first half of May, 1244.[22]

While the master-general with his companions continued
their journey to Bologna to the general chapter which opened
on May 22, Thomas now found himself completely in the
power of his family who were not yet reconciled to the idea
of seeing him a mendicant friar.

He was shut up under strong guard, says William da
Tocco,[23] in the castles of Montesangiovanni Campano [24] and
Roccasecca, or only in that of Montesangiovanni Campano,
according to the *Vitae Fratrum*, Bernard Gui, and Ptolemy of
Lucca,[25] until the return of his elder brothers.[26] Montesangio-
vanni, on the top of a hill in the limestone region between
Frosinone and the Cistercian abbey of Casamari, looks over
the valley of the Amaseno.[27]

On behalf of the Order, this armed aggression, made with
the emperor's consent against members of the Order, was re-
ported to the emperor by the master-general, John the Teutonic. The report was either made directly or by way of Pope
Innocent IV [28] (who had been elected on July 25, 1243), so
that he himself could demand satisfaction from Frederick.
Now the emperor was anxious on the one hand not to alienate
the clergy and on the other not to " queer the pitch " with the
d'Aquino. So he summoned the brothers who had arrested
Thomas, giving a chance to the Dominicans, if they wished,
to start a lawsuit against them. But in view of the increasingly

difficult relations between the imperial and the papal parties, and for the avoidance of scandal and even of acts of violence against themselves, the Dominicans decided that it was wiser not to take the matter to law, and in this they were encouraged by the fact that the young Brother was showing himself firm and constant in trial, and remaining true to his vocation.[29]

The *Vitae Fratrum* relates that every effort was made by the family to induce Thomas to leave the Order.[30] Thomas of Cantimpré adds a further detail, stating that certain women were put to lodge with Thomas.[31] Tocco, who divides the imprisonment into two periods, says that attempts were made to seduce him in both periods.

With regard to Thomas' treatment during his detention, William da Tocco distinguishes the periods before and after the return of his brothers. During the first period—at least so Tocco would have us believe—Theodora tried in various ways to test her son's attachment to the Order of Preachers, and this not only to try his constancy but still more to prove to herself the truth of the prophecy she had received about him. But it was more than a mere test when by arrangement of the mother herself, one of Thomas' own sisters was sent to him to corrupt him. But he " with his words and example brought her to the love of God and the contempt of the world." This was the sister named Marotta.[32]

But the worst trials came when the brothers returned. First of all, they at last succeeded in ripping off the Dominican habit which he was still wearing. This insult he bore with great patience, feeling that the tearing of his habit brought him the joy of sharing the insults offered to Christ. But worse than this were the systematic attacks on his chastity, by which they hoped to turn him from his constancy. A woman's wiles, they thought, would be the easiest way to arouse the passions of a young man of little over eighteen. But they did not reckon with the grace of God. In fact, the girl who was to seduce him had hardly entered his room, when Brother Thomas, startled by so unexpected a sight and feeling the passions suddenly surge up within himself, seized a firebrand from the hearth and indignantly put her to flight. He returned to his room, traced with the point of the firebrand, his victorious weapon, a large cross on the wall, fell upon the floor, and prayed.[33]

A recent author [34] claims that this story is but fiction: he says it is no more than the story of his sister's visit, elaborated and coarsened by legend. It does seem unlikely that St. Thomas' brothers, who are spoken of as outstandingly upright men,[35] would ever have recourse to anything quite so base. And there may be some truth in the first part of this explanation, for the first to recount the incident is William da Tocco, who has a certain liking for legends and does not hesitate to paint the simplest events in quite exaggerated colors; but with regard to the second part, there can be no doubt that Thomas' brothers, " serving in Frederick II's army, led disordered lives in common with most of that soldiery." But since these brothers later " abandoned the cause of Frederick II, returned to the strait way and suffered persecution in defense of the Faith and fidelity to the Holy See," we need no longer be surprised that the ecclesiastical author calls them virtuous men.[36]

The young Thomas had had the victory, but at the cost of a hard battle. He lay on the floor, exhausted. Presently sleep overcame him and he was consoled by a wonderful dream: " from heaven two angels came to him and girded his loins." They spoke to him: " On God's behalf we gird you with the girdle of chastity, a girdle which no attack will ever destroy." So it happened that Thomas acquired his first title *Angelicus*,[37] a title not only well-deserved from the above event, but later universally used when his great works appeared whose lucid composition suggests an angelic mind.

Present-day historians agree with Mandonnet, who sees in the account of Tocco and Gui of the girdle of chastity not a material reality but rather the expression of an inner meaning. But the story is of course the reason why a cord is given to members of the Angelic Warfare, the sodality that is placed under the patronage of St. Thomas.[38]

The stay of Thomas in the castle of Montesangiovanni was short, as is explained by Scandone and Toso,[39] and still more by Mandonnet,[40] who makes this stay to be no more than a halt on the journey to Roccasecca, though he has not noticed that the elder brothers did not accompany Thomas, and that the episode of the temptation did not occur until after their return.

After his detention at Montesangiovanni, Thomas was moved to Roccasecca, but it is not known when.

The location and description of Thomas' room in the castle of Montesangiovanni are given by Mancini in a special treatise.[41] The young friar was not kept a close prisoner, as is shown by the friendly relations with his sisters,[42] to whom he was able to give spiritual advice. He also received frequent visits from Father John of San Giuliano, the one who at Naples had first guided him towards a Dominican vocation and now was encouraging him in it.[43] The *logotheta* Bartholomew even says that he was a fellow-prisoner with Thomas. And furthermore, conditions were such that they allowed Thomas to give himself to prayer and study. Tocco writes: " There he read the Bible, learned the text of the *Sentences,* and, it is said, compiled the tractate on the fallacies of Aristotle." [44]

The date of this last-mentioned *opusculum* seems most unlikely. His work *De fallaciis* and the cognate *De modalibus propositionibus* belong to altogether another period of his life.[45]

In 1768, a manuscript written at Modena in 1347 was brought to light. It contains a sonnet attributed to the youthful Thomas. It would be the only extant piece of his verse written in his native tongue; but its authenticity is, to say the least, doubtful.[46]

With these various occupations, however, he managed to foster and develop his Dominican vocation. He effected the union of progress in virtue with that in wisdom: a thing indispensable to those whose desire and whose task it is to benefit not only their own souls, but also the souls of others.

For two whole years,[47] 1244–1245, he was interned in the castles of his own family. But the whole time he showed such manifest and indisputable signs of perseverance in his vocation that it would have been not only useless, but cruel, not to set him free. So at last he was allowed to have his way, and was sent back to the Friars Preachers " who received him with joy and brought him back to Naples." [48]

The *Vitae Fratrum* has a most sober account of his departure: " dimiserunt eum "; and Thomas of Cantimpré simply says: " fratres fratrem solverunt," but Ptolemy of Lucca has an exciting account of how the Friars came to rescue him at dead of night by means of a rope, something like St. Paul's escape from Damascus.[49] Tocco wrote in his *Vita* that Thomas was let down from a window by a rope; [50] yet while giving evidence at the Process for Canonization, he stated that the parents and brothers restored him to the Order. If we wish not entirely to disbelieve Ptolemy, and Tocco in the *Vita*, we have to take the view of De Groot and Toso of a liberation that was like a flight (which Toso even describes as pretended).[51] This notion leads to a realistic, obvious, natural, and therefore likely explanation: the family, having realized the uselessness of incarceration, simply did their part by bringing him out of prison. This is what is stated by the *Vitae Fratrum*, by Cantimpré, and by Bartholomew of Capua,[52] who further explains that Landulf, the father, had a bigger part in the imprisonment and the various attempts to bend the will of Thomas than Tocco's account suggests. This is also borne out by the bull of canonization.[53] But, on the other hand, Mandonnet and Leccisotti maintain that Landulf was already dead.[54]

In addition to all this, the political circumstances were favorable to the family's decision: for Innocent IV, after having stayed for a short time in Italy, went to France to assemble the Council of Lyons, and on July 17, 1245, declared Fred-

erick II to be deposed from the imperial throne.[55] This marked
the beginning of the end for the fortunes of the Swabian
monarch, and many who had till then been on his side now
found it easier to abandon him.

Among these were also the d'Aquino.[56] They were impli-
cated in the Capaccio plot against Frederick's life in 1246, and
this brought death in 1248 to Count Thomas of San Severino,
with his eldest son William, the husband of Thomas' sister
Mary. Roger of San Severino succeeded in fleeing to the Papal
States.[57] Thomas' own brother, Ronald d'Aquino, was put to
death by order of Frederick, and therefore earlier than 1250.
And, if the story is true, Thomas added: " Without any sem-
blance of justice." [58]

Thomas, then, was free once more round 1245.[59] Once more
he was able to devote himself to a full religious life and to
make great progress therein. The bonds which his own family
had set upon him were broken largely through the new political situation. They had not been too burdensome, but they
were certainly unpleasant. Now, however, he was free to
follow his vocation, and even his family considered that his
freedom would be greater within a worldwide religious order
than it would be at home. But he was not to remain long at
Naples,[60] whither his brethren had conducted him after his
release from Roccasecca. His superiors considered " that it
would not be advisable to keep the young aristocrat in his
native district, even though his family after realizing his firm-
ness had ceased to molest him, so they sent him to Rome," for,
taking into account the future, they desired to send him as
soon as possible to a *studium generale*.[61]

The interrupted novitiate presented no serious problem. In
the priory where he stayed after his release he could easily
fulfil his obligation to the regular period of trial. And in view
of the young friar's proved tenacity of purpose, the period of
novitiate could not but be full of promise for a glorious future.
Should a dispensation for Brother Thomas d'Aquino have been
necessary, it could easily have been obtained, even of the Holy
See, especially since the master-general usually dealt with
these matters personally at the Roman Curia.

Chapter Five

Student at Cologne

1245/8–1252

THE STUDY OF THEOLOGY — THEOLOGICAL SCHOOLS
IN ITALY AND BEYOND THE ALPS — THOMAS TRAVELS
TO COLOGNE VIA PARIS — THE STUDIUM ON THE RHINE
— SAINT ALBERT THE GREAT — SIGNS OF THOMAS'
FUTURE GREATNESS IN THE WORLD OF STUDIES —
NEWS FROM HOME — EVENTS IN COLOGNE AT THIS
TIME

ANY attempt to establish an accurate chronology of St.
Thomas' years as a student involves problems that are no less
difficult than those encountered so far. In particular there is
the intricate matter of deciding at which study-houses of the
Order he received his theological formation.[1]

The first precaution is to observe, with Fr. Denifle,[2] that the
ancient biographers were so much occupied with relating his
precocious and mighty intelligence and his enormous and
rapid progress in wisdom, that they neglected to mention both
his novitiate (which he certainly had to make) and his preliminary studies in the Order.

So it happened that St. Thomas' biographers speak at once
of his departure for the pursuit of higher studies, without
recording any studies in his own priory or province. But success in such preliminary studies was a necessary condition for
proceeding to higher studies. Of course, Brother Thomas had
made a good start, for he had attended the lectures of the

41

philosophical faculty at Naples even before he was clothed, but he would certainly have received further instruction either at the priory of Naples, where he lived, or somewhere else in that province of the Order. These local centres of studies in the Order were often very important, though they have never received the attention they deserve because of the overwhelming glory of the *studia generalia,* especially that of Paris. But every Dominican priory had to have its theological school. Next to the prior, the most important member of the community was the " doctor " [3] who was responsible for the continuous instructions of the brethren in sacred science. At the local *studium* the curriculum included matters of dogma, moral, exegesis, canon law, and homiletics. The best students at the local schools were selected and sent to the great centres, where they could receive a more complete technical training. This arrangement existed from the very beginning of the Dominican Order, and is described by the master-general Humbert de Romans in his work *De officiis Ordinis,* in the chapter (XII) on the office of master of students: " Cum autem fuerint aliqui in conventu, de quorum profectu in studio multum speretur, et sunt bene morigerati, [magister studentium] debet laborare ut detur eis occasio et adiutorium ad proficiendum in studio, iuvando eos ad hoc in quibus potest per se, et innotescendo hoc maioribus; et intercedendo pro eis ut provideatur eis in libris, ut mittantur ad studia meliora . . . et similia, quae possunt ad promotionem valere praedictam." [4] It should be noted that the word " profectus " does not imply any change of residence [5] or of status,[6] but refers to the intellectual progress involved in the pursuit of higher studies, and in particular such as lead to academic degrees as the lectorate.[7]

Of course, there were notable theological schools in Italy— one has only to think of the great teachers at Bologna, and also of the centre of studies at the Dominican priory in that city, which began in the time of the founder of the Order himself.[8] But the most renowned schools of the twelfth century were to be found beyond the Alps. The cathedral schools of Chartres, Laon, and, above all, of Paris, were famed for their scholarship, for their development of teaching methods, and for the great number of first-class teachers who attracted students from all parts of Europe. Paris, on account of its *studium*, was called by Albert the Great "the city of philosophers," and by Armandus of Belvezer "the first seat of theological learning." [9] The scholarship of the schools of France is sufficiently manifested by names like Anselm of Laon (✝1117), William of Champeaux (✝1121), Hugh, Count of Blankenberg, usually known as Hugh of St. Victor (✝1141), Abelard (✝1142), or Peter the Lombard (✝1160). The principal theological school in England was that of Oxford,[10] and in Germany the most outstanding was the cathedral school of Cologne.[11] The question of the origins of scholasticism and of these schools, and the cognate historical problems, have received full treatment from distinguished writers such as (to name but a few) Denifle, Rashdall, Ehrle, Mandonnet, Gilson, Grabmann, Geyer, Pelster, Masnovo, D'Irsay, De Wulf, De Ghellinck, Van Steenberghen, and others.

The same voice of Divine Providence that called Thomas d'Aquino from the world to the cloister now summoned him to the pursuit of advanced theological studies: he was about to move into new surroundings which offered him the best instruction and the services of the most illustrious masters of the day.

Tocco is very brief: "The said Thomas, whom John the Teutonic, master of the Order, treated as a well-beloved son, was taken by him to Paris and then to Cologne, where he flourished exceedingly at the *studium generale* directed by Brother Albert, master in theology, who was considered by all to excel in every field of knowledge." [12]

These few unadorned words hide many problems indeed. What was the route of the journey of the master-general and the student friar who accompanied him? Where did the latter stay to study? Who were his masters? The many questions have not yet received a unanimous answer from either the historians of scholasticism or the biographers of St. Thomas.

The first task is to distinguish three main problems: Thomas' association with the master-general, his journey to Paris, and the young friar's place of residence for study beyond the Alps. Recent research has brought to light the varying witness of the ancient sources and the early biographers on the presence of the master-general. The *Vitae Fratrum* and Ptolemy of Lucca say that the first journey of 1244 was made in the company of John the Teutonic,[13] but came to an end at Acquapendente. Tocco, Gui, and Calo, on the other hand, claim his presence on the second journey, which did indeed bring St. Thomas to the lands of the North.[14] These opposing views are not, however, irreconcilable. It is possible that Thomas made the latter journey in the company of the head of the Order at least for a part of the way, if not for the whole. They might have been together, for instance, from the Mediterranean to the Seine.

Tocco relates that when Thomas left Rome he went to Paris, and from there to Cologne, where he studied under Albert the Great. But Thomas of Cantimpré, who was his contemporary, says that he went from Italy to Cologne.[15] The important evidence of Ptolemy of Lucca adds that he went from Rome to Cologne "where he remained a long time" with Albert.[16] And St. Thomas' niece, Gaitegrima or Catherine San Severino, told William da Tocco in February, 1318—as he himself stated categorically on August 4, 1319—that she had learned from Thomas' own mother that Thomas, already a cleric in the Order of Preachers, after spending some time with his family, had been sent from Italy to Cologne for studies.[17]

Bernard Gui states that Thomas was brought to Paris by the master-general, but was then sent on to Cologne.[18] In the same way Peter Calo writes that John the Teutonic took Thomas with him, but later sent him on to Cologne.[19] The same thing is repeated by John Flaminio[20] and Anthony of Siena.[21]

Furthermore, according to John Colonna [22] and Henry of Herford,[23] Thomas was at Cologne as Albert's disciple after the latter's return there from Paris. All this evidence goes to show that Thomas' abode for studies was none other than Cologne. None of the above-mentioned authors, not even the famous letter of the Paris professors of philosophy written at the death of Aquinas, nor the bull of canonization, say that he studied in Paris and still less that he studied in Paris under Albert. The value of these witnesses must not be underestimated. When we bear in mind the Angevin sentiments of those who promoted the cause of canonization, their very negative evidence is significant enough. It is only Thomas of Cantimpré who refers to Albert's move from the studium of Cologne to that of Paris, and it might therefore be supposed that his student, Thomas, also removed from the banks of the Rhine to those of the Seine. But Cantimpré makes no such direct assertion; and anyway, too much weight cannot be given to his remarks, since his information about St. Thomas is generally so vague, and his observations so notably inadequate on the particular matter of St. Thomas' studies,[24] which quite certainly involved a fairly long stay at Cologne after Albert's return from Paris.

It appears that Thomas only spent a very short time in Paris on his arrival there from Italy, since some authors do not even mention this stay, as we have seen. Moreover, Ptolemy of Lucca says that the first time he went to Paris was when he was already a graduate,[25] and he does not even consider it worth while noting the brief halt he made there on his way to the studium generale on the Rhine.

The precise dates of these journeys cannot be ascertained.

On the supposition that Brother Thomas was granted his freedom in 1245, the journeys could be placed in that year or shortly after. This would allow for the period of novitiate, which he probably made in Italy, and perhaps also for a period of study in a local studium at one of the priories, unless of course such studies were dispensed with in view of the university course he had already taken. He seems to have made some of the journey to Paris by sea, for William da Tocco [26] relates that "while Thomas was upon a journey to Paris there arose a terrible storm, and although the very sailors were in fear of death at any moment, he alone remained unperturbed during the whole storm." It seems obvious that the reference is to the first journey, since on the second he followed the road from Milan across the Alps.

The sea-route was not unusual. It is known, for instance, that Blessed Jordan of Saxony in 1229 left Lombardy for Genoa, where he took a ship to Montpellier and so proceeded to Paris.[27]

The general chapters in which John the Teutonic took part, and to which he might have taken the young Thomas with him, were those of Bologna in 1244, of Cologne in 1245, of Paris in 1246, of Montpellier in 1247, of Paris in 1248, and of Trier in 1249.

There is no difficulty in admitting that Thomas went to Paris and on to Cologne in 1248, for at that time, according to all the historians, Albert was at Cologne,[28] and the *studium generale* there had already been definitely established. If, on the other hand, Thomas' arrival in Cologne is to be placed in 1246, it is necessary to suppose that there was at that time at least a project for the erection of a *studium generale* there, even in the absence of Albert. In point of fact, it was in 1247 that the project received official approbation, with confirmation in 1248 and the solemn inauguration of the *studium generale* of Cologne.[29] There is also a possibility that Thomas had been destined for the *studium generale* of Paris, but had been unable to remain there because that institution was just being divided and reduced, owing to the excessive burden that it was imposing on the Paris priory. He might well have been sent from there to the new *studium* at Cologne belonging to the German province. This movement of decentralization from the Dominican house of studies in Paris was the direct cause of the foundation of *studia generalia* on the same pattern in various provinces of the Order, notably at Montpellier in Provence, Bologna in Lombardy, Oxford in England, and Cologne in Germany. From this time onwards these were centres of the most intense zeal for learning.

The later hagiographers—perhaps owing to the obscurity of the historical problem itself—all record Thomas' going from Italy to Cologne, without any explicit mention of any stay or studies in Paris. This is the line taken by Rudolf of Nijmegen [30] in 1488, by Pizamanus [31] in 1497, by Claudius of Rota in the Life of St. Thomas printed at Lyons in 1555,[32] by the compiler of the biography in the *editio piana* of 1570,[33] by Ferdinand Castillo [34] in 1584, and by Serafino Razzi [35] in 1588. And in 1690 the editor of the chronicle of the masters-general [36] still insists on opposing the seventeenth century writers who claimed that Thomas studied in Paris. Then came Echard,[37] who held that Thomas studied at Cologne round 1245, in Paris 1245–1248, and then again at Cologne. This theory was followed by almost everyone until about 1885, the year in which Fr. Denifle published his history of the universities, and demolished Echard's hypothesis that St. Thomas ever studied in Paris before he went to Cologne.[38]

The opinion of Fr. Denifle was, however, revived by De Groot, Pelster, and Toso.[39] Pelster for his part shows that St. Thomas' study in Paris could not be historically proved and he grants a longer stay at Cologne [40] than Denifle, who limits that period to about four years, only long enough, that is, for Thomas to be publicly promoted to the degree of Doctor.[41] Pelster [42] holds that Thomas studied under Albert at Cologne in 1245, and again from 1248 until 1252.

In view of the fact that St. Thomas' studies in Paris cannot be proved from historical data, other modern writers—on the grounds that a journey to Paris could only have been undertaken for purposes of higher studies—take refuge in the theory of mere probability or hypothesis. Among these are Mandonnet,[43] Grabmann,[44] Castagnoli,[45] and Glorieux.[46]

If St. Thomas did study in Paris, he had many opportunities

in addition to attending the lectures of St. Albert in the school for "externs." He would have met many learned men, such as Fr. William d'Estampes, who taught in the Dominican school of the province of France, the Franciscans De la Rochelle and Odo Rigauld, the secular priests Aimeric of Veire, Peter Lambelle from Château-Thierry, Peter (known as, *dictus*) the Archbishop, Stephen of Poligny, Rudolf of Mondidier, John Pagus, Peter (*dictus*) Parvus, and also important people like the Bishop of Paris and Cardinal Odo of Châteauroux. It was the last-mentioned who took part, in 1247, in the lawsuit of the lecturers Raymund and John Brescain, and in the following year, in the condemnation of the Talmud. The same cardinal also preached the crusade which was led by Louis IX in 1248.

In the metropolis on the Rhine (Cologne was at that time the greatest city in Germany) the Dominican *studium* was for many years at the celebrated priory of Holy Cross.[47] It was here, according to De Loe and Pelster, that Albert was lecturing before being transferred to Paris,[48] and hither later he returned. In fact, so close was his association with the city that before ever he was called "the Great," he was known as Albert "the Teutonic" or "of Cologne."[49] Surely he must have loved this city before all others. Furthermore, while the *studia generalia* of the Dominicans at Montpellier, Bologna, and Oxford were all erected in cities where universities were already established, at Cologne the entire scientific authority reposed in Albert, the "Doctor universalis,"[50] who held a quite unique position of esteem both as a man and as a teacher. His own contemporaries, such as Pope Alexander IV,[51] scholars like Roger Bacon[52] and Ulrich of Strasburg,[53] and historians like Ptolemy of Lucca and the biographers of St. Thomas, all speak of him in the most remarkable terms of praise. For these last, while St. Augustine was the greatest doctor of the past,[54] Albert was that of the present. He was "the man of blameless life, who held the undisputed primacy among the doctors both in every branch of knowledge and in his manner of teaching."[55]

From his youth Albert had always had a passion for the countryside, the woods and fields and animals, and for the River Danube that flowed through his Swabian homeland. As a student in Italy he had become a careful observer of nature, of its physical and mineral characteristics. In Paris he had made a skilled examination of the Spanish prince's collection of sea-shells. All his life he had taken a keen interest in the forms and phenomena of nature. Now, as a philosopher, this training received its fulfilment in his championship of Christian Aristotelianism. This work indeed became his principal activity. Further, as a theologian, he was able to build up his system of sacred science with the most apt illustrations and observations. It was while he was lecturing in Paris that he began work on the great scientific encyclopedia, which was nearing completion in 1256 and was finished during the years that followed. Albert was indeed a noble spirit, intensely alive to every problem that confronts the mind. He was a great and generous master, an indefatigable worker in all that concerned the schools as well as in his priestly ministry, and, as a true son of the Order of St. Dominic, he never divorced his work as a scholar from that of the priest and religious. In addition to all this, he had the most remarkable personal gifts as a peacemaker both in the Church and in the state, and as a healer of dissensions between various cities and institutions as well as between private individuals.[56]

In the school of Albert the Great were found that Master and Disciple, sons and brothers in that " holy flock, obeying that Dominic, who hath a pathway shown " (Dante, *Paradiso*, X, 94–95, tr. Bickersteth), who, by the scholastic method, were to lead the mind of man to its highest conquests.[57] The poet places these word of wonder on the lips of Thomas:

> Questo che m'è a destra più vicino
> Frate e maestro fummi; ed esso Alberto
> È di Colonia, ed io Thomas d'Aquino.

My brother and my master, of Cologne,
neighbours me on my right: Albert his name,
and Thomas, called Aquinas, is my own.

Dante, *Paradiso*, X, 97–99 (tr. Bickersteth).

Fra Angelico painted the school of Albert with the young
Thomas sitting at the feet of the master.[58] The claims made by
medieval writers that science received so exceptional an im-
petus through the work of Albert and Thomas, were most
happily and explicitly confirmed by Pope Leo XIII when he
gave such warm commendation to the wisdom of the school-
men,[59] and again by Pope Pius XI when he canonized St. Albert. And memorable indeed were the words of Cardinal
Pacelli in his panegyric in the church of the Minerva in Rome
on April 10, 1932: " The giant tree of the *Summa Theologiae*,
planted by St. Thomas in the garden of the Church, and reaching out to the very heavens, has its mighty roots deep in the
fertile earth of the school of Albert the Great." [60]

The *studium* at Cologne was growing and now needed more
room. In the public archives at Cologne we find the fact mentioned that in 1248 a house near the Dominican priory was
acquired in the street called the Stolkgasse.[61] This can only
mean that the increased number of students now assigned to
this *studium generale* called for an enlargement of the living
quarters of the priory. The friars, some of them already ordained priests, some still only clerics, who came to pursue their
studies at the *studium generale* of Cologne, and who included
Thomas d'Aquino in their number, came from all parts of the
German province of the Order, which extended from the Alps
to the North Sea and the Baltic, and from Austria to Flanders.
In addition, there were probably already at this time students
from other provinces, from Denmark, Hungary, and England,
while Thomas represented the Roman province.[62]

Thomas, writes Tocco, " had no sooner heard him [Master
Albert] expound every science with such wondrous depths

of wisdom, than he rejoiced exceedingly at having so quickly found what he had come to seek: one who offered him so unsparingly the fulfilment of his heart's desire. And as if to show his very eagerness in attaining his goal, he began to be more than ever silent, more than ever assiduous in study and devout in prayer, storing up in his memory the learning he was later to pass on to others. And it happened that his utter simplicity and silence concealed all that he was learning from the master and all that God's own mercy taught him, so that his companions began to call him the ' dumb ox,' little knowing what mighty sound was later to come forth in his teaching." [63]

Ptolemy of Lucca [64] merely says that from this time onward he outstripped his fellows, but Tocco and Calo [65] give two special instances that show Thomas' progress during his student days at Cologne.

The first occurred while Master Albert was expounding the book of the Pseudo-Denis *De divinis nominibus.*[66] " A certain student, unaware of the hidden intellectual powers of Brother Thomas, offered in a kindly way to do him the service of a little coaching. Thomas in his humility accepted with every expression of gratitude. But the student had scarcely started when he lost the thread. So the learned Brother Thomas, as if God himself had given him authority to speak, went right through the argument step by step and even added a number of things that the master had not explained." Thereupon the student asked Brother Thomas to be his coach instead, to which Thomas willingly agreed, but on condition that no one should be told about it.

Soon enough, however, the master of students, as was only right, got to know about this remarkable facility in learning and store of knowledge which Thomas possessed.

The second instance is the story of the sheet of notes, which Thomas had made for his own use, on a question which Albert was at the time treating in his lectures. Thomas dropped this bit of paper by mistake in the passage just outside his own

room. One of his brethren picked it up and took it to Albert,
who was so much impressed by the intelligence and speculative power that these notes betrayed, that he decided to put
Thomas to the test on the next important occasion. This led
to the third instance of Thomas' remarkable intellectual attainments, for in the disputation that followed he fully manifested his brilliance.

Albert therefore called upon Thomas to make his first appearance in a scholastic disputation in which the student had
to uphold a thesis against the master himself. Thomas
acquitted himself so well that Albert, overcome with admiration for him, and quoting the nickname that the student from
Naples had been given, but using it now in a very different
way, suddenly exclaimed with the voice as of a prophet:
" We call him the dumb ox, but the lowing of that ox, when
he comes to teach, will resound throughout the whole world."
From then onward Albert always called upon Thomas to expound the more difficult scholastic problems. Scheeben looks
upon the above-mentioned solemn disputation before a select
public as an occasion of particular importance, marking the
end of Thomas' period of studies and his promotion to the
office of lector or *baccalaureus*.[67]

During St. Thomas' residence at Cologne, there is record
not only of his progress in study, but also of the abundant
fruits of his vast knowledge. William da Tocco observes:
" Then the aforesaid Master Albert began to expound the book
of the Ethics, adding certain enquiries of his own on the matter. Brother Thomas took careful note of the lectures and
proceeded to write out the whole himself . . . in the most
graceful manner and with the greatest subtlety of argument,
as was indeed possible when the work was drawn from the
springs of knowledge of so great a teacher who surpassed in
learning every man of his time." [68] This flow of moral teaching
from master to disciple and their agreement in matters of
moral science has been noticed in many and various ways in
their writings, first by John of Freiburg (†1314), and then

ever since down to our own times.[69] Msgr. Pelzer and Fr. Meersseman have in recent years carried out a fuller investigation of these commentaries on Aristotle's *Nichomachean Ethics*, and have compared the explanations given by St. Albert himself with those preserved in the notes taken by Brother Thomas.[70] It appears that in the commentary on the *Nichomachean Ethics*, St. Albert, contrary to his usual opinion, taught that the soul is not a *compositum* but a *simplex forma*. It would seem that this is the opinion of the disciple rather than of the master,[71] and if it is really contrary to the rest of Albert's teaching, it is a most valuable indication of the future trend of the disciple's teaching; for the latter took up the thought again later in more detail in his *De ente et essentia*. It may be that the *De ente et essentia*,[72] the date of which varies between 1250 and 1256 according to the chronology adopted, is no more than an elucidation of an original idea of St. Thomas, in which he disagreed with his master. The facts of the aforementioned disputation, of his scientific and literary output of the time, and of his long residence at Cologne, have inclined some modern authors, De Groot,[73] Berthier,[74] and Pelster,[75] to admit, at least as a probable opinion, that Thomas was a lector at the *studium* on the Rhine. Scandone, by an evident confusion, claims that he held the post of regent under Albert,[76] while Scheeben,[77] more exactly, admits that Thomas was Albert's *baccalaureus*. Denifle, however, in his notes, sets aside this view, basing himself on the authority of Bernard Gui and others who say that Thomas only studied *audiendo magistrum* at Cologne, and never taught there.[78] One may nevertheless take leave to differ from Denifle on this point.

There is good reason to suppose that it was during his residence at Cologne that Thomas was ordained priest. There is only one piece of historical evidence that can give us any indication in this matter, and that is the phrase in the Bull of Canonization which states that after his profession " he made

such progress both in science and in the things of the spirit
that he was raised to the priesthood while he was still
young." [79] And it was precisely at Cologne that his remarkable
progress in studies became manifest.

Various items of news reached Thomas from his distant
homeland while he was at Cologne: notably the death, on
December 13, 1250, at Castle Fiorentino, of Frederick II, who
had been called " stupor mundi et immutator saeculi," [80] and
who died, it appears, in the bosom of the Church.[81] Thomas
then remembered Frederick's benevolence during the better
years toward the d'Aquino and toward many of his Dominican
brethren,[82] and he pardoned the persecution and trouble that
the defunct sovereign had so many times brought upon the
friars and upon his own brothers.

Thomas of Cantimpré and Ptolemy of Lucca relate that
while Thomas was at Cologne the Pope offered him the dignity
of the abbacy of Montecassino.[83] This position in the Benedictine arch-abbey was twice vacant during the years from
1240 to 1254. The first time was at the death of Abbot
Stephen II on January 21, 1248,[84] and the second after the
short-lived rule of a certain Nicholas, who appears in 1251,[85]
and who was followed by an interregnum of three years. " In
point of fact," observes Inguanez, " the Cassinese documents
between 1251 and 1254 . . . are made out in the name of an
official of the abbey . . . without mention of an abbot. But
by December 24, 1254, Montecassino seems to have had an
abbot once more: " [86] a certain Richard, who was made a
cardinal by Alexander IV, and not by Innocent IV, as has
sometimes been thought. Richard was deposed by Alexander IV in 1259.[87] According to Ptolemy, it would have been
Alexander IV (1254–1261) who offered the abbacy to Thomas
d'Aquino. But at that time he was no longer at Cologne; and
Ptolemy is therefore contradicting himself. But if we admit
that Cantimpré is right, Thomas was invited to the pontifical
court and offered the abbacy by Pope Innocent IV (1243–
1254).

Behind the papal offer of this prelacy lay motives quite other than the desire to confer special distinction on Thomas Aquinas. The family was to reap considerable material benefits from the appointment. Some of the d'Aquino who had rebelled against Frederick had been put to death (like Ronald), and others, it is to be presumed, suffered exile or various other trials. These exiles, driven from the Kingdom of Naples, would have taken refuge at Montesangiovanni in the papal territory, with their income, however, seriously diminished. Herein lies the reason for steps being taken to get for one of the family some ecclesiastical benefice which could provide for their needs.[88] Ptolemy states this quite plainly. The fact that Innocent IV in 1254 appointed Marotta, the sister of Aimo d'Aquino, " most devoted to him and to the Church," as abbess of the Benedictine nuns of St. Mary's at Capua, is one more indication of the Pope's effort to repay the services rendered to him by the d'Aquino of Roccasecca.[89]

But anyway, Thomas from his youth had refused ecclesiastical dignities, and was going to continue to do so. He had no wish to abandon the life of a friar.[90]

It is possible that Thomas was already in Cologne when the first stone of the new cathedral was laid, and he may therefore have assisted at that solemn ceremony. The famous cathedral " in which are preserved the bodies of three holy Magi " had been twice destroyed by fire, and the Cologne chapter decided to rebuild it in the grandest possible manner. Pope Innocent IV encouraged the faithful to assist in this work by granting an indulgence which bears the date of May 21, 1248.[91]

The first stone was laid on August 15, 1248, and work was pushed on with eagerness. Thomas could have assisted at the preparations, and watched the House of God rising before his eyes, as day by day he was being prepared and guided by Divine Providence to raise the mighty and wondrous edifice of his scholastic teaching. On November 1, Archbishop Conrad of Hochstaden, who had begun the work, crowned William of Holland as King of the Romans at Aachen.[92]

On the feast of the Epiphany in 1249 King William passed through Cologne, and we may well believe that Thomas, together with the other friars of Cologne, was present at the civic honors offered to him on that occasion, especially since the king was entertained as the guest of Master Albert at the Dominican Priory.[93]

Chapter Six

Graduate in Paris

1252–1255

THE UNIVERSITY OF PARIS — DOMINICAN LECTURERS
— THE POSITION OF A "BACHELOR" — HOSTILITY TO-
WARD THE MENDICANT ORDERS — THOMAS' LECTURES,
WRITINGS, AND DISPUTATIONS — HIS COMMENTARY
ON THE "SENTENCES" — HIS NOVEL APPROACH TO
PROBLEMS AND THEIR EXPOSITION — HIS APPOINT-
MENT TO A PROFESSORIAL CHAIR

THE famous letter of February 4, 1254, addressed by the University of Paris to the hierarchy of the Church and to all students, is a plentiful source of information on the history of that great centre of studies in the Middle Ages. In this letter we read that "it was God's own right hand that planted in Paris this venerable *Studium*, a fountain of wisdom, divided into its four faculties: theology, law, medicine, and philosophy (the last being divided into its three parts: rational, natural, and moral), which like the four rivers of paradise directed to the four quarters of the world, water and enrich the whole earth, so that inestimable advantage both spiritual and temporal is brought to Christendom." [1]

To this centre, especially of theological and philosophical studies, which was at the time truly international, St. Dominic, the founder of the Order of Preachers, had sent his sons, who arrived in Paris on November 12, 1217.[2] At first they fixed their residence at the hospice of St. Mary opposite the bishop's

57

palace, but at the insistence of their protector, Master John
of Barastre, dean of Saint-Quentin, they exchanged it for a
place near the church of St. James. August 6, 1218, when the
Friars Preachers took possession of their new house near
St. James', can truly be considered the birthday of that famous
priory and of the first *studium generale* of the sons of St. Dominic. At Paris, John de Barastre with his authority and his
learning was a very great help to the Dominicans and gave
them continuous encouragement; the university gave them the
most invaluable aid [3] when once they " began to apply themselves zealously to the study of theology " [4] and to earn for
themselves an excellent name by their life and their scholarship alike. A proof of this is in the academic degrees that they
took, thus shedding glory also upon their own Order. The
first of them to rise to the position of professor, or master, in
about 1229, was Roland of Cremona,[5] who after a short period
of teaching was assigned to Toulouse and left the university
chair to his fellow Dominican, Hugh de Saint-Cher.[6] The
Order of Preachers obtained another chair when the English-
man John of St. Giles, master of theology and of medicine,[7]
joined the Order, according to Mandonnet in 1230, according
to Ehrle about 1232.[8] When the Order had thus obtained two
professorships, the continuity of its teachers and professors
in the University was assured by the timely dispatch of graduates, or bachelors (*baccalaurei*) to Paris, while the masters
of theology trained in Paris were sent elsewhere as professors,
to the great advantage of the Church and the Order. So it
happened that the Dominicans were gradually beginning to
carry weight in the learned world, both at the *alma mater* on
the Seine, and elsewhere. Now that the Order was committed
to filling two chairs at the University, the formation of suitable
subjects in the Order became a prime necessity. This formation was assured by the rules governing the conferring of
university degrees, laid down for the theological faculty in
the foundation-statute of the Cardinal Legate, Robert de
Courson, in 1215, which decreed that " no one shall teach in

Paris unless he is at least thirty-five years old, has studied for at least five years, has followed the courses of exposition of the books of theology, and has attended theological lectures for five years before ever giving public lectures himself." [9] This means that before a man could be authorized to give public instruction, he had to have completed eight years of study, three in the Arts and five in Theology.[10] At the conclusion of these studies he could graduate to the baccalaureate, and so enter upon an intermediate stage in which he was no longer an undergraduate, but not yet a master.[11] In the *Chartularium* of the University of Paris the first mention of such graduates is in 1231.[12] Blessed Jordan, who was a graduate of Paris in 1220, speaks in his letters of graduates or bachelors at Paris and Vercelli.[13]

The work of a bachelor of theology, especially during the first half of the thirteenth century, consisted in the exposition of the Scriptures or of the *historiae, i.e.,* biblical history, but later, about the middle of the century, also of the *Sentences.*[14] At any rate, in early times no formal examination was required for admission to the baccalaureate, and selection by the master who directed the candidate's studies was sufficient.[15] The master had to form a judgment on the intellectual attainments of his candidate, and on his aptitude for teaching, and he then had to take the responsibility himself.[16] Among the mendicant orders, the head of the order also had the right to present a candidate. Thus we have John of Parma, minister-general of the Friars Minor, giving to Brother Bonaventure the task of teaching in Paris,[17] and in 1251 or 1252 we find John the Teutonic, master-general of the Order of Preachers, appointing a bachelor of theology for the *studium* of Paris.

It appears, in fact, from an explicit statement, that John commissioned Master Albert the Teutonic, resident in Cologne, to choose a suitable friar for the post of bachelor in the *studium* of Paris. And Albert, having not only no doubts, but even remarkable evidence of the intellectual powers and praiseworthy life which appeared in his disciple Brother

Thomas d'Aquino, could not possibly hesitate in his choice, and " wrote to the said master [general of the Order], urging him to call upon Brother Thomas d'Aquino to be bachelor in the aforesaid *studium* [of Paris], at the same time describing to him his suitability both with regard to his learning and his manner of life." [18] According to the statute of Cardinal de Courson, an exemplary life and sufficient learning were the first necessities for a teacher in Paris.[19] But the general of the Order did not see his way to accepting this candidate straight away, even though he was proposed by a professor of such distinction, since Brother Thomas' " merits were as yet unknown " to the master-general.[20] This fact sheds considerable light upon certain events in the earlier period of Thomas' life, in particular upon the matter of the " double " journey which some authors maintain was made in the company of the master-general John in 1244 and 1245, either from Rome to Acquapendente or from Rome to Paris. On these occasions John would have had ample opportunity to discover not only the mode of life but also the intellectual capacity of Thomas, and would have had no reason for doubting Albert's word. It should be observed in addition that the problem of appointing a bachelor involved taking into account not only the person appointed, but the difficulties of the position itself, especially in view of the delicate situation in Paris, of which we shall speak presently.

However, in spite of the objection raised, Albert did not give up his proposal, but began to urge it with renewed vigor. He found an unexpected supporter of his plan in Cardinal Hugh de Saint-Cher, who had been regent in Paris.[21] The cardinal had been chosen by Innocent IV as papal legate to deal with the affairs of the German Empire, and in the summer of 1251 he was traveling from Burgundy through Alsace and Hesse [22] to the Rhenish capital. It seems that the Dominican master-general, John, met the legate, Cardinal Hugh, twice: the first time probably when both of them were visiting the camp of William of Holland, the King of Germany, near

Rüdesheim, during the August of that year, and the second time in 1252 at Soest in Westphalia.[23] At one of these meetings, Cardinal Hugh, urged by a letter from Albert, so far influenced the master-general that he approved Thomas Aquinas as bachelor in Paris. In fact, " at the instance of the Lord Cardinal Hugh, the master accepted him [Thomas] as bachelor in the aforesaid *studium* [of Paris], writing to him and ordering him to proceed at once to Paris and prepare himself to expound the *Sentences*." [24] This vital decision on the part of the master-general of the Order of Preachers was taken on the advice and urgent recommendation of none less than Albert the Great. Now begins Thomas Aquinas' public life, which was to be so full of problems, upon all of which, however, he was to bring to bear the power of his mind and the generosity of his spirit. Until now his path of religious life had lain within the sheltered walls of God's House, be it in the abbey of Montecassino or in the mendicant priories at Naples or Cologne, under the guidance of masters who led him on to the science of the saints and to the summits of human and divine wisdom. Now Divine Providence was requiring him to find his own path, to look into the future and to overcome its problems, although remaining dependent upon his superiors and in close collaboration with his own brethren. This thought must surely have softened the blow of separation from Albert, the master he loved so well. Now, although he was to preserve his filial devotion to him, he was to leave the very master who had decided the matter of his promotion to Paris.

With regard to the route of Thomas' journey from the Rhine to the Seine, the historians can do no more than conjecture. Some of them maintain [25] that Thomas traveled by Aachen, Maastricht, and Louvain, and on the way passed through a part of the Duchy of Brabant, for he later dedicated a theological treatise to the duchess. The precise time of the year when he reached Paris cannot be decided.

Thomas Aquinas was certainly in Paris by 1252. In his inaugural lecture, then called the *principium*, he took as his text the words of the prophet Baruch (4.1), *Hic est liber mandatorum Dei et lex quae est in aeternum.*[26] From henceforth he so organized his life that his entire energy was devoted to his public lectures, and by his astonishing application to the work in hand, by the profundity of his thought and the clarity of his exposition he showed himself to be a model of the university lecturer.

But it was a very turbulent and difficult time for the mendicant friars at Paris University.

It was in the year of Thomas' arrival in Paris, in 1252, that there arose in the university a great struggle between those theological lecturers who belonged to the secular clergy and those of the mendicant orders.[27] The struggle was to continue for a good twenty years, and several times Aquinas was to find himself in the very midst of it.

This struggle had various causes. The first was a certain friction between the two groups, which arose from a feeling among the seculars that they had been overshadowed by the powerful influence of the mendicants' teaching during the previous fifteen years. Denifle observes in this connexion [28] that there must have been some points of irregularity in the conduct of the mendicants, and perhaps even of Albert and Thomas themselves, with respect to existing practice in the university. A further reason is suggested by Halphen for this animosity, namely, that the seculars looked upon the friars as exponents and instruments of Vatican policy with regard to university affairs.[29] In this they cannot be said to have been wrong. It is sufficient to read d'Irsay's account of how the Holy See with inexorable logic and with consistent success was gradually taking control of the universities of Europe.[30] Coulton calls the friars " a papal militia." While King Louis IX was away in the East (1248–1254),[31] there was more hope of success for those lecturers who were opposing the mendicants, and a better chance of putting a check upon their rapidly growing influence in the university.

Thus, in a statute published in February, 1252, the theo-

logical faculty limited the number of religious to be admitted
to a lectureship, and decreed that the friars might have but
one master of theology as regent over a single school of
theology.[32] Apparently the religious orders paid no attention
to this decree, which had been drawn up without their being
consulted. In March, 1253, a police intervention infringed
upon the privileges of the university and many of the lecturers
proposed to withhold their courses. The three professors from
the mendicant orders refused to take the oath prescribed by
the decree,[33] but it is certain that the Dominicans would have
taken the oath if their two schools had been recognized. The
secular professors were greatly irritated by the whole situation,
and decided not to admit into the Corporation of the Masters
anyone who had refused to take an oath accepting not only
the papal ordinances relative to the University of Paris, but
also the statutes of the Masters themselves. This meant that
the Friars Preachers were thrust out of the teaching body.
The religious orders immediately appealed to the regent of
the kingdom and to the pope. Pope Innocent IV took the
matter much to heart, and began by repeated insistence on
the rehabilitation of the mendicant professors.[34] But later he
changed his mind. William of Saint-Amour in the Franche-
Comté, professor of theology in Paris and chief mover of the
opposition to the mendicants,[35] used all his evil skill to blacken
the reputation and the purity of doctrine of the friars, especially when a certain Franciscan, Fr. Gerard of Borgo San
Donnino, a lector in Paris, published in 1254 a somewhat
unfortunate work entitled *Introductorius in evangelium aeternum*. In this " introduction " to the three principal writings
of Joachim da Flora, which Gerard called the " everlasting
gospel " (although Joachim himself only thus described his
general teaching), the secular professors found thirty-one
errors.[36] William of Saint-Amour, as the delegate of his colleagues, hastened to the papal court, where he arrived in July,
1254, to secure the condemnation of Gerard's book. He then
proceeded to elaborate his accusations. It was now no longer

merely a matter of the mendicants having university professorships; it was their ideal of poverty and even the legitimacy of
their exercise of priestly functions that was at stake.[37] Already
in May, Innocent IV had curtailed certain rights of the regular
clergy, but now, in the bull *Etsi animarum* of November 21,
he canceled the privileges of the mendicants.[38] However, when
he died (on December 7), the hopes of the regulars were
raised once more. And in fact, Alexander IV's bull *Quasi
lignum vitae* of April 14, 1255, revoked the previous decision
of Innocent IV,[39] restored the former juridical position, and
composed the affairs of the university in a just and compre-
hensive way.

William of Saint-Amour was furious. In March, 1255, he
had produced a pamphlet entitled *De periculis novissimorum
temporum*,[40] and now in June, 1255, in order to evade the
papal ordinances, he proposed that each of his colleagues
among the university professors should resign individually,
and that in the autumn the courses of lectures should be suspended.[41] But Alexander IV did not withdraw his good will
toward the mendicants, even though he had to make a pronouncement upon the *Introductorius* of Gerard of Borgo San
Donnino. Actually, the writings of the Franciscan, together
with those of Abbot Joachim, were examined by a commission
of cardinals, with the result that on October 23, 1255, the
pope condemned the *Introductorius*. The author was pun-
ished with perpetual imprisonment in his own province.[42]
But Alexander IV remained the friend of the religious. The
leaders of the faction in Paris, however, were far from inactive.
They even went to the length of not only trying in every way
to impede the apostolic and scientific work of the Dominicans,
but of attempting to take away their good name by every kind
of calumny, so that the brethren, " who lived solely on the
charity of the faithful, were so haunted by the fear of those
clerics that they hardly dared to set foot outside their priory
to go and buy something to eat." [43] In sermons popular feeling
was roused against the friars. The climax of these troubles

came in December, 1255, and January, 1256. It was at the beginning of 1256 that the king, St. Louis IX, had to place a military guard near St. James' to ensure the personal safety of the friars.[44]

The master-general, Humbert de Romans, wrote a celebrated letter, manifesting his worry over the Paris crisis, and asking all members of the Order to rally round him and implore the divine assistance in bringing the affair to a happy conclusion. He writes: " The fact is that many of the masters in sacred theology in Paris have become jealous of the great number of our teachers, of our large audiences, and of our success in teaching, and so one day they formed a party, and although they were unable to take legal proceedings against us, they began a great campaign of serious and dangerous accusations against us and against all the religious orders "; and he concludes: " We desire to recommend to your charitable prayers these matters which briefly [we have described to you], so that, being made aware of the true state of affairs, you may be moved by supernatural compassion and pity, and, while an attempt is being made by diabolical intrigue to bring ruin on the whole Order, you may multiply your own prayers to Christ, to his Virgin Mother, our Order's special advocate, to our blessed Father Dominic, and to the holy and glorious martyr Peter, whose blood so recently shed cries (we hope) to Heaven for the defense of his Order . . . and so that you yourselves, when the need arises, may hasten to our defense by proclaiming our innocence." [45]

Fr. Thomas was an eye-witness of these troubles. He saw their beginning, followed carefully the development of the struggle, and eventually put into writing his own judgment on the matter in his *Contra impugnantes Dei cultum et religionem*.[46]

Meanwhile he was carrying on diligently his work as bachelor. He taught under the master Elias Brunet, who was at the head of the " school for externs " from 1248 to 1256.[47]

At the beginning the task of the bachelor was to give classes upon two books of Scripture. Although this is not in fact recorded by William da Tocco, who does not mention in detail the material taught by St. Thomas at the beginning of his bachelorship, the rules of the University of Paris are well known, and according to these the bachelor (who was the *cursorius biblicus*) began with a year's lectures upon two books of Scripture, and then proceeded to a two years' course on the *Sentences*.[48] But the record of Aquinas' course on the Scriptures given as bachelor during the year 1252-1253, or, as others[49] maintain, during the two years 1252-1254, seems to have been lost, unless, as Pelster holds, it has been preserved in the expositions of Isaias, Jeremias, and Lamentations; the commentary on the *Sentences* of Peter the Lombard is to be assigned to the following two years, 1253-1255.[50] The opusculum *De principiis naturae ad fratrem Silvestrum* is usually placed in the year 1255.[51] But let us return to the commentary on the Lombard. In his course on the work of the Master of the *Sentences*, Thomas devoted a prologue and then a series of questions to the exposition of the 182 distinctions contained in the four books of the Lombard. The autograph of Thomas' commentary on the third book of the *Sentences* is preserved in the Vatican Library, in Cod. Vat. Lat. n. 9851.

The great *Commentary on the Sentences*, writes Grabmann,[52] is a youthful work (and consequently one or two points were understood more correctly later on); it is an excellent and more or less organically conceived exposition of the text. It is the result of the lectures given by Thomas as bachelor in the University of Paris (1254-1256), and it was held in great esteem by the early Thomists. There is more evidence of the influence of the Augustinian school and of Avicenna in this work than in Thomas' later writings. An examination of the *Commentary on the Sentences*, which treats of many questions at greater length than the *Summa Theologiae*, helps us to understand St. Thomas' intellectual progress and the definitive maturity which is represented in the *Summa Theologiae*.

Apart from his lectures, it was Thomas' duty as bachelor to appear at disputations and defend theses indicated by the master under whom he worked, as well as to answer objections put by selected members of the audience to these theses.

Now, a scientific affirmation is arrived at by means of the exposition of the truth and the confutation of error, and St. Thomas from his youth showed in his scientific affirmations not only an extraordinary clarity of insight but also a wonderful personal conviction and devotion in the matter of truth. Thus it was that these qualities, which from now on were to meet with so much adversity, were noticeable in him from his first entrance into the academic world. This explains, on the one hand, the definite feeling that an innovation in teaching was being introduced by the school of Albert and Thomas, and the traditional school especially of the Franciscans, with the consequent alertness to all possible opposition or hostile trends in doctrine. It also explains, on the other hand, the recognition that was to come later of the new attitude in teaching that Thomas was taking up in the formal disputations of the schools. This is particularly clear in the account given by William da Tocco,[53] even though his view of the Saint's early days is doubtless to some extent colored by the impressions of his later triumphs.

Tocco says: "Thomas began to bring forth in his teaching that which he had formerly kept hidden under the cloak of silence, for God indeed infused into him such wisdom, and such was the learning imparted from his lips, that he seemed to outstrip all, even the masters themselves, and the lucidity of his teaching more than that of any other incited the students to a love of learning. In his lectures he started new enquiries, found new and brilliant solutions, and brought new arguments into the disputations. None who heard him propound this novel teaching and overcome difficulties by his new methods was able to doubt that God himself was illuminating him with rays of hitherto unknown light; for he had shown at once so sure a judgment that he had been able without any hesitation both to teach and to write novel opinions, on which God must certainly have deigned to give him special inspiration. Thus, during his bachelorship and the first period of his mastership, he composed a work upon the four books of the *Sentences,* which was at once elegant in style, profound in doctrine, lucid in exposition, and rich in novel enquiries."

After this glorious success, he had to be presented to the chancellor of the university to receive permission to preach and teach in public: the degree of "licentiate." [54] But before this permission would be granted, the chancellor had to have time to seek information from the professors and other eminent persons about the candidate, his capacities, and his chances of success. [55] This was done by means of certain regular enquiries.

Then the chancellor, acting according to his conscience, granted or refused the permission. [56] In the case of Fr. Thomas there cannot have been the slightest doubt about his capacities. The chancellor, Aimeric of Veire, [57] when he had granted the licentiate to Fr. Thomas d'Aquino, was duly congratulated by Pope Alexander IV in a special letter dated March 3, 1256. And, indeed, if the chancellor had not of himself granted the licentiate in this case, the pope would have compelled him to do so, for he ordered him to make arrangements that the aforesaid friar should thereupon start teaching in the theological faculty of his university. [58] It was this degree that gave to Fr. Thomas d'Aquino as a bachelor the right to teach in public, to preach, and to exercise the functions of a master, as well as to join the *consortium* of the masters.

The first duty after receiving the licentiate was to take an oath to observe the statutes of the faculty, drawn up by the college of the masters. [59] The next duty was to give an inaugural lecture, known as the *principium.* [60] And the chancellor then directed the prior of the Dominican house in Paris to "order the aforesaid Brother Thomas in his name to prepare himself without further ado to receive the degree of master in sacred theology." [61]

So the date was fixed on which Fr. Thomas, licentiate in the faculty of theology, should deliver his *principium*. But life in the University of Paris was far from tranquil, and the Dominicans were ready, in order to preserve peace, even to renounce this claim to a second professorial chair, had not the pope expressly forbidden them to take such a course. In these circumstances it is not surprising that there were certain people anxious to foment trouble and dissension who placed all kinds of obstacles in the way of those who intended to be present at St. Thomas' discourse. This is evident in a letter of Alexander IV, written on June 17, 1256, in which among other things we find this passage: " The aforesaid masters and students have had no care, as we well know, to preserve that concord which the thorns of discord have assailed. They have opposed in the most unworthy manner those who desired to attend the lectures, disputations, and sermons of the friars, and in particular those who wished to be present at the inaugural lecture of our beloved son Fr. Thomas d'Aquino." [62] There was now no more question of preventing Thomas Aquinas from entering upon his career as professor.

Chapter Seven

Professor in Paris

1256–1259

IN the period between the pope's letter of March, 1256, and that of June, Thomas held his solemn inaugural lecture or *principium*,[1] after Aimeric, the chancellor of the university, had obtained the approval which gave Thomas preference over others who were senior to himself: *non servato ordine secundum anticipationem temporis consueto*, as Tocco puts it.[2] Thomas had not reached the age of thirty-five, as prescribed by the university regulations. It is recorded that he began by excusing himself, but was then ordered under obedience to give the inaugural lecture, and so implored the divine assistance—according to some, before the altar,[3] according to others, in the privacy of his cell[4]—and "besought the Lord with tears that he should give him wisdom and grace worthily to begin and continue the office of master." Among other prayers he recited Psalm 11, which begins with the words: "Save me, O Lord, for there is now no saint: truths are de-cayed from among the children of men." And he had the privilege of receiving from a heavenly messenger, who was attired as a Friar Preacher, the suggestion of a text for his lecture,[5] namely v. 13 of Psalm 103: *Rigans montes de superi-oribus suis:* "Thou waterest thy hills from thy upper rooms: the earth shall be filled with the fruit of thy works." "And these words were not only the theme of that discourse, but were a presage of all that lay in him to do." [6]

This episode is already to be found in the *Vitae Fratrum,* that record of edification and history.[7] Fr. Peter Capotto, O.P., of Benevento, recounts that he was much struck by this pas-sage when he heard it read during the customary periodic cupping, on August 13, 1319, while he was a student in Paris. He adds that it was commonly said in Paris that the messenger who appeared to Thomas was none other than St. Dominic himself.[8] Be that as it may, there is no doubt that the sober account of the *Vitae Fratrum* and of other sources [9] took definite form in the story as told by Capotto.

After Thomas had delivered his *principium,* he now received a professorial chair as doctor and master, and thereupon be-came regent of a regular school. But on account of the dis-sensions between the seculars and regulars, the newly-created doctor did not receive full membership in the university Corpo-ration of Masters, which was usually granted by the College of Professors.[10] Like St. Bonaventure, who had received the degree in 1253 but had not yet been admitted to the Corpora-tion,[11] so also Aquinas had to wait. It is obvious that this pro-cedure of the Parisian Masters in relation to professors from the mendicant orders does not reflect any honor upon their College. It was only by papal authority of Alexander IV, ex-pressed in a bull of October 23, 1256, that the Parisian masters belonging to the secular clergy were compelled " to accept the friars Thomas d'Aquino of the Order of Preachers and

Bonaventure of the Order of Friars Minor, masters in sacred
theology, both being explicitly mentioned by name." [12] This
was carried out in the following August, when " in the year of
Our Lord 1257, on the Sunday preceding the Assumption of
Our Lady, in plenary session convoked in the Franciscan
Friary of Paris, Master Christian of Verdun," [13] in the presence
of the delegate of Reginald Mignon, Bishop of Paris (1250–
1268), [14] made the formal declaration that Fr. Thomas
d'Aquino and Fr. Bonaventure were admitted to membership
of the teaching body and the University of Paris." [15] Later,
Bonaventure was made general of his Order, but Thomas
remained in the profession of teaching.

The fact that the College of Professors so unjustly and un-
warrantably delayed in publicly recognising Thomas and
Bonaventure, and excluded them from full membership of
their body, made no difference to their position as teachers, [16]
for as soon as the degree was conferred upon them, they both
began their work in public as regular and independent lecturers, Bonaventure in 1253 and Thomas at the latest in 1256.

The moment when Thomas was approved as master, and
had the degree conferred upon him, marks the end of the
period of his education and scientific formation. The noble
city of Paris, the *alma mater studiorum,* was now no longer
responsible for his intellectual upbringing and education: it
was he who was now to give her " of his own unspeakable
riches." [17] These words of the famous letter of the Paris faculty
of philosophy are understood by Denifle [18] to refer exclusively
to his position in the university as bachelor and professor,
while Mandonnet and others consider the reference to be to
his time there as a student, as well as a bachelor and professor. [19] A bachelor was at once a disciple and a teacher, who
began his work by teaching " in sacra pagina " and went on to
become a regular public lecturer. [20] The news that Thomas
d'Aquino was now a Master in Christendom's supreme centre
of studies was received with particular joy and satisfaction in

his own Roman province of the Order, which was then governed by Fr. Thomas Agni or by his immediate successor.[21]

It has been already explained how the Dominicans ran two schools in Paris, the one being known as the "internal" and reserved for members of the French province, and the other "external," in which there were teachers from other provinces. Of course Thomas taught in the "external" school.[22]

From henceforth Thomas devoted himself to fulfilling the duties of a Master, which meant lectures, disputations, and sermons. These things constituted the task of a doctor or professor in the university. The lectures were his routine work; from time to time there were the official scholastic disputations; and preaching was regarded as an integral part of the work of teaching.[23]

The academic year began in September and continued until the Feast of SS. Peter and Paul, and although not every day was "legibilis," yet the course of lectures amounted to 42 weeks. The masters gave their classes in the morning between the hours of Prime and Terce; these were followed between Terce and Sext by the bachelors' classes on the *Sentences.*[24]

Thomas, during his professorship, lectured principally on the Scriptures, since the Bible was the foundation of all theological teaching. According to Mandonnet it was at this period that he gave classes on the Book of Isaias and on the Gospel of St. Matthew.[25] His commentary on Isaias has been preserved for us in the form of an *expositio,* that is, notes written by the lecturer himself, while the commentary on St. Matthew exists at least in part as a *lectura,* that is, in the form of notes taken down by one of the students [26]: in this case Peter of Andria and Leger of Besançon.[27]

As professor, Thomas also had to preside at disputations.[28]

Disputations were of two kinds: the regular ones, and the extra ones (de quolibet). The *quaestiones disputatae (ordinariae)* are the records of the regular disputations, held by the professor of theology several times in the course of the year on the main problems of theology and philosophy treated in a connected series. They usually represent the maturer results of the professor's learning, and special points are discussed from a central point of view with great depth and subtlety of reasoning.[29] The procedure of a disputation was as follows: the professor would propose a thesis to the students and the general audience. The thesis was expounded and defended by the *respondens,* who most frequently was the bachelor. Objections could then be put by students and by the professor, who had the right to intervene when he wished, and finally to sum up. In his next lecture the professor could draw up the material of the disputation in proper form. A *quaestio disputata* was the result of such a formulation of the material after a regular disputation. The problem chosen by the professor for discussion might extend over a number of disputations. St. Thomas' *quaestiones disputatae* on the soul number 21.

Among these serial disputations, there were sometimes intercalated separate ones, such as that of St. Thomas *De opere manuali religiosorum,* which was held in 1255 or 1256, when he was writing his *Contra impugnantes.* It was afterwards included among his *quodlibetales* or extra disputations, although it does not strictly belong to these.[30]

The *quaestiones disputatae* are "a large collection (63 *quaestiones* comprising 400 articles) of very profound treatises on all the most important arguments in theology," and St. Thomas here gives a fuller and more complete treatment of the various problems than he does in his other works. They are in consequence the key to the understanding of all his writings, since more than any others they show us his manner of thought, expression, and development. They were composed at various times as occasion arose, and they have been collected, unhappily not too methodically, under the following headings: *De potentia, De malo, De spiritualibus creaturis, De virtutibus,* and *De veritate.* A more satisfactory arrangement would be in three groups: *De ente et potentia, De veri-*

tate et cognitione, and *De bono et appetitu,* which would provide a fairly complete survey of *Ontology* from both the theological and philosophical points of view, of the *Theory of Knowledge,* and of *Ethics.* In great part the *quaestiones disputatae* run parallel to the growth of the *Summa Theologiae,* and are therefore the most valuable and sure commentary on a considerable part of the latter work. They supply, by their extent and their thoroughness, further explanation of many passages in the *Summa* where Thomas is brief and concise, according to the confessed object of this work, which was to provide beginners with a simple textbook.[31]

The *quaestiones quodlibetales* are the records of disputations held by the professor of theology twice a year, before Christmas and before Easter, in which were discussed random questions from the most varied fields of theology and cognate sciences. The *Quodlibeta* demonstrate most forcibly the unity of the whole of medieval theology (Exegesis, Dogma, Moral, Liturgy, Canon Law, and the discussion of particular *Casus*), and reflect a very fine period in the history of thought and culture at the time.[32] The *Quodlibeta* deal with problems of the moment, apologetics, and even personal matters.[33] Only masters who were regents, that is regular professors, were entitled to preside at these disputations, though anyone present was able to put forward problems for discussion. Under the aegis of his master, the bachelor answered the questions. The master helped him and either confirmed or corrected his answers.

Mandonnet wished to see in St. Thomas the originator of this kind of disputation. But the facts provided by other historians show clearly that already before St. Thomas' time disputations *de quolibet* had been held by Alexander of Hales, Warrick of Saint-Quentin, Robert Grosseteste, and Walter of Château Thierry.[34]

The teaching and the disputations of Thomas Aquinas earned universal praise. He always had great crowds of students at his lectures, as William da Tocco observes: " When

he was declared a Master, the mighty doctor began his classes
and disputations, and so great was the multitude of students
who flocked to hear him that the lecture-hall could scarce
contain them, for the instruction of so great a master drew
them, nay, drove them, along the path of progress in study." [35]
It is difficult, however, to mention by name many who were
among his students. One certainly was Brother Nicholas of
Marsillac, a small village in the département Haute-Loire, who
later, round 1306, was counselor and chaplain to the King
of Cyprus. Brother Nicholas noticed especially St. Thomas'
spirit of poverty and his purity of mind.[36] When he was writing the *Summa contra Gentiles,* Nicholas tells us, he only used
" schedulae minutae," scraps of notebooks or poor quality
paper, for he had no good paper. Others of his students were
of course the note-takers, Peter of Andria and Leger of
Besançon.[37]

Time passed quickly for the master, always busy with intellectual preoccupations, but the fragrance of his holiness did
not pass unobserved. William da Tocco makes a brief reference to the interior life of the young professor: " Witness to
the purity of mind and of body of this doctor is given by
Fr. Raymund Severi of the same Order, who more than once
affirmed on oath that when he was in Paris with the aforesaid
doctor, he did not remember a single occasion during the
seven years that they were together, when he mentioned in
confession having ever given consent to a fleshly temptation,
and that he hardly ever had even any ' motus primi-primi,'
and that during that time they always went to confession to
each other and served each other's Masses. And the aforesaid
Fr. Raymund was a very religious and honorable man, whom
we are entitled, through his long intimacy with the holy doctor, to consider a saint." [38] This Raymund Severi entered the
Order of Preachers in 1250, and so was probably a little
younger than Aquinas. During the seven years (1252–1259)
that they could have been together every day, Raymund
seems to have been appointed a sort of companion to the

bachelor and later to the master. In 1267 we find him assigned as lector in theology to the priory of Béziers in his own province, that of Provence, and finally in 1277 and again in 1302 he was proclaimed a preacher-general. At one time he was subprior at Montpellier, where he was known to Peter Capotto, one of the witnesses at St. Thomas' process of canonization.[39]

Doubtless Thomas, as master, would have been on friendly terms with the bachelor who taught under him and for whom he was responsible. This was probably Annibaldo degli Annibaldi during the years 1258–1260.[40] He would, of course, also have known intimately his colleagues who were at the time teaching in the "internal" school belonging to the Paris province and reserved for French masters. Among these would have been Florentius of Hesdin, Hugh of Metz, and Bartholomew of Tours.[41] The future professors, Blessed Peter of Tarentaise, William of Alton, and Annibaldo degli Annibaldi, would naturally have been among his friends,[42] and they must certainly have often talked and exchanged ideas with their Neapolitan colleague. He must often have had learned discussions with Vincent of Beauvais, who had been the tutor of Prince Louis of France and was still held in the highest esteem by his royal disciple.[43] He would have enjoyed the company and the kindness of the provincials of the province of France: after Humbert de Romans (1244–1254), Theodoric of Auxerre (1254–1258) and William of Séguin (1258–1261).[44]

Outside his own Order, Thomas was especially friendly with the sons of the seraphic patriarch St. Francis, and this for several reasons, not the least of which was the fact that the Franciscans and Dominicans found themselves united in the same cause, being equally embroiled in the question of the mendicants which was troubling the whole university at the time. It was surely not merely fortuitous nor without advantage to Christendom as a whole, that on February 2, 1255, the generals of the two Orders, John of Parma and Humbert

de Romans, wrote a most beautiful joint letter on peace and
unity between the friars of their respective Orders.[45] There
was a special link between St. Bonaventure and St. Thomas,
and their names appeared together more than once, as we
have seen, in papal and other public proclamations. Although
history has left us but few indications of the holy and friendly
relations of these two saintly and learned men, there is no
doubt that there existed between them a godly friendship
based upon the highest religious and intellectual interests in
common, a friendship which was portrayed with such charm
and such nobility by the later writers. Lemmens has preserved
for us all that legend has recorded of their friendship. We are
compelled, however, to admit, with Grabmann, that the historical sources tell us nothing whatever about the mutual
personal relations between St. Bonaventure and St. Thomas.[46]
Grabmann further considers it certain that Thomas already
during this first residence in Paris made the acquaintance of
various professors of the " facultas artium," among whom the
most eminent were Nicholas of Paris and John of Sicca Villa,
who wrote a treatise *De principiis naturae.*[47] We have already
mentioned a work of this name composed by St. Thomas.

It must not be forgotten that Thomas Aquinas, probably
already during this first sojourn in Paris, was on friendly terms
with the pious and excellent King of France, who was so
great a protector and friend of the mendicant orders. Louis
was indeed a son worthy of his mother, Queen Blanche, of
whom the Blessed Jordan (at the time master-general of the
Dominicans) could write to the Blessed Diana, a nun at
St. Agnes' at Bologna: " The queen herself dearly loves the
friars, and has often spoken to me in a very friendly way of
her own affairs." [48] Louis, who was an exemplary administrator
of a Christian realm, and who " kept before his eyes those
principles according to which the whole of human life is to be
regulated according to the will of God," was always anxious
to seek the counsel of wise men in difficult matters, thus showing himself to be a person who sought always to do what is

right and just. Several times, therefore, during both the first and the second period of Thomas' teaching in Paris, Louis IX had recourse to the wisdom and prudence of the master for the solution of his own problems. On one particular occasion he was going to hold on the morrow a council of state in his palace, to deal with certain difficult and urgent matters, and that evening he sent word to the doctor, asking him carefully to study the case in question during the night, and in the morning to give him his advice as to what should be said at the meeting. The obedient friar did exactly as he was asked.[49]

Some [50] would assign to this first period of teaching in Paris the episode of Thomas' discovery of the argument against the Manicheans while he was at luncheon with King Louis. But we prefer to place the story at a later date.

Among the personal matters of Thomas during this period is recorded his concern about the death of his sister and the fate of his brother who had already died some years before. It was while he was in Paris that he received the news of the death of his sister Marotta, who was abbess of St. Mary's Convent at Capua until 1257. She appeared to her Dominican brother and asked him to say a certain number of Masses in order that her soul might be freed from Purgatory. He then asked his students to pray for the repose of his sister's soul. Marotta also told Thomas that their brother—probably Ronald —was already in Heaven. These details of family affairs are all the more to be treasured, since we have them on the sound authority of the *Vitae Fratrum*,[51] the first edition of which dates from 1259 or 1260. Tocco confirms the story of apparitions and heavenly communications, but not without his own typical embellishments.

While we are discussing Thomas' personal contacts at this time, mention must be made of the troubles endured by the mendicants from the secular professors who became so hostile to them. During this conflict of words, both spoken and written, St. Thomas' authority in the matter emerged and became established through the publication of his opusculum *Contra impugnantes Dei cultum et religionem,* which was an attack on the accusations and unjust statements contained in William of Saint-Amour's treatise on the dangers of the Last Times. Glorieux has made a special study of the circumstances, thought, and characteristics of this work of St. Thomas.[52]

In point of fact, on March 1, 1256, before Alexander IV's instructions had reached Paris, the Friars Preachers had arrived at an agreement with the opposing faction: the friars were to keep their two professorial chairs, but the admission of friars to the College of the Masters was to be decided by the masters themselves.[53] This arrangement brought a short respite, although the position of the mendicants was still in danger, and in spite of the agreement of March 1, the Dominicans were still afraid that they might lose their Parisian schools. The letters written by the master-general, Humbert de Romans, early in April to the prior and community of Orléans, describing the trials of the Fathers in Paris, are still preserved.[54] And according to Gerard de Frachet, " the Order was threatened with a grave disaster." [55] Further, it was not without reason that the general chapter, which met in Paris in 1256, directed [56] " that until further orders every priory shall recite weekly the seven penitential psalms, the litany and prayer to Our Lady, the prayer to St. Dominic, and the prayer *Ineffabilem* with versicle, for the safety of the Order." People outside the Order also helped the Friars Preachers in their hour of need with their prayers: we read in the revelations of the Venerable Mechtilde of Magdeburg,[57] whose spiritual directors were Dominicans: " At one time certain false teachers and other lovers of sinful avarice started a great persecution of that beacon of truth that is the Order of Preachers. And I, feeling in the depths of my soul so great a compassion for them, prayed to the Lord that he preserve in prosperity this Order which is so necessary to the good of the Church." And God gave to this chosen soul the consoling reply that the Order would not succumb, but would overcome the danger.

Meanwhile William of Saint-Amour's pamphlet came to the notice of the papal court, and on June 17, Alexander IV rescinded the agreement made between the Dominicans and the other masters in sacred theology in Paris, deprived William and his associates of their benefices, and decreed their expulsion from France.[58] The pamphlet itself was then handed to a specially appointed commission in the Roman Curia, where it was read, examined, and received judgment. The pope himself, in the bull *Romanus Pontifex* of October 5, declared its condemnation.[59] The small work that St. Thomas wrote on the matter could not have been known by the commission at Anagni. What St. Thomas Aquinas was doing on behalf of the Friars Preachers, St. Bonaventure and Bertrand of Bayonne were doing for the Friars Minor. It is in the works of these authors that we have the first systematic study of the nature and ideals of the two mendicant orders.[60]

It would be well here to enquire whether or no Thomas had any part in the discussions at Anagni about the adversaries of the mendicants.[61] It appears impossible to answer in the affirmative, for although on the one hand there are serious historians who claim that he was present, others on the other hand fail to find any such indication in the historical records.[62] The *Vitae Fratrum* is content to limit Thomas' participation in the discussions at Anagni to a dream which he had in Paris and in which he was fully assured of the satisfactory results of the controversy going on at the papal court.[63] Further, Thomas' biographer makes no sufficiently clear reference to his having taken part in the sessions of the Curia. William da Tocco, when dealing with the period from Thomas' receiving the degree of master to his death, that is, from 1256 to 1274, speaks of " two returns to Italy and two journeys to Paris," which would not include a journey to Anagni in 1256; in any case, he states in another passage that he refuted and destroyed the error of William of Saint-Amour while remaining in Paris.[64] Too much stress should not be laid on the evidence produced in 1319 by Fr. Conrad of Sessa Aurunca, from which it is argued that Thomas was in Italy in 1257.[65] The most important person on the Anagni commission was Albert the Great, who had been specially summoned from his distant province of Germany, of which he was at the moment provincial.[66] Yet there are many details [67] supplied by Thomas in his *Contra impugnantes Dei cultum et religionem* which throw much more light on the matter than does Albert's treatise on the same subject. But one must bear in mind that Albert had not been present at the later stages of crisis in Paris. Albert's position was rather one of personal prestige, which was still further enhanced by his contribution to present case. It was this that caused the members of the Curia to keep the learned Dominican for a time at the papal court, in order to profit by his wisdom and his prudence; he was asked to lecture, and his advice was often sought.[68]

The papal pronouncement from Anagni did not, however, finish the matter, for we find Humbert, master-general of the Order Preachers, speaking at the general chapter of 1257, still referring to the trials which the Order had to face, especially in Paris, and exhorting all the friars to give the Order their energetic support; but it eventually happened, through the good offices of the pope and the King of France, that these trials were turned rather to the advantage than to the injury of the Order.[69]

When finally the troubles in the university subsided, Fr. Thomas d'Aquino got full recognition as master and was duly received into the College of the Professors. And the master-general of the Order was able in 1258 to assure his friars that they had at last reached the end of the troubles which had been afflicting them in so many parts of the world.[70] Yet it was not quite the end, and all was not yet quite calm. For not only was the pope's order for the destruction of William of Saint-Amour's pamphlet not carried out, but the pamphlet was circulated " afresh both in Latin and in the vernacular with the addition of popular ditties and unseemly songs."

And Master Thomas himself was to endure a bitter experience. It happened on Palm Sunday, April 6, 1259. Thomas was preaching, and suddenly the bedell of the students from Picardy had the effrontery to get up and read out, in the presence of all the clergy and the people, a pamphlet supporting William and attacking the Bishop of Paris and the Friars Preachers, although the pamphlet had already been publicly condemned by the bishop under pain of excommunication for those who composed, kept, or distributed it. On June 21 the pope himself wrote and imposed the severest punishment on the bedell and his companions.[71]

This papal pronouncement closed the first phase of the contest in Paris between the secular professors and the mendicants as far as St. Thomas was concerned.

Thomas was very diligent in occupying his free time with writing scientific works. The following fruits of his unremitting study flowed from his tireless pen during the present period.

Besides the pamphlet *Contra impugnantes,* Thomas wrote other notable works during his first professorship in Paris: in particular his commentaries on Boethius' books *De hebdomadibus* and *De Trinitate,* of which the latter contains the classical exposition of St. Thomas' theory of knowledge, and is also important for the problem of the introduction to dogmatic theology.[72] The original manuscript of the commentary on the *De Trinitate* is preserved, together with that of the commentary on Isaias and the *Summa contra Gentiles* in the Vatican Library (Cod.Vat.Lat.9850).[73]

The beginning, at any rate, of the elaboration of the *Summa contra Gentiles* is usually placed in this period. Fr. Motte dates its beginning in the year 1258.[74] Fr. Maxime Matthew Gorce [75] put forward the theory that the *gentiles* were the last representatives of Averroism in Paris, who had been installed there in the time of Albert the Great and defeated by Thomas in 1270. However that may be, the usual opinion, corroborated by the studies of Salman and Van Steenberghen,[76] remains the most likely. Van Steenberghen says that the *Summa contra*

Gentiles marks the first appearance of Thomism. Grabmann [77] describes this work of the Angelic Doctor as follows:

The *Summa contra Gentiles* (in the manuscripts: *Liber de veritate fidei christianae contra errores infidelium*) was written by Thomas at the instance of St. Raymund of Peñafort for the missions among the Moors in Spain. It was begun toward the end of his first period of lecturing in Paris and was finished at the court of Urban IV at Orvieto before 1264. The object of the work is to discuss in the first three books the philosophical and religious questions which Christianity and Islam have in common, and then, in the fourth book, to treat of the mysteries proper to the Christian Faith (the Trinity, the Incarnation, and the sacraments). The *Summa contra Gentiles* is a splendid example of a method that is at once apologetic and restrained; it makes fairly clear to us Aquinas' attitude to the philosophy of the Arabs; and it contains the clearest expression of his harmonious conception of the relations between Faith and Reason, and between the natural and the supernatural order. The full importance and grandeur of this work have recently been made evident by the superb edition that has been made on the basis of the original manuscript. The erasures, corrections, and marginal notes in the original reveal to us the growth not only of the text itself, but also of St. Thomas' own thought, and permit us to observe the very birth of Thomistic teaching. The greater part of the *Summa contra Gentiles* is concerned with matters of philosophy, although it actually only treats of those which have some connexion with theology. The general aim is simply to provide a mass of arguments and a complete defense against every kind of unbelief; but in point of fact the argumentation always throws new light on the subject. This *Summa* is divided into four books: the first two treat of the essence and nature of God and of creatures, that is, of metaphysics; the third of the movement of creatures toward their ultimate end, which is God, that is, of their intimate union with him by the contemplation of his essence, and therefore also of God's *super-*

natural providence. This latter section forms a transition to the fourth book, in which the mysteries connected with the creature's supernatural union with God, either with regard to God (such as the Trinity) or with regard to the creature (original sin, the Incarnation, sacraments, and resurrection), are proved from the Scriptures against infidels and heretics, and are theologically explained and defended. The form of exposition is not by question and answer, but the stating and proving of theses.

To this learned author's description of the *Summa contra Gentiles* we might add a remark upon the systematic completeness of the work. That there is nothing haphazard about its construction is shown by the fact that both parts are divided in the same complete way, that is, according to the causes: the first three books treat of God, according to unaided reason, as he is in himself (I 1), as efficient cause (I 2), and as final cause (I 3), while the fourth book treats of God, according to faith, as he is in himself (c. 1–26), as efficient cause (c. 27–78), and as final cause (c. 79–97). Fr. Clement Suermondt, president of the committee for the Leonine edition, has made a masterly analysis of the plan and contents of the *Summa contra Gentiles*.[78]

An important date in Thomas' life is June 1, 1259, when he was present as *socius* of the delegate from the Roman province [79] at the general chapter gathered at Valenciennes. It was at the request of this meeting that a committee of experts drew up and fixed the programme of studies to be observed in the Order of Preachers. The master-general and the diffinitors entrusted five masters in sacred theology with the task of drawing up a set of proposals for the furtherance of studies in the Order. The five masters were Bonhomme of Brittany, Florentius of Hesdin, Albert of Cologne, Thomas d'Aquino, and Peter of Tarentaise, and their proposals were approved by the same chapter and inserted into its minutes.[80]

The most important part of this programme of studies was the inclusion, so long keenly advocated by the wisdom of

Albert the Great, of philosophy as an essential part of Dominican formation.[81]

It was Thomas more than any of the others who supported Albert's proposals, insisting that an important place should be given to the study of philosophy.

Aquinas was now to go to Italy, and his place in the professorship of theology in Paris was taken for the academic year 1259/60 by an English friar, William of Alton,[82] who was in turn succeeded for the following two years, 1260/62, by a compatriot of Thomas, Annibaldo degli Annibaldi.[83]

Italy

1259–1269

PTOLEMY of Lucca in his Church History informs us, under the heading *De reditu fratris Thomae in Italiam tempore huius Pontificis* (Urbani IV) *et qualia fecit suo mandato et scripsit,* that "Brother Thomas then returned from Paris for quite specific reasons, and did many things and wrote much at the request of Urban." [1] Later he says more precisely: "After three years' lecturing as master, he returned to Italy at the time of Urban IV, under whose pontificate he wrote many useful works." [2]

Ptolemy's second statement carries more weight, for critical reasons, among recent biographers; and according to this statement, Thomas apparently left Paris for Italy in 1260,[3] or already in 1259,[4] at the end of his three years' teaching, while

87

Alexander IV was still reigning. And the move took place "for quite specific reasons."

What can these reasons have been? Because of the hostility of the followers of William of Saint-Amour at the University of Paris? [5] Or an order from Thomas' own superiors with a particular task in view? Or the wish of the Roman curia? Or because the Roman province was eager to achieve distinction at the papal court through the glory of the young and promising theologian, Fr. d'Aquino? Masetti quite rightly calls St. Thomas "provinciae Romanae decus." [6] Or was it because they wished to give another member of their province a chance of succeeding to the professorial chair in Paris? Or it may have been that Cardinal Hugh de Saint-Cher or some other suggested that Thomas' noble birth as well as his renowned and solid learning made him an obvious candidate for some post in the papal curia, or even for the purple, all the more since Alexander IV had not so far created a single cardinal, and in fact never did so, leaving the College of Cardinals reduced to eight members. [7]

As to the places of residence of the holy Doctor after his return to his homeland, it is only possible to make conjectures by indirect evidence. If we suppose with Mandonnet [8] that he was called to the papal court after the summer vacation of 1259, he would have stayed at Anagni—probably for two years. What is not explained, however, is how Mandonnet makes out Ranieri Maturo, of Pisa, who in 1274 lived at the priory of Anagni, to be Thomas' student at Anagni from 1259 to 1261, while Tocco only claims that he was Thomas' friend during the latter's lifetime. [9] It is more likely that it was another person who was Thomas' student during this period: Thomas de'Fuscis, from Rome, who in 1273 became a preacher-general. [10]

Grabmann numbers among Thomas' students at this time in Italy Fr. Tomasello of Perugia. [11]

From the scattered evidence of Thomas' activities either in the Order or at the papal curia, we can trace with a fair probability all his places of residence. Thus from Masetti's statement that " in the year 1260 the provincial chapter was held at Naples . . . and that at this chapter various Fathers were made preachers-general, among whom was Fr. Thomas d'Aquino, lately returned from Paris with the degree of master in sacred theology," [12] several conclusions may be drawn. In the first place, he would now have a vote in provincial chapters which included priors and preachers-general,[13] at a time when masters in sacred theology were not yet, as such, admitted to these meetings.[14] From this we can legitimately presume that St. Thomas was able to take part in the chapters of his own province. In fact, the only reasons which could have excused him from attending would have been illness or pressure of work in the schools.

Another conclusion that we may draw from the fact of Thomas' nomination to the rank of preacher-general in 1260 is that at the time of the provincial chapter held in Rome in September, 1259,[15] either Thomas was not yet resident in the province, or that there was so much business to be transacted that the nomination was not thought of; but this last supposition seems unlikely.[16]

Since the holy Doctor was now obliged to attend the provincial chapters, we can reconstruct some sort of itinerary, apart from the places where he had a more or less permanent abode during his sojourn in Italy at this time.

In fact the provincial chapters of the Roman province during those years were held [17] as follows:

1261 at Orvieto, on the feast of the Exaltation of the Cross, September 14;

1262 at Perugia, during the octave of SS. Peter and Paul, July 6;

1263 in Rome, probably in September;

1264 at Viterbo, on the feast of St. Michael, September 29;

1265 at Anagni, on the feast of the Nativity of Our Lady, September 8;

1266 at Todi, on the feast of St. Dominic, August 5;

1267 at Lucca, probably in July;

1268 at Viterbo, on Pentecost, May 27.

When we notice in how many different places the provincial chapter was held, each time requiring a journey on the part of Thomas, we are better able to understand the references to his many travels and residences in various cities and districts. The first of these is that of the Dominican, Conrad of Sessa Aurunca, who stated " that he lived with him for several years, at Naples, in Rome, and at Orvieto, in the time of Pope Urban of happy memory." [18] The second reference is that of William da Tocco, who says of Thomas that " he was not accustomed to traveling, being so absorbed in divine contemplation, but he was always of such ready obedience, for he knew that obedience comes even before humility and is the mistress of all the virtues." [19]

At these gatherings, and on the provincial council, St. Thomas' collaboration was illuminating and effective, and the provincials of the Roman province were not slow to appreciate the advantage both spiritual and intellectual that accrued to the widespread territory under their care. The provincials of that period were, from 1260 to 1262, Fr. Troiano del Regno; from 1262 to 1268, Fr. Aldobrando de'Cavalcanti, who became Bishop of Orvieto in 1269; and from 1268 to 1278, Fr. Sinibaldo of Alma.[20]

When we come to examine the various topographical notices of Thomas' residence in various towns of central Italy, we find that with regard to his stay at Orvieto, apart from the aforementioned statement of Conrad, evidence is plentiful. We have evidence of a period in Rome from the fact that the diffinitors of the provincial chapter directed him to lecture at the Roman house of studies, beginning in the autumn of 1265.[21] There is perhaps a connexion between this assignation of Thomas to Rome and the avowed intention of Charles of Anjou to set up a *studium generale* in Rome, a plan which was, however, later abandoned for political and financial considerations—things which Charles cared about much more than he did about scholarship.[22] We then find Thomas preaching at Viterbo under Clement IV.[23] Thence, as the Dominican chronicler Galvano della Fiamma relates, he went as diffinitor for the Roman province to the general chapter at Bologna in July of 1267.[24] This gathering is noted for the translation of the relics of St. Dominic that took place during the chapter. But unfortunately the statement of Galvano is not confirmed by the acts of the provincial chapter of 1266, which appointed Fr. Hugh of Siena as diffinitor and Fr. Sinibaldo of Alma as socius.[25] However, the possibility remains that Thomas was summoned to the chapter in some other capacity, perhaps at the desire of the master-general himself. There seems to be an indication that Thomas was indeed absent from the papal court during that July and present among the many friars assembled for the general chapter, in the fact that Clement IV on July 14, 1267, entrusted him with the task of seeing that the chapter provided two friars to act as companions and attendants to Walter of Calabria, O.P., Bishop of Jibleh in Syria.[26] Furthermore, there is an admonition issued by the same general chapter of Bologna, which some writers [27] understand as an order that Thomas should resume his lectures in the city where the papal court resided, i.e., at the *studium* which had been erected at Viterbo, after he had concluded his period of teaching in Rome at Santa Sabina. The text of this admonition is as follows: " The provincial of the Roman province is to take special care that the priory in the place of residence of the papal court be equipped with friars who are competent to meet the requirements of the curia; this applies particularly to the prior and the lector." [28]

St. Thomas, therefore, on his return to his own land, by no means interrupted his labors of teaching, though he doubtless continued them on a more modest scale than in the refined and distinguished society of Paris. But just as he had become an outstanding figure among his fellows and among the masters in Paris, so also now in Italy his quite exceptional brilliance must have given him a great authority in the eyes of his own brethren and of the clergy as a whole; and the possession of the degree of master in sacred theology, a rare enough honor in those days outside Paris, would have earned him the highest recommendation.

The authors are divided on the problem not only of where Thomas was teaching, but also of the kind of teaching in which he was engaged. Echard and De Rubeis [29] maintain that he followed the popes from place to place, wherever they chose to take up their residence, and that in each place he held the position of regent in the school of theology at the Dominican priory there. However, Masetti observes that Thomas did not give public lectures in every place he stayed in, nor did he everywhere teach even privately. Masetti goes on to speak of the Palatine Schools, and notes that Urban IV gave a new impulse to the hitherto neglected study of philosophy and with this object entrusted to St. Thomas the interpretation of Aristotle.[30] Finally, the great historian Fr. Denifle, after a careful enquiry into the history of the school of the papal curia, made the important distinction between the *studium generale* attached to the papal court and founded in 1245 by Innocent IV, a sort of traveling university (complete with faculties of theology, canon and civil law, and later also of medicine and arts), which followed the curia on its many wanderings of this period, and the Roman University founded by Boniface VIII in 1303.[31]

The recent profound researches of Fr. Creytens into the nature and working of the school of the Sacred Palace have been highly illuminating, and they certainly do not confirm the suggestion that Thomas was connected with that institution.[32]

If we examine carefully the two pieces of evidence, the injunction of the provincial chapter of 1265 and the admonition of the general chapter of 1267, according to which Aquinas was appointed either to the provincial *studium* (quite apart from the residence of the pope) or (if the second document really does refer to St. Thomas) to the priory " in the place of residence of the papal court," it appears that he did not undertake any teaching outside the Order. There are, however, arguments the other way, for at any rate the second document could refer simply to any competent conventual lector who might have been somebody quite else. We must therefore leave open first the question whether or no St. Thomas was ever lector or regent in the *studium* attached to the papal court, and secondly the more general enquiry into exactly in what capacity he was teaching in the various cities of Italy. We shall pass on to an examination of his scholastic activities during this period.

It is well known that during this residence in Italy St. Thomas was occupied with the usual work of a professor, which included lectures, disputations, sermons, and literary work. In addition to this his advice was widely sought.

It was at this time that he gave his scriptural lectures on the Book of Jeremias, on the Lamentations,[33] and on St. Paul's Epistles starting from the eleventh chapter of First Corinthians.[34] Various writers have attributed to St. Thomas a commentary on the Canticle of Canticles which has been lost,[35] though Fr. Suermondt regards it as unlikely that any authentic work of St. Thomas could remain down to the present untraceable in the manuscript tradition. It has also been claimed that he composed a second commentary on the *Sentences* of Peter the Lombard; but Dondaine has definitely placed this claim among the unfounded assertions.[36]

The holy Doctor also held a number of disputations on various questions, both *ordinariae* and *quodlibetales*. The following famous *quaestiones disputatae* were held at this time:[37] the *De potentia* in Rome between 1265 and 1267; the *De spiritualibus creaturis* at Viterbo between 1266 and 1268; and the *De anima, De unione Verbi incarnati, De virtutibus in communi,* and *De caritate* during his stay in Italy.[38] Mandonnet found in Cod.Vat.Lat.784 a *quaestio disputata* entitled *De natura beatitudinis*, which he attributed to St. Thomas and assigned to the year 1266 in Rome. But Dondaine has shown this *quaestio* to be spurious and has rejected it from the list of St. Thomas' works.[39] A few *quaestiones quodlibetales* belong to this period in Italy.[40]

St. Thomas' commentary on the *De divinis nominibus* of the Areopagite is usually assigned to this period.[41]

Meanwhile he never interrupted his labors in the noble ministry of preaching, as befitted a Friar Preacher and a professor of theology, and he did so with great zeal, yielding abundant fruit. For example, not only did he deliver "the Maundy Thursday sermon on the Eucharist in the consistory before Pope Urban and the cardinals," [42] but he also preached to the people of Viterbo at the command of Clement IV.[43] About the same time he preached occasionally in Rome. It was here, in the church of St. Mary Major, that he preached a series of sermons in Holy Week on the Passion of Our Lord and moved the people to tears, but on Easter Sunday caused them to have transports of joy at Our Lady's gladness over her Son's resurrection, just as his account of her sorrow had caused them to weep with her before. This was also the occasion on which a woman, who had long suffered from an issue of blood and been unable to obtain relief by medical treatment, drew near to St. Thomas as he came down from the pulpit, touched the hem of his cappa, and instantly felt herself cured. She followed him to Santa Sabina and told Fr. Reginald, the holy Doctor's companion, of the grace she had received. Fr. Reginald told the story several times to several people, among whom were Fr. John of Caiazzo, the Roman provincial from 1285 to 1288, Fr. Angelo of Termoli, prior of San Sisto Vecchio in Rome, and Fr. Leonard of Gaeta, who afterwards during the process of canonization gave witness that he had heard it about 35 years before.[44]

Let it be observed, however, that Fr. Leonard in his evidence places St. Thomas' sermon in the basilica of St. Mary Major, while Tocco says it took place in St. Peter's.[45]

When we consider the importance and the number of scholarly works with which St. Thomas enriched Christian

letters between 1259 and 1269, in addition to those which he
wrote as part of his duties as professor, we can hardly express
the warmth of our admiration. His arguments touch so many
questions, enter into them so deeply, and treat of them so
fully, that at every step our wonder increases at the intellectual power of a man who composed so many works of such
outstanding value.

At the desire of Urban IV, and in fulfilment of the duty
which he laid upon him, St. Thomas undertook a work which
was greatly admired by his contemporaries. It was entitled
A continuous exposition of the Gospels, or, as it began to be
called in the fourteenth century, the *Catena aurea*. He was
able to dedicate the *catena* on St. Matthew to Urban IV and
present it to him,[46] but the sections on other Gospels he completed only after the pontiff's death, and dedicated them to
his friend Cardinal Annibaldi, who from being a Paris professor had been raised to the purple in 1262, created by Urban
IV cardinal-priest with the title of the Twelve Apostles.[47]
In this work Thomas reveals both his assiduous study and his
tenacious memory, for "living as he did now in one priory
and now in another, he would read various volumes of the
Fathers and would retain in his memory a great part of their
authoritative commentary, which he would later incorporate
[into his exposition of the Gospels]."[48] Further, in order to
render more complete and homogeneous this exposition, based
entirely on the writings of saints, he had some of the commentaries of the Greek doctors translated into Latin.[49]

It was during the pontificate of Urban IV that the holy
Doctor finished a work he had begun in Paris, the great
Summa contra Gentiles in four books, which was written
"against the errors of the infidels, and by which the mists of
darkness might be removed and sunshine of true doctrine be
revealed to unbelievers."[50] With this *Summa* he brought aid
to missionaries who were preaching the Faith especially
among Mohammedans, but he also brought similar aid by the
light of his learning and his energetic holiness to the labor of

gathering souls into the one true fold, in the business of the
union of the eastern schismatics with the Church of Rome.
What happened was that the Eastern Emperor, Michael VIII
Palaeologus, in 1261 drove Baldwin II from the throne of
Constantinople and restored Greek power; then, in order to
ensure the position of his empire, from 1263 onwards he sought
to obtain from the Holy See the union of the Churches.[51]
Many discussions, diplomatic and controversial, ensued for
the attainment of this object. In the midst of all this, the pope
received a *Libellus* containing various authorities on the universal Faith of the Church. According to Uccelli,[52] who is
followed by Loenertz,[53] the author of this pamphlet, or at
any rate the person who presented it, was the Bishop of
Cotrone in Calabria, Nicholas of Durazzo,[54] a Greek by origin,
who had, however, been brought up in the Latin Church.
Urban IV wished this pamphlet to be examined by a competent theologian and therefore handed it to Master Thomas
d'Aquino, who carried out his task most carefully and exactly.
The result of this examination was the opusculum *Contra
errores Graecorum.*[55] The edition of both the *Libellus* and
St. Thomas' opusculum was still in manuscript when Uccelli
was overtaken by death, but was published in 1880 by Fr. Vincent Ligiez, O.P.[56] Unfortunately, the editing of the *Libellus*
is somewhat unsatisfactory, and there is still work to be done
on the question of the literary form of the *Libellus* and the
Contra errores Graecorum, as well as on the controversies
which were involved, a work that is especially necessary since
Reusch and others have confused the issue on the point of the
aims and the findings of St. Thomas' investigation of the
matter.

St. Thomas devoted another special opusculum to the controversies with the Orientals, a work entitled *De rationibus
fidei contra Saracenos, Graecos et Armenos* and written at the
request of the Cantor of Antioch. It is possible that this cleric
was recommended to go to Aquinas by his own bishop, the
Dominican Christian Elias.[57]

Various important personages, as well as private individuals, submitted problems to him, and the Master, always ready to help, wrote several treatises, some long and some short, in answer to these enquiries. Thus for the Archbishop of Palermo, Leonard de Comitibus, he wrote the opusculum *De articulis fidei et sacramentis ecclesiae*,[58] and for his brother in the Order, Fr. James of Viterbo, Lector in Florence, he wrote the *De emptione et venditione* about the year 1263.[59] He also wrote an exposition of the first and second chapters of the dogmatic decrees of the Fourth Lateran Council (the decrees *Firmiter* and *Damnamus*) for the Archdeacon of Todi,[60] who perhaps had approached him while he was at the provincial chapter at Todi in 1266.

While St. Thomas was at Orvieto, he received a special commission from Urban IV, as Ptolemy of Lucca, Tocco, and Gui bear witness, the result of which was the treasure which is the complete office of Corpus Christi, including the hymns *Pange lingua*, *Sacris solemniis*, and *Verbum supernum*, and a proper Mass with its sequence *Lauda Sion*.[61] We shall not discuss here the hymn *Oro te* or *Adoro te*, whose literary and textual problems have received fully adequate treatment from Dom Wilmart.[62]

The Bollandists did not accept St. Thomas as author of the office of Corpus Christi, but in this they were opposed in 1679 and 1680 by the Dominicans John Maison and Noel Alexandre. Since then, St. Thomas' authorship has been generally recognised, even by Huf,[63] and this may be called the traditional view, although the discussion is still open today, especially with regard to the hymns. No less glory is reflected upon the writer by the fact that he evidently took inspiration from already existent liturgical texts: the opening words and the metre of the *Pange lingua* follow those of the Passiontide hymn *Pange lingua gloriosi proelium certaminis;* the hymn *Verbum supernum* corresponds in many passages closely to the office used in the Cistercian Order; and the sequence *Lauda Sion* borrows the metre and occasionally exact words

from the " versificator egregius," Adam of St. Victor. All these
are indications of the considerable problems of literary de-
pendence or at any rate influence. We shall not go into the
matter of the melodies which were used for these texts: suffice
it to say that a choice was made of existing tunes, some of
which were already centuries old.[64]

The whole office of Corpus Christi combines in a wonderful
way the expression of the highest truths of the Faith with the
most exact propriety of words and with all the strength and
warmth of a fine poetic spirit. Various elements will have had
an influence on the composition of this office, and not the
least among them is the astonishing event which occurred at
Bolsena during the Mass celebrated by a Bohemian priest
named Peter in the year 1262 or 1263,[65] which greatly contributed to the institution of the feast and apparently decided the pope to extend it to the universal Church,[66] for he
already knew and loved the feast since his days at Liége.[67]
Another important element was surely the remarkable geographical position of Orvieto, which inspires noble spirits with
the sublimest thoughts. But the chief source of the rich inspiration shown in these hymns was the divine gift of a shining
faith, a firm hope, and a perfect charity unhindered and un-
darkened, strongly rooted in the soul. According to the traditional view it was granted, as was fitting to one so adorned
with these particular virtues, to the Angelic Doctor to express
the devotion and the desires of Christian men in the liturgical
prayer of the feast of the Blessed Sacrament, just as it was
reserved for him at the end of his life to devise the complete
theological treatise on the same Sacrament. It is indeed a
special glory of the Master, Thomas Aquinas, *doctor communis*
of the Catholic Church, to have composed this admirable
office of Corpus Christi, whose antiphons, prayers, and hymns
are the regular prayers of all Christian men whenever the
Blessed Sacrament is exposed for public veneration or distributed to the faithful. He is therefore justly called the poet and
theologian of the Eucharist. These thoughts are developed in

a magnificent manner in Pius XI's encyclical *Studiorum ducem*.[68]

Traditional Christian art reflects the same idea. The fresco of Ugolino di Prete Ilario of 1360, which adorns the Blessed Sacrament chapel in the cathedral of Orvieto, represents St. Thomas in the act of presenting the office of the Blessed Sacrament to Pope Urban IV. And later painters also depicted St. Thomas as the poet and theologian of the Eucharist.

After the pontificate of Urban IV, St. Thomas wrote the following works: to his well-beloved companion Fr. Reginald he dedicated the *Compendium theologiae (De fide, spe et caritate ad Reginaldum)*, in which he intended to treat, as in St. Augustine's *De fide, spe et caritate*, of the content of revelation in relation to these three virtues, and almost in the order of Deharbe's catechism. The only complete section is the first, which deals with the Creed (*De fide Trinitatis creatricis et Christi reparantis*), while the second, on the *Pater noster*, only reaches the second petition, which expresses the object of our hope. The treatment is by no means uniform; but as the work proceeds, the exposition gradually becomes fuller and of greater weight, so that certain things here receive a more adequate treatment than in his major works. The *Compendium* is much to be recommended to beginners in theology.[69] This opusculum, which is often assigned to Aquinas' last years, is probably more correctly to be placed in this period of his sojourn in Italy. The same may be said of the opusculum, also dedicated to Fr. Reginald and also incomplete, entitled *De substantiis separatis seu de angelorum natura*.[70] These works were doubtless broken off by a change of residence on the part of the author.

Blessed John of Vercelli, who was elected master-general of the Dominicans on June 7, 1264, at the general chapter of Paris, who probably got to know the holy Doctor at the general chapter of Valenciennes, if not before, and during whose period as master-general Thomas died, consulted him several times from the beginning of his period of office.[71] Between

1264 and 1267, or 1265 and 1266, St. Thomas examined, at the request of John, the master-general, the commentary on the *Sentences* written by Peter of Tarentaise, or more precisely, 108 propositions taken from that commentary and published anonymously. Thomas made an examination of the propositions one by one, and wrote a suitable note on each.[72] In fact he supports Peter of Tarentaise, and deals somewhat severely with the anonymous author whom he even accuses of deliberate false interpretation.[73]

It was the eastern Mediterranean that was to receive the *De regimine principum ad regem Cypri*, an important work from the point of view of St. Thomas' social and political theory. He only reached the fourth chapter of the second book, the rest being by Ptolemy of Lucca. The King of Cyprus to whom the opusculum is dedicated was either Hugh II or Hugh III.[74] The opusculum *De regimine iudaeorum ad ducissam Brabantiae*, which is also, and probably more correctly, entitled *Ad comitissam Flandriae Margaritam*, is to be assigned to the period between 1261 and 1272.[75] Either of these ladies was a deserving recipient of the help and advice of the Dominicans: the Duchess Adelaide of Brabant, like her husband before her, was very well-disposed toward the Order, and there were still polite exchanges of letters between her and the master-general John of Vercelli in June, 1264;[76] Margaret of Flanders (†1271) was the daughter of Louis IX.

Under the pontificate of Clement IV, to be precise in 1266, St. Thomas began his famous *Summa theologiae,* which had already been in his thoughts for some time.[77] The way was prepared for this great work by his other major works such as the commentary on the *Sentences,* the greater number of the *quaestiones ordinariae* and the *Summa contra Gentiles.* Grabmann [78] explains as follows: The *Prima pars* was written in 1266 during St. Thomas' stay in Italy. The *Secunda pars* was begun not earlier than March, 1266. He worked upon this part after he had left the papal court and right into the period of his second professorship in Paris (1268–1272). The *Tertia*

APOTHEOSIS OF SAINT THOMAS
(Seville, Museum)

by Francisco Zurbaran

(Spanish School, mid-seventeenth century)

pars was composed at Naples, where he began teaching in the autumn of 1272, and work upon it continued until, at the latest, 1273. The *Summa* represents St. Thomas' own system, organically arranged. It is concise and practical, and does not set out to be an exhaustive discussion of the various points for the learned reader, but rather a straightforward manual for beginners. Unfortunately it remained unfinished, and reaches only to the sacrament of Penance (including part of this tractate), the rest being added by another hand from extracts from other works of the Saint. In order to make this work a satisfactory help to teachers and a guide for "incipientes," Thomas made several notable improvements on the defective method and arrangement of material which prevailed in the theological literature of the time: he eliminated questions, articles, and arguments that were superfluous; he insisted on clarity and order in exposition; and he excluded useless and boring repetition. In this way he made his *Summa theologiae*, which in its restraint and, as it were, its architectural qualities far exceeds all the other *Summae* of Scholasticism, a peak in theological writing, which has so far never been equalled. Lacordaire likened the *Summa theologiae* to the pyramids, by reason of its majestic simplicity. The theological *Summae*, which belong almost exclusively (including that of Aquinas) to the thirteenth century, can also be likened to the great gothic cathedrals, both for their delicacy of construction and for the fact that they have remained more or less unfinished.[79]

We shall give here a brief outline of the structure of the *Summa*,[80] so as to make reference easy to this work which has become the classical manual *par excellence*.

The *Summa* is divided into three parts, the second being again divided into two (the *Prima secundae* and the *Secunda secundae*); each part consists of a series of questions, and each question of a number of articles. The *Pars I* treats of God as he is in himself and as the *principium* or beginning of all things; the *Pars II* and *Pars III* treat of God as the *finis* or end of all things: in particular, the *Pars II* in so far as the end is attainable through our own actions ("de motu creaturae rationalis in Deum"), and the *Pars III*, in so far as God brings us to himself through the Incarnation and the sacraments, and unites us to himself in glory. Compared to the Lombard and to Alexander of Hales, this arrangement has a notable advantage over that of the earlier masters, for their treatment of moral questions comes several times, being scattered among the questions on creation and on the redemption, while St. Thomas places them all together in a connected exposition in the *Secunda pars.*

The *Prima pars* therefore treats of A) *God in himself,* in his own Being (q. 2–13), with reference to his own inner operations (q. 14–26) and to his own inner life in the Holy Trinity (q. 27–43); B) *God as first cause of all creatures,* a) as universal cause (q. 44–49), b) as particular cause of each principal division of creation (and here he treats of the origin of each: c) of the Angels (q. 50–64), d) of the material universe (q. 65–74), e) of man (and here he treats of the nature of man and of his original state (q. 75–102), and finally f) he treats of God's *control* of creation and of creatures' share in this control (q. 103–119).

The *Secunda pars* treats of *the rational creature's movement toward God:* A) in general in the *Prima secundae:* a) man's final end (which is beatitude) (q. 1–6), b) human actions as such and the natural condition of man (q. 7–48), c) the formation of mental habits in man, which either lead him toward his final end (virtues), or away from it (vices) (q. 48–49), and d) God's influence upon this formation, which is regulated by means of *law* and raised to the supernatural order by means of *grace* (q. 90–114); B) in particular in the *Secunda secundae:* a) with reference to *the object of the various virtues,* theological (q. 1–47) and moral (q. 48–170), and b) with reference to *particular persons,* that is, a study of certain special graces, of the active and contemplative life, and of the duties of those who hold particular offices (q. 171–189).

The *Tertia pars* treats of A) *Christ* a) in himself (q. 1–26), and b) his life and work (q. 27–59); B) the *Sacraments* of Christ, as far as the sacrament of Penance (q. 60–90).

Of particular value is Fr. Chenu's explanation of the plan of the *Summa theologiae* of Aquinas.[81] For a synthesis of the division of the whole work according to St. Thomas' own plan the schematic table drawn up by Fr. Suermondt should be consulted.[82]

To make our study of St. Thomas' teaching and scientific writing complete, after dealing with his theological works, we must glance at his philosophical writings. William da Tocco says [83] that "he wrote upon natural and moral philosophy and upon metaphysics, had these books newly translated so that the genuine thought of Aristotle should be more clearly expressed, composed many works on philosophical questions as well as a few on logic, and with God's help was able to interpret everything that he read. In this way God showed how he had chosen him to investigate every truth, for he gave to him a clearer understanding than to any other man." From this quotation we can see not only how much the new philosophical learning owed to him, but how the Latin translation of Aristotle and the interpretation of his thought and works were in great measure due to his efforts. At the time the popes had several times forbidden that the works of Aristotle should be read in the schools, and the masters of arts were not permitted to make use of them unless they had already been revised—a prohibition that was once more issued on January 19, 1263.[84] At a providential meeting, however, of Albert the Great, Thomas d'Aquino, and William of Moerbeke in Brabant, the papal penitentiary, the matter was discussed and effective action was taken in favor of Aristotelianism.

If St. Thomas, as some authors hold,[85] knew no Greek, or, according to others, had but an elementary knowledge of this language,[86] he would certainly have been glad of this opportunity of meeting an outstanding Greek scholar. In fact, he made considerable use of the erudition of his confrère, William of Moerbeke.[87] William was born about 1215, and became a Dominican probably at Louvain. After spending a certain amount of time in Greece, he was called to the papal court, where during the reigns of Urban IV, Clement IV, and Gregory X, he held the office of papal penitentiary and chaplain. In addition to his work in the sacred ministry, he applied himself to translating the works of Aristotle, and also those of other authors such as Proclus. In 1278 he became Archbishop of Corinth, and died about 1286. These translations of Greek books enabled Aquinas better to understand the contents of Greek sources for the purposes of the commentaries which he was proposing to write.

The problem of the Latin versions of Aristotle and the use of them made by medieval students have been studied by Pelzer, Franceschini, and others, and finally by Msgr. Grabmann,[88] to whom reference should be made. It should be observed that the dates proposed by Mandonnet for the commentaries by St. Thomas on Aristotle are for the most part too early.[89]

The commentary on the *De anima* is probably to be assigned to the year 1266, or even later.[90] There is a chronological connexion between this commentary and those on the *De sensu et sensato* and *De memoria et reminiscentia,* which are therefore also to be placed between 1266 and 1272.[91]

When we consider St. Thomas' literary output during this period in Italy, we must bear in mind that he was much freer from teaching labors than he was at the university, either in Paris or Naples, and was thus able to complete several works of considerable size. Apart from this, he must now have had opportunities for quiet study and writing which the agitations of the great city never allowed him. Lastly, his almost daily contact with the most eminent personages of the ecclesiastical world must have brought much mutual advantage.

An acquaintance with these people and with the current

affairs of the time will help us considerably to understand
Thomas' personal relationships at this period, for the Roman
curia, to which at least for a time St. Thomas was attached,
was a meeting place of many people and was in touch with
most of the political movements of the time.

First of all, he was in frequent contact with the popes themselves on matters of religion and scholarship. Thus " at the
request of Urban he did many things and wrote much." [92]
And Clement IV " held the aforesaid doctor in great affection."
He had even offered him ecclesiastical preferment, such as
the archbishopric of Naples with the notable revenues of the
abbey of St. Peter ad Aram.[93] The reason that prompted the
pope to offer so exalted a dignity to Thomas d'Aquino was
most likely—as for a previous pontiff—a consideration for the
saint's family, which at that time was in great distress owing
to political disturbances. But Thomas " refused to accept the
honor, preferring to remain poor and humble . . . O the
blessed doctor . . . who despised the things of this earth as
if he already had a pledge of the heavenly things which he
was awaiting." Petitot considers that this proposal of Clement IV is no more than a confusion on the part of Tocco with
the offer made by Innocent IV or Alexander IV of the abbatial
dignity of Montecassino. But although Tocco does sometimes
make mistakes, there is no justification for supposing, with
Petitot, that there is a confusion in this case.[94]

There is a remarkable contrast between St. Thomas' utter
peace of mind and recollected life and the spirit of agitation
which pervaded the public and private life of the rulers both
religious and secular of the time. This contrast only shows
how absorbed he must have been in the contemplation of
God and of heavenly things. The question of the kingdom of
Sicily was the centre of incessant troubles between popes and
kings. It was this question that caused several popes to adopt
a new policy altogether, and to throw themselves into the
arms of the dynasty of France. The papal objective of bringing about the downfall of the last Hohenstaufen, who were

still in Italy, was the reason for this close alliance with France; and the object was only attained at an enormous price.[95] It was a time of political agitation and strife, marking the fall of Swabian power in southern Italy and the gradual control there of the house of Anjou.

Urban IV decided to invite Conradin himself to Italy, rather than come to an agreement with Manfred, although St. Louis, King of France, and Baldwin, the ex-Emperor of Constantinople, both present at the papal court, had urged him to effect a reconciliation with Naples.[96] Finally, when the armies of the King of Sicily were drawing near to the papal residence, and revolts were breaking out in Orvieto, Pope Urban, without going to Rome or ever setting foot in the Lateran, fled in great haste to Perugia, where he died shortly afterwards, on October 2, 1264.[97] " As a ruler he did not achieve greatness, nor success as a statesman." [98]

Clement IV followed the policy of his predecessor,[99] thus placing the Church and the papacy in a more awkward position than ever the Hohenstaufen had done with regard to the spiritual power. What happened was that Charles of Anjou was received in Rome in May, 1265, by Cardinal Annibaldo [100] and other cardinals, who gave him their full support.[101] He was then invested with the kingship of Sicily by four cardinals who had been charged by the pope to perform the ceremony. The chief of the four was Cardinal Annibaldo. " From then onwards Charles considered himself King of Sicily, although the pope seems to have turned round, for he did not confirm the acts of the investiture until November 4." [102] Charles' behavior soon brought to the pope the bitterest disillusionment, and he could do nothing but repent his action.[103] Even the superiors of the Dominican Order, and especially those of the Roman province, which was more favored by the prince of Anjou, had to impose, by means of obedience, silence upon their subjects who spoke ill of the actions of Charles.[104]

Charles left Rome on January 20, 1266, accompanied by the cardinal legate, Richard Annibaldi. The battle that took

place at Benevento on February 26 showed plainly, wrote
Morghen, the outstanding nobility of Manfred, the Swabian.
" Betrayed by his own, he preferred to die a valiant death
than to live a miserable life, whereupon he cast himself into
the melee and battled till his last breath." [105] Manfred's great-
hearted friend, Theobald Annibaldi, stayed with him to die
with him, while Thomas of Acerra, his brother-in-law, took to
cowardly flight. Roger of Sanseverino, St. Thomas' brother-in-
law, was fighting bravely at the side of Charles of Anjou in
the same battle of Benevento. In 1267 Conradin landed in
Italy. In the summer of 1268 he received a triumphal welcome
in Rome, but his short-lived glory came to an end on August
23 in the disastrous battle near Tagliacozzo, when he was
betrayed into the hands of Charles of Anjou.

When Conradin was publicly executed in the market-place
at Naples on October 29, 1268, a shudder went through the
whole of Europe. Clement IV died at Viterbo on November 29
of the same year.[106]

The echoes of these troubles also reached the ears of Thomas
and brought him distress. His own family was being involved,
for in July, 1264, his brother Aimo, " patron of the churches
of St. John within the territory of the castle of Montesangiovanni and of St. Mary of Gallinaro," was placed in the difficult
position of receiving orders not to allow Manfred's soldiers
entrance to the castle of Montesangiovanni. In return for this
awkward prohibition Aimo received certain favors from the
pope.[107]

These facts make it clear why William da Tocco [108] explains
the political attitude of the d'Aquino family entirely from the
Angevin point of view. But the facts and the records tell the
story differently. Tocco speaks repeatedly of the oppression
of the house of Aquino by Frederick II, as if it were a permanent state of affairs. One would also suppose from Tocco that
not one of them was ever on good terms with the Hohenstaufen, and that no relative of St. Thomas ever opposed the
Angevins; while in point of fact, even apart from Thomas

d'Aquino, Count of Acerra and joint-owner of the castle of Montesangiovanni, who in 1264 set himself against the pope, we find a number of close relatives of the holy Doctor who were styled, in the official language of the time, " enemies of the Holy Roman Church," being at the same time enemies of Angevin rule in the Kingdom of Naples. Among these we could mention, for example, St. Thomas' brother Adenulf, who made peace with Manfred about 1260 and received back his property together with that of his wife.[109] Among the family of his brother Philip there were also adherents of the Swabian party: Philip's son Pandulf who fell fighting for Conradin in the battle of Tagliacozzo in 1268, and his daughter Frances together with her husband, Annibaldo of Ceccano.[110] This niece of the holy Doctor will appear again in these pages.

While Thomas was in Rome, he received—according to Tocco—another vision of his sister Marotta, now a blessed soul in heaven, who told her brother that soon he would be coming to join her in paradise.[111] From this word " soon," attempts have been made to fix this apparition either on the occasion of his passing visit to Rome in 1272, or during his last stay in Rome during the provincial chapter of 1273, or else during the years 1265–7, especially since Tocco mentions the vision before the vision of Fr. Romano, which took place in 1273. It is, however, wiser not to discuss chronology with Tocco. Tocco also relates that Thomas asked his sister for news of his two brothers who were already dead, and received the reply that Landulf—and let us repeat that there is no record of a brother of that name—was in purgatory, and Ronald in heaven.[112] This last fact we knew already from the *Vitae Fratrum*, where, however, there is no mention of the special vision about Ronald.[113]

It was at this time, perhaps after the provincial chapter of Rome in 1263, or that of Anagni in 1265, that Thomas spent some time with his niece Frances, wife of the lord of the castle of Maenza, not far from the monastery of Fossanova, if indeed this is the meaning of the statement of Peter of Montesangiovanni, who said he had known Thomas for ten years (1264–1274).[114] But what is certain is that this visit took place before Annibaldo and his wife and brother-in-law, who were all faithful to the Swabian party, were driven out by Charles of Anjou.

St. Thomas will have taken part with great devotion in the religious functions of the curia, in the solemn liturgy, in the ceremonies of canonization, and in other sacred festivals. It should be noted that in 1262 the canonization took place of Richard, Bishop of Chichester (✝1253), and in 1267 that of Hedwig of Merania, Duchess of Silesia (✝1243).[115]

At the papal court and within his own Order Thomas will have met many eminent churchmen, and he will have welcomed these contacts in his courteous way as profitable occasions both from the point of view of piety and of learning.

Among these must be mentioned the cardinals, Hugh de Saint-Cher, a man of moderation and justice in politics, who died at Orvieto on March 19, 1263,[116] Annibaldo degli Annibaldi, who has been mentioned several times, and Odo of Châteauroux, Bishop of Frascati, a person with remarkable gifts both for scholarship and administration.[117] St. Bonaventure also appeared at the pontifical court.[118] And from 1261 to 1263 St. Albert the Great was there: he had been made Bishop of Regensburg in 1260; and after having reorganized the diocese, he arrived in the spring of 1261 at the papal court in order to ask to be relieved of his episcopal office. Urban IV, a lover of philosophical discussion, kept him at the curia. The philosophical genius of whom Henry of Würzburg speaks in his poem *De statu curiae* is identified with St. Albert by Grabmann, Eckl, Pelster, and Scheeben, although an identification with St. Thomas is proposed by von Grauert, who is not, however, so well acquainted with St. Albert's chronology.

> Est illic aliquis, qui si combusta iaceret
> Inventor fieret, philosophia, nove.
> Erigeret meliore modo novus editor illam
> Vinceret et veteres artis honore viros.

Albert left Orvieto in the spring of 1263 with the commission to preach the crusade across Germany and Bohemia.[119] It goes without saying that St. Thomas talked with these representatives of the University of Paris about theological and ecclesiastical affairs. The same must be said of his meeting with William of Moerbeke and Witelo, the learned naturalist from Silesia, whose father was a Thuringian and his mother a Pole.[120]

Another acquaintance was Bernard Ayglier, who had been Abbot of Saint-Honoré at Lerins and came from France with Charles of Anjou. In March, 1263, he was appointed Abbot of Montecassino in place of Theodinus (1262–3), who had been installed by Manfred and was now deposed. It was an ecclesiastical promotion with a purely political motive. Bernard's brother also came to Italy, and by the favor of Clement IV became Archbishop of Naples.[121] Both brothers took a prominent part in the war of the Angevins against the Swabians. Bernard, after giving financial assistance and valued counsel to Charles in his struggle with Manfred, finally, toward the end of his life, wearied of this tiresome prince and turned against him.[122] It was to the Abbot Bernard I (1263–1282) that Thomas dedicated his last written work.

Thomas will also have come in contact with the principal men in his own Order, and in particular with the master-general, John of Vercelli, who had been urged by Urban IV and Clement IV to get his friars not only to preach for the crusade to the Holy Land,[123] but also to preach throughout Italy against the Swabians.[124] And then other important people in the Order, provincials, Dominican bishops, priors, lectors, and inquisitors will have visited either the cell or the lecture-room of d'Aquino in the various places of his residence in Italy.

But there is one more person who must receive special mention, and that is the simple, hard-working, and congenial confrère, Fr. Reginald (or Ronald) of Priverno, who was appointed as the Master's habitual companion or " socius continuus " [125] after his return from Paris,[126] and henceforth was always with him. It was the practice in both the Order of Friars Minor and in the Order of Preachers for lectors and masters in sacred theology to be always attended by such companions.[127] They held no academic office, but their duty was to be the personal attendants of the lectors or masters, to be at hand by day or night, at home in the priory or away on journeys, and to assist them in preparing and writing up their lectures. It is not therefore surprising when we find the masters much attached to these brethren of theirs who were their *socii,* and inspired by a special feeling of gratitude toward them.

St. Albert's most faithful companion was Godfrey of Duisburg,[128] and St. Thomas calls Reginald his "most dear companion" in the dedication of several of his opuscula: the *Compendium theologiae,* the *De substantiis separatis,* and the *De iudiciis astrorum.* There is no doubt that they were real friends: Thomas used to go to confession to him [129] and offered him the fruits of his learning in these opuscula. It is also thanks to Reginald that we possess several books and treatises of his: for example, the first book of the *De anima,* the explanations of the Psalms, and some of his lectures on the Gospel of St. John and on the Epistles of St. Paul, and perhaps the Supplement to the *Summa theologiae* is also due to him.[130]

It seems probable that we should place during Thomas' period in Rome the visit which he paid to the castle of Molara or Molaria, which stands below the Colle Iano to the west of Frascati, on the southern slope of the Alban hills along the Via Latina. He came here at Christmas time in 1256,[131] at the invitation of Cardinal Richard degli Annibaldi, the owner of that castle, who had come into possession of this and other properties previously belonging to the counts of Tusculum, in 1254.[132] The cardinal was "on affectionate and intimate terms" with Thomas, the friend of his nephew Cardinal Annibaldo. Now, Cardinal Richard had also invited other guests, and among them were two Jews, both very learned men, "very rich, and friends of the aforesaid cardinal." In their presence the cardinal asked his dear friend Master Thomas to address to them a few kind and edifying words, which he knew so well how to do. Thomas replied most politely that "he would be delighted to say anything he could, if they were willing to listen." And in order to talk with them more freely, the three of them withdrew to the chapel and began their discussion. "Brother Thomas was able completely to settle their doubts, and seeing that they were satisfied with what he had to say, he said to them: 'Go and think these things over, and come back here tomorrow . . . and explain to me any further doubts you may have.' . . . The next day, which was the Vigil of Christmas, the aforesaid two Jews returned, and again had a discussion with Brother Thomas in the chapel. After a long conversation the sound came from the chapel of the voice of Brother Thomas and that of his companion, singing the *Te Deum laudamus*. Upon hearing this, the cardinal, who was unable to walk because of his gout, had himself carried into the chapel, and all his clergy and members of his household also hastened to the chapel and joined in the conclusion of the aforesaid canticle, after which the two Jews were baptized." On Christmas Day there was a grand luncheon to which many of the cardinal's distinguished parentage were invited and the two convert Jews declared that from the moment that they met Thomas, they felt themselves interiorly changed and ready to embrace the Christian Faith.[133]

After these various apostolic labors and activities, both religious and scientific, which he performed in Italy, St. Thomas was in 1268 sent by his superiors once more to Paris to take up duties as professor of theology.[134] It was rare that anyone ever had more than one period of teaching in Paris—although there were occasional exceptions, like Peter of Tarentaise and William of Alton [135]—and the fact that Thomas was reappointed is a sign that there were quite special reasons.

Mandonnet was under the impression that the reason was to provide a successor to the master, Gerard Reveri, who died, he said, in February, 1269.[136] But a more exact chronology has established that Reveri was already dead in 1259.[137] It would seem that the authorities of the Order took into consideration both the person himself and the very difficult psychological and doctrinal aspects of the question (of which we shall speak in the next chapter), when they decided to put a man of such outstanding prestige into the professorial chair which was probably occupied at the time by Gilbert van Eyen. The Flemish master of the school for " externs " [138] was apparently no longer able to cope with the situation which had now arisen. So John of Vercelli began by approaching Albert the Great, who was much the most famous teaching authority that the Order possessed. But the holy man declined the invitation,[139] doubtless for his own serious reasons, and once more recommended his own student d'Aquino for the post. The master-general therefore turned to Thomas, who accepted and set off without delay.

St. Thomas probably began his journey at Viterbo, accompanied, we can suppose, by his usual companion, Fr. Reginald of Priverno, and by Fr. Nicholas Brunacci, whom we know to have followed him " from the Roman province right to Paris." [140] An argument on which Fr. Mandonnet insists [141] suggests that this academic mission stopped at Bologna and Milan. For it is recorded that St. Thomas preached at either Bologna, Milan, or Paris on the first, second, and third Sundays of Advent, so that if we leave aside the mention of Paris it becomes obvious that on the first Sunday of Advent he was at Bologna, and on one of the following Sundays at Milan.[142] And these dates fit in well with his journey to Paris.

It is perhaps to this journey that we should assign the following incident recorded by his biographer as follows: " While the aforesaid Doctor was stopping at Bologna in the course of a journey, and, as was his wont, was pacing up and down the cloister deep in thought, it happened that one of the brethren from another priory, who did not know Thomas, had obtained the prior's permission to go out on business and to take with him the first brother he should meet. This chanced to be Thomas, who was approached by the other with the words, ' Fr. Prior has told me to take you with me.' Thomas bowed his head and followed. But the other brother walked quickly, and Thomas was unable to keep up and humbly apologized for this, after the other had several times expressed his annoyance. Some people in the street, however, recognised Thomas and were much astonished that so eminent a professor should be acting as companion to a mere ordinary friar to whom he was far senior. Supposing that some mistake had been made, they mentioned to the friar the identity of his companion. He therefore turned to Thomas and apologized for his ignorance, and the people then ventured to approach Thomas and compliment him on this beautiful example of humility, but he simply replied: ' In obedience religious life is made perfect.' " [143]

With the help of the dates of the four sermons it is possible to state that St. Thomas was at Bologna on December 2 and at Milan on the 9 or the 16 of the same month. In the Lombard capital he did not fail to venerate the tomb of St. Peter of Verona, the Dominican martyr, in the church of St. Eustorgius. [144] There is no serious foundation for Mortier's date, 1260, for this visit " on the way " to the general chapter in London in 1263, which in fact he never attended, [145] nor for his date for another visit in 1265. [146]

From Milan he proceeded to Christendom's great centre of studies in the French capital, probably passing through Vercelli and Aosta and so over the Pennine Alps. He will have arrived in Paris together with his Italian companions probably in January and certainly before Easter of the year 1269. [147]

Chapter Nine

Paris Again

1269–1272

IN 1269, the year in which B. Peter of Tarentaise, regent of studies at St. James' in Paris, was once more elected provincial of the French province,[1] Peter of Dacia, a Swede who had previously studied at Cologne, wrote to Christine of Stommeln, a Servant of God who lived in Germany, and described his manner of life since May 10.[2] He wrote: " I must tell you about the devout novices here in Paris, the cultured students, the exemplary friars and the kindly superiors. Living as I do among these men who have a radiance like glowing coals, I feel indeed like the reproach of men and the outcast of the people." [3]

In this admission one easily discerns the ardor and expansiveness of youth, but even if this ardor and eagerness was joined to the simplest humility, there is no doubt that

115

Peter's joy at finding himself in Paris, the great city of studies, was the thought that was uppermost in his mind. And he had every justification, for Peter, at the age of only twenty-nine, was a very keen student.[4]

In the same year, round the month of January, St. Thomas, summoned by obedience from his own Roman province, arrived once more in Paris. But we cannot suppose that this learned man, ordered by his superiors to take up his abode here again after the experience of a busy and varied life, can have been caught by the same prevailing enthusiasm of Paris. Surely his mind was rather filled with serious thoughts, and indeed there was a certain seriousness about him that was instantly noticeable. He was "heavily-built, tall and upright as befitted his upright spirit; his countenance was of wheaten hue, bespeaking the fineness of his fibre; his head was large, for his mighty intellect required a mighty brain; he was also slightly bald."[5]

The reasons for his reappointment to Paris were serious, and it was with grave steps that he approached the city. The saintly scholar had become accustomed to facing difficulties and overcoming them ever since his youthful battle for his own religious vocation, and he was gradually discovering for himself the truth of the words, "The life of man upon earth is a warfare."[6] He was preparing himself for the struggle: he was going to use spiritual weapons—virtue and scholarship, as well as the authority which he already wielded.

The fortunes of the Dominican Order were so closely linked with the University of Paris that if relations became hostile or even tense, the matter was bound sooner or later to come to a head. At the present important juncture in this vital centre, the defense of the interests of the Order was entrusted to the person who, after Albert, held the position of greatest authority in the Order, that is, to Thomas.

Toward the end of the sixth decade of the thirteenth century troubles arose within the university which threatened to upset the established order of things: there was, for instance, the aftermath of the struggle with the mendicants, which in point of fact had never been settled; then there was another trouble which arose from the fact that different professors at the university had been putting forth doctrines that were mutually irreconcilable; and finally dissensions broke out in 1266 when the French members of the faculty of philosophy cut themselves off from those of the other three " nations." [7]

Mandonnet believes that the chief motive for St. Thomas' return to Paris was the doctrinal crisis, that is—according to Gillon's explanation [8]—the " Averroist " crisis. It seems to us, however, unlikely that the Order would have recalled to Paris its most distinguished lecturer to deal merely with a point of doctrine, but on the other hand more probable that the general policy of the Order with regard to university life was to keep a firm hold on the place that they already held in the academic world, without unduly emphasizing attachment to any of the views on doctrine which were under discussion at the time.

Opposition to the friars in the university broke out afresh. William of Saint-Amour, although driven into exile, did not cease as long as he lived to molest the mendicants in every way he could. In Paris his friends and supporters included Gerard or Gerald of Abbeville,[9] Nicholas of Lisieux, and others, who were all known as the " Geraldines " after their leader. In 1269 Gerard wrote a book *Against the adversaries of Christian perfection*,[10] the vehemence of which was only exceeded by William of Saint-Amour's own pamphlet *On the dangers of the last times*. Apart from this, Gerard spared no effort in his preaching, teaching, and writing, to cause trouble against the mendicants, and he was assisted by Nicholas.

Those who entered the battle on the side of the Franciscans and Dominicans were John Peckham,[11] St. Bonaventure,[12] and St. Thomas Aquinas.[13] The latter produced in 1269 a work entitled *De perfectione vitae spiritualis*,[14] which was an answer to Gerard's *Contra adversarium*, and in the next year, 1270, the *Contra pestiferam doctrinam retrahentium homines a religionis ingressu,*[15] which was a reply to Nicholas' pamphlet *De perfectione et excellentia status clericorum.* The two monographs of Aquinas are much maturer works than the pamphlet *Contra impugnantes* which he had written thirteen years previously, during the first phase of the struggle.

The concluding words of the *Contra retrahentes* should be well weighed, for they fully express the gravity of the situation, saying that these problems are not solved by simply discussing them with the young, and thereby misleading them, but should be worked out in writing, according to strict reasoning and after careful consideration.

In the *quodlibeta* I, III, IV, V, and XII, the holy Doctor also treats of the question of vocations to religious life and to that of the mendicants in particular.[16] But St. Thomas was not content with writing and teaching: he also expressed his point of view in his university sermons, examining and demolishing the Geraldine position, by showing how far it was removed from the traditional idea of Christian perfection through the evangelical vows.[17]

Käppeli, on both external and internal critical grounds, has attributed to St. Thomas certain sermons, which have been preserved in a Spanish collection noticed also by Beltrán de Heredia, Grabmann, and Glorieux. One of the internal criteria is the similarity of matter and treatment in two of these sermons with the thought of the *Contra retrahentes* and of questions 23 and 24 of *Quodlibetum IV,* so that Sermon V in the collection can be placed in Advent, 1270, shortly after the composition of the *Contra retrahentes* (October, 1270), and Sermon VI on February 1, 1270, which was Sexagesima Sunday, a little before the two questions *De ingressu religionis,* which are questions 23 and 24 of *Quodlibetum IV.* In the Advent sermon, "the reader becomes at once aware that the preacher has passed rather suddenly from the exposition of the theme to the attack—a sure sign that the struggle was at that time at its height, and that the preacher felt compelled by the maneuvers of his opponents to give an answer to their arguments, to fortify his hearers against their dangerous propaganda, and at the same time to convey to them the Church's traditional teaching." The Sexagesima sermon ("Exiit qui seminat seminare semen suum") was a good opportunity for speaking of disseminators of false doctrines, and the preacher makes good use of it, both in the morning sermon and in the afternoon conference or "collatio."[18]

However, in spite of all the writing and preaching of the mendicants, Nicholas of Lisieux would not give in, but wrote a special pamphlet entitled *Contra Peckham et Thomam*.[19]

For the details of the struggle and the long development of the controversy we must refer the reader to the most recent studies made of the question by Bierbaum, Hirschenauer, Glorieux, and Clasen.[20] The battle, from the theoretical aspect and also in so far as it featured in the public eye, only began to die down with the death on November 8, 1272, of Gerard of Abbeville himself. The aftermath, however, remained. But the Church for her own part recognised publicly and officially, in canon 23 of the Second Council of Lyons in 1274, her debt to the Order of Preachers and to the Order of Friars Minor.[21] The great champions of the mendicants, Thomas and Bonaventure, had won a complete victory in this second phase of the struggle for their very existence.

The Dominicans and the Franciscans made common cause in repelling attacks upon their religious profession, their priestly ministry, and their rights as teachers. But they were divided on certain technical points of teaching.

The Dominicans favored Aristotelianism in philosophy, and made great use of philosophy in theology, without prejudice to the many Dominican teachers who preserved their Augustinian tendencies. But St. Bonaventure, together with the other Franciscans, stood for the mystical tendency, following the traditional "Augustinist" theology. St. Bonaventure himself describes this double current as follows, the first allusion being to the Friars Preachers and the second to the Friars Minor: "Some lay the principal emphasis on speculation, and then upon unction; while others emphasize first unction and then speculation." [22]

This difference of emphasis was gradually becoming more and more sharply defined, until finally the two schools came into conflict, on the famous occasion when John of Peckham, regent of the Franciscan school in Paris, after bringing out his vain arguments with all the impetuousness of his warrior's soul, was halted and compelled to retreat before the force of the arguments brought forth with the greatest calmness by Thomas Aquinas. The occasion was probably a *disputatio quodlibetalis*, held at Eastertime in 1270, at which the secular masters were continuing to put their objections on the matter of the clerical and religious states, when Peckham and others made their attack on the Aristotelian position. What is certain is that the Franciscan regent, who was known to hold a different view from Thomas on the unity of the substantial form in man, was not only unable to uphold his contention, but made matters worse " by his puffed-up and pompous words." [23]

Almost at the same time another party appeared: these were the followers of an unorthodox Aristotelianism, whose teaching had for the previous ten or even fifteen years remained unknown to the public and was now making its first appearance.[24] The peripatetic doctrines, so well understood by Albert, Thomas, and others, had also other interpreters of a very different kind, who were much attached to certain ideas of Averroes and upheld certain theses inimical both to science and to general morality. This party was now taking up a position as a rival Aristotelian school among the Latins. The matter became more complicated by the intervention of certain of the " Augustinists," on whose behalf St. Bonaventure from 1267 or 1268 onwards spoke against the excesses of the Averroists of Paris. The result was a great feeling in the university not only against this unorthodox Aristotelianism, but also against that of Albert and Thomas, which certain of the professors were eager to see defeated.[25] On all these problems and tendencies, on the conflict of words, both spoken and written,

between the opposing interpreters of Aristotle in the thirteenth
century, and on the eventual defeat of this Latin Averroism,
some most interesting researches, discoveries, and studies have
been made in recent years, which are to be found in the elaborate volumes of Mandonnet and especially of Grabmann and
Van Steenberghen. The merits of Mandonnet's work are well
known,[26] even though it had to be retouched in several
places [27] in the light of later research. It was Grabmann who
had the good fortune to unearth some forgotten material of
Siger, which provided twelve or fifteen times more evidence
than Mandonnet had to work upon.[28] Van Steenberghen gives
a most careful and exact account of all the work of previous
scholars,[29] and Nardi's recent publications on Siger have
earned for the author great distinction.[30]

Gilson had already shown that St. Thomas' intervention
against Siger had been preceded by the violent dissension with
Peckham, so that Thomas found himself in fact less occupied
with attacking new doctrines than with defending his own
Aristotelian position by clarifying his own principles and dis-
sociating himself from the new unorthodox Aristotelianism.[31]

The great leaders of the two Aristotelian parties in Paris at
the time were on one side Thomas Aquinas and on the other
Siger of Brabant,[32] canon of Liége and professor in Paris, who
appears in 1266 as the sponsor of the movement known as
radical heterodox or "Averroist" Aristotelianism. Each side
challenged the other in various disputations, and Thomas set
about composing a fundamental refutation of heterodox Aristotelianism, of which we shall speak presently.

We have (according to Mandonnet) an echo and an indication of the situation in Paris during the spring of 1270 in
the letter written by the Dominican Giles of Lessines to
St. Albert at Cologne, who was still regarded as the principal
authority in the Order on philosophical matters. From this
letter we gather it was not only the errors of unorthodox
Aristotelianism that were attacked, but even certain theses
that come directly from Aristotle himself. Albert answered

Giles' enquiries in an opusculum entitled *De quindecim problematibus,* declaring that all fifteen propositions, with the exception of two, were unorthodox. Van Steenberghen, however, would place this letter in the years 1273–1276.[33] These thirteen theses were in point of fact the matter of the thirteen articles condemned on December 10, 1270, by the Bishop of Paris, Stephen Tempier.[34] The two theses which escaped condemnation were the two Aristotelian theses upheld by Thomas. The holy Doctor at this time was sparing no effort to use every means that his position offered him, in his teaching, disputing, preaching, and writing, of rebutting the attacks of the Averroists, of clearly demonstrating the soundness and the breadth of Aristotelian principles, and of proving the falseness of certain conclusions which his opponents drew from them. The appearance of Thomas' treatise *De unitate intellectus contra Averroistas* [35] was the great event of 1270 in the academic world of Paris.[36]

In this work, after a survey of the Averroist movement in general, the holy Doctor shows that Aristotle's own teaching about the soul excludes the Averroist interpretation, proves that the rational soul is itself the *forma substantialis* of man, and launches an attack against the theory of the one single intellect, which was held by his opponents. At the end he calls attention to the method he used, namely the use of pure philosophical reasoning, without recourse to the authority of Faith. In conclusion he has an appeal for the serious conduct of scientific controversy, in almost the same words as he used at the end of the *Contra retrahentes,* though here the phrases are somewhat stronger.

In the same year, 1270, we find a work which resulted from a not unimportant discussion on a particular point, which shows the writer's great speculative ability and is written in an extremely strong and decided manner: the opusculum *De aeternitate mundi contra murmurantes.*[37] While the Arab *Mutakallimûn* (or teachers of the word), Bonaventure, and most of the scholastics reject the possibility that the world was created from all eternity, Thomas here defends the thesis that, although we know by Faith that the world had its origin in time, we cannot demonstrate from pure reason the impossibility of creation *ab aeterno*. Thomas arrived at this position under the influence of Moses Maimonides, and still more through his preoccupation with the danger that comes to religion, when attempts are made to prove the truth of a revealed doctrine by means of a rational demonstration, which in point of fact is unconvincing (*Sum. Theol.* I 46 3). In many passages in his works St. Thomas has denied, as being contrary to the Faith, the affirmation of the eternity of the world and of motion, which was one of the principal tenets of the Latin Averroism of Paris, and is traceable through Averroes to Aristotle.[38]

Thomas' action was quick to have its effect among the radical Aristotelians, as is shown by the changed attitude, the amendments and hesitations that we can observe among them after Thomas came upon the scene. Siger's own work, *De anima intellectiva*, of 1272 or the next year, not only takes into account many of the criticisms leveled by Thomas Aquinas in his *De unitate intellectus* at heterodox Aristotelianism, but also takes up a position of respect towards the teaching of Christian revelation. And in this work Siger makes important modifications of his previous positions.[39] The day was to dawn when he should become a fervent admirer of Aquinas, after having been his philosophical opponent.

Amid all these philosophical agitations, scientific storms, and academic battles, Professor d'Aquino, so renowned for his intellectual self-discipline, was quietly going on with his work: his lectures, disputations, and occasional sermons.[40]

We have seen how during the troubles with the Geraldines the holy Doctor sometimes referred to current problems in the pulpit. A collection of sermons preserved in two Spanish codices contain these and other sermons of St. Thomas, preached in Paris between 1270 and 1271.[41]

For his theological course he probably chose the book of

Job, on which he drew up a commentary,[42] as well as the Gospel according to St. John, the notes on which exist in part as a commentary, but in greater part in the form of lecture-notes written up by Fr. Reginald of Priverno at the request of the Provost of Saint-Omer, Adenulf of Anagni, who was a lecturer in Paris and a nephew of Pope Gregory IX.[43]

For the *quaestiones disputatae* of this period Thomas chose the following subjects: *De malo, De virtutibus cardinalibus, De correctione fraterna,* and *De spe.*[44] Among the *quodlibetales* we find reflections of the various problems and controversies of the moment, and indications of the current tendencies in theology and philosophy.[45] Fr. Jacquin has given a very vivid description of a disputation held by St. Thomas in the March of 1270.[46]

Dom Lottin has called attention to the close affinity of thought between questions 9 and 10 of the *Prima Secundae* and the corresponding articles in *De malo.*[47] The Master was making tireless progress meanwhile with his work on his *Summa theologiae.*[48]

During this period in Paris he also continued his series of commentaries on Aristotle, in particular *In libros III De anima* (the first book of which dates already from 1268/9), *De sensu et sensato, De memoria et reminiscentia,* though some writers hold that these three works were at least begun while he was still in Italy; he then wrote the commentaries *In XII libros Metaphysicorum, In VIII libros Physicorum, In X libros Ethicorum, In libros Meteorologicorum, In libros Perihermeneias, In I et II Posteriorum Analyticorum,*[49] and finally *In libros Politicorum,*[50] at least as far as lectio 6 of book III, the work being completed to the end of book VIII by Peter of Auvergne. He also compiled a commentary on the *Liber de causis* from the *Elementatio theologica* of the neoplatonist Proclus.[51]

The part played by Albert the Great and Thomas Aquinas in these philosophical discussions, the clear and decided position that they took, the mass of valuable monographs and commentaries which they produced, and the keen encouragement they gave to philosophical studies, all these things had a most important result in their contribution to the formation of a Faculty of Philosophy in the University of Paris. Now true and authentic philosophy appeared in the curriculum in addition to the "artes." D'Irsay quite rightly insists on the university's indebtedness to the Dominicans for the establishment of a real Faculty of Philosophy in Paris.[52]

The most famous "artists" or representatives of the Faculty of Arts at this time were Siger of Brabant, Boethius of Dacia, Bernier of Nivelles, and John of Meung.[53] It is perhaps to this period that we should assign Thomas' treatise *De fallaciis ad quosdam nobiles artistas,* which Grabmann observes to have many affinities with the unpublished work *Tractatus maiorum fallaciarum* by Peter Hispanus, who later became Pope John XXI (✝ 1277).[54]

The friendly relations that were growing up between Fr. Thomas d'Aquino and the lecturers in the Faculty of Philosophy are nowhere more plainly described than in the joint letter [55] which the latter wrote after the Saint's death. Here we can see how his utter goodness, his humility, and his readiness to be at any time of service, had placed him on the best of terms with them. He had promised to send them, at their request, some philosophical writings which he had not yet finished when he left Paris, and which would be of interest to them. He also explicitly undertook to get for them certain works, such as Simplicius' commentary on the *De caelo et mundo,* the exposition of Plato's *Timaeus,* and the book entitled *De aquarum conductibus et ingeniis erigendis.* Finally, they were eager also to get anything he should write on the problems of logic. The friendly tone of this famous letter and the expressions of esteem and veneration for the person, the virtues, and the teaching of Aquinas show clearly how things had changed, even in technical scientific points, since Thomas had entered the field of philosophical controversy and eventually overcome any dangerous and erroneous doctrines and placed philosophical studies on a basis of sound reason.

Various Paris professors had become supporters of St. Thomas: in particular Ralph the Breton, Peter of Auvergne, James of Douai, and Simon of Faversham.[56]

Even during this period in Paris, Thomas found himself called upon, because of his prudence, authority, calmness, and goodness, to deal also with questions and difficulties that arose within the Order of Preachers and had been submitted either to a general chapter or to the master-general. Thus the general chapter, which in 1269 was held in Paris, submitted to him and to certain other professors six moral problems. It was a matter of *casus conscientiae:* whether or no a religious superior was in certain matters entitled to compel a subject to reveal secrets. The commission which was appointed to examine the cases in question gave their reply in a document which bears the following title in a Paris manuscript: *Responsio fratris Thomae de Aquino cum quibusdam aliis magistris ad aliquas quaestiones eis propositas de occultorum vel secretorum revelatione.* The other members of the commission were the Breton Bonhomme, Peter of Tarentaise, Bartholomew of Tours, Baldwin of Maflix, and Gilbert van Eyen. The report is not the work of Thomas in particular, for it is only in the answers to two out of the six *casus* that his personal opinion appears as such, differing from that of the others and favoring the solution of obedience.[57]

Another matter of minor importance arose, which was a dispute between two of the brethren, one an Italian and the other a German, both called John of Cologne, about whose was a certain commentary on the *Sentences.* This affair was also referred by the general chapter of Paris in 1269 to a special committee composed of the same six masters for investigation. Aquinas decided in favor of Fr. John of Cologne, from San Faustino near Viterbo, while Bonhomme the Breton, Peter of Tarentaise, Bartholomew of Tours, Baldwin of Maflix, and Gilbert van Eyen were in favor of the other party. The conclusion was that " the title should remain unaltered, with no indication of the friar's native land, Italian or German, and should be known as the Joannine edition made by Fr. John of Cologne, for this was undoubtedly true and wronged no one." [58]

Yet another case required investigation and judgment before the general chapter met in Milan in 1270. It was a matter concerning the master in sacred theology, Fr. Bartholomew of Tours. Since 1266 St. Louis IX had been making active preparations for a crusade, and the Friars Minor, and still more the Friars Preachers, were greatly assisting him in this work by their preaching. The master-general, Fr. John of Vercelli, had appointed Fr. Bartholomew to be vicar-general over the Dominicans who were to accompany the crusade overseas. " But since even the wisest among us are sometimes not careful enough, he let something slip about some business of a will, which very much displeased the master-general." To make matters worse, Bartholomew attempted to excuse himself by bringing an accusation against the master-general, thereby damaging his authority and giving rise to a double scandal. John of Vercelli therefore called for an investigation and submitted the matter to the judgment of three of his most learned and competent friars, Thomas d'Aquino, Robert Kilwardby, and Latino Orsini. These three eminent men studied the case and made a report to the master-general in a letter which indicates that the guilt of Bartholomew of Tours had also been established by an investigation carried out on behalf of Fr. Michael, the prior of Lille, and the famous preacher Lambert of Liége. In view of these reports the chapter of Milan imposed severe penalties on Bartholomew, took away from him certain privileges, and removed him " from the office of vicar-general over the friars who were to go overseas with the crusaders, which had been entrusted to him by the master-general." [59]

B. John of Vercelli himself did not fail to consult the illustrious master during this period. The first time was when he passed on to him a text, which Thomas examined and corrected in January or February, 1270, in an opusculum entitled

De forma absolutionis.[60] A year later the master-general submitted to two of his friars, Thomas Aquinas and Robert Kilwardby, a collection of forty-two articles or questions chiefly
concerned with problems of cosmology and eschatology. Since
all that was required was a brief and concise answer,
St. Thomas at once set about working out his reply in sum-
mary fashion: *praetermissis aliis occupationibus.* The following
day he gave his report to the master-general. We cannot but
admire Thomas' prompt obedience in acceding to a request
made to him by authority, and notice his reverence for the
head of the Order. St. Thomas, as it were, apologizes for the
brevity of his reply, adding in conclusion that this particular
task was one outside his professorial routine, and only undertaken at the special order of his superiors. Robert Kilwardby,
who was also recognized as a great master in the world of
theology, made a fuller report than Thomas, but it must be
remembered that the latter was at the time much preoccupied
with the doctrinal conflicts in Paris, and had little time to
delay over matters not directly concerned with his position
as professor. Fr. Chenu has made an interesting study of the
two replies of Thomas Aquinas and Robert Kilwardby to the
enquiry of John of Vercelli, comparing the two different atti-
tudes and methods of answer.[61]

With the holy king, Louis, that man of wonderful integrity
who led the crusade of 1270, St. Thomas continued in the
friendly relations which had begun during his first period of
teaching in Paris. It was probably now, in 1269 or early in
1270, that the event occurred which is at once a splendid testi-
mony to the friendly relations between the saintly king and
the saintly Dominican,[62] and to St. Thomas' absorption in his
studies. The story goes that " St. Louis once invited him to
luncheon, but that he at first humbly excused himself on account of his work on the *Summa theologiae,* which he was busy
with at the time. Upon receiving an express command, however, from both the king and the prior [of Paris], he left his
studies and went to the king. But his mind was still full of

the idea that he had begun to work out in his cell, and as he
sat near to the king at table, all of a sudden he had, as it
were, an inspiration about a certain truth of the Faith, banged
down his fist upon the table and cried: 'That's finished with
the Manichean heresy!' The prior touched him, saying: 'Remember, Father, that you are at luncheon with the king,' and
he began to pull at his cappa to bring him back from his abstraction. Thomas seemed to come down to earth again,
bowed to the king, and asked him to pardon his absent-
mindedness. But the king was much impressed and edified,
for Thomas, being of noble birth and upbringing, might have
been expected to derive special pleasure from such a royal
invitation and to leave his speculations aside for a short time,
while on the contrary not even a royal entertainment was
able to distract his soaring spirit. The holy king then took
measures that the thought which had so absorbed the holy
Doctor should not be lost, and he sent for his scribe, and
ordered him in his presence to take down on paper what was
hidden in the Doctor's mind." [63]

Since St. Louis left the capital in March, 1270, it was certainly before this time that Thomas was invited to the royal
table, that is, during 1269 or early in 1270.[64] At this time
St. Thomas was busy dictating the *Summa in theologia*, in
particular the I–II. In this matter the account of Tocco and
the chronology of the Saint's writings are in agreement.[65]
The editors of the Leonine edition,[66] in connexion with the
words of the last paragraph of chapter 15 of Book III of the
Contra Gentiles, "per hoc autem excluditur error Manichaeorum," mention the Master's exclamation, "Modo con-
clusum est contra haeresim Manichaeorum!" There are, however, two important facts recorded by Tocco with regard to
the composition of the above-mentioned text. St. Thomas took
a lot of trouble over that chapter and wrote it all out with
his own hand, while he was in Italy during the years 1261–
1264: not, therefore, in Paris or at the King of France's table.
On the other hand, the Master composed the *Summa the-*

ologiae by dictating. This also explains why St. Louis immediately called his secretary to take down his learned friend's idea even during the court luncheon. The use that Thomas made of secretaries during his second period of teaching in Paris is an indication of the position which he enjoyed. It only remains, therefore, to find among Aquinas' writings, lectures, or disputations of the time an argument against the Manichaeans. When, however, we know the particular style of Tocco, it is not impossible to suppose that " contra Manichaeos" means rather " contra monopsychistas," " contra murmurantes," or even " contra Averroistas."

But to return to the luncheon at court to which Thomas was invited: this was perhaps the last conversation upon earth of these two true princes of piety and holiness. St. Louis died of plague near Tunis on August 15, 1270, while fighting the infidels. The sad news was announced to Europe, together with a request for prayers addressed to certain religious people and communities, by King Philip III, who chose as bearers of his letters the Dominican Godfrey of Beaulieu, who had given the Last Sacraments to St. Louis, William of Chartres, O.P., John dei Monti, O.F.M., and other friends. In addition to the request for prayers in this letter of September 12, the same king, during the next year, having in between lost his brother, his wife, his sister and his brother-in-law,[67] turned once more to the Friars Preachers, writing a letter dated May 6, asking the Fathers who were about to assemble for their general chapter at Montpellier (May 24) to remember in their prayers and sacrifices the souls of his dear ones who had died. The chapter dispatched a gracious reply to this royal request, to which there is also a reference in the acts of the same chapter, among the directions about suffrages for the dead to be said by the friars: " For my lord the King of France and for my lord the Count, his son, and for the young queen, each priest is to say four Masses." [68]

Another announcement, this time from Italy, brought no small sorrow to Thomas while he was still perhaps in Paris.

This was the death at Orvieto, before June, 1272, of Cardinal Annibaldo, with whom he had at one time lived as friend and brother. The general chapters of Florence in 1272 and Siena in 1273 [69] ordered as suffrages for the soul of this eminent churchman that every priest should celebrate one Mass. We can well imagine Thomas' own feelings as he fulfilled this obligation.

When we look at Thomas' social relations with his colleagues and disciples, we cannot help noticing the outstanding authority which he enjoyed among his contemporaries. His profound and subtle, yet solid, doctrine, his sureness and modesty in teaching, his shrewdness and prudence in judgment and discussion, his earnestness and piety of life—these things had given him an authority, both as a man and as a teacher, which was not only not denied even by his adversaries, but on the contrary willingly recognised, as witness the remarks of Nicholas of Lisieux and of Siger. The former speaks of Thomas as a great master,[70] while the latter praises equally Albert and Thomas as the most outstanding philosophers: *praecipui viri in philosophia.*[71] Not even Peckham refuses his veneration for Thomas, but claims that he supported him as far as he could.[72]

A special honor was conferred on him by his colleagues in the Faculty of Theology, when they asked him to "make an authoritative pronouncement on the problem of the dimensions of the Body of Our Lord Jesus Christ and of the accidents subsisting without a subject in the Sacrament of the same Body and Blood of the Lord."[73] He would, of course, be closely connected with the lecturers in the theological school of the province of Paris, who at the time were probably John of Varzy, William of Quinchy, and William of Luxeuil.[74]

The majority of the members of the Faculty of Arts, who expressed their mourning at Thomas' death in a quite exceptional way, had paid him no less honor during his lifetime. It could not have been otherwise with a man who was at once so learned and so lovable and humble.

These virtues were especially evident at the examination

of a certain religious, who was already a " licentiate " and so was hoping to proceed to the degree of master. It happened that the candidate held an opinion opposed to that of the examiner and to the truth, and Master Thomas had not succeeded in making him change, but nevertheless bore with him with great patience and calm. But as his students were returning with him to the priory, they said to him: " Master, we feel much offended on your behalf, because that master should not have contradicted you, and you should not have tolerated this injury to the truth in front of all the masters of Paris." " My dears," St. Thomas is supposed to have replied, " I thought I would make allowance for a new master at his *principium*, and not cause him confusion. But if the brethren think otherwise, I can always put straight tomorrow what I did not do today." In fact, on the next day, Thomas and his students arrived with this in mind, and the same audience being gathered in the hall of the bishop's palace, the candidate repeated without any correction the very same arguments and conclusions. So Fr. Thomas in the quietest way pointed out a discrepancy between the candidate's opinion and the words of one of the Councils, and then proceeded very gently but most methodically to overwhelm the headstrong young man in argument. When he finally yielded to the truth, Thomas in his goodness felt that he had achieved his object, and simply said to him in an affectionate way: " Now you've got it right." [75]

From this story we can see with what respect and gentleness Thomas dealt with people, and how he by these social gifts won over young people, who were always ready to go about with him. In the above story we find Thomas surrounded by a group of students.

There is another incident, which is better known especially for a famous answer of St. Thomas: he made a trip with some young people, to go on a pilgrimage to the abbey and sanctuary of St. Denis. On the way back, as they drew near to Paris, the students exclaimed: " Look, Master, how lovely Paris is! Wouldn't you like to be the owner of it? " They said this hoping to get some edifying answer. What he said was: "I'd rather have the homilies of Chrysostom on St. Matthew. And if I owned that city, the trouble of governing it would take me away from the contemplation of divine things and I should be miserable." [76] And so it is believed that when occasion arose Thomas gladly talked in a friendly manner with his students on things either academic or spiritual. [77] With reference to the homilies of Chrysostom, Dom Germanus Morin [78] is of the opinion that he did not mean the authentic homilies of the Greek Father, but the *Opus imperfectum in Matthaeum* of the author who adapted the works of Origen on the Gospel of St. Matthew.

Among the people in close contact with him—in addition to the bachelor, Fr. Romano Orsini of Rome, [79] who taught under his direction—it is possible to name several who were either certainly or most probably his students. [80] Thus, for example, from the Order of Preachers we find Peter of the province of Dacia (Scandinavia), [81] Peter of Andria, [82] John of Caiazzo, [83] Remigius Chiaro de'Girolami of Florence, [84] Nicholas Brunacci [85] of the Roman province, and a certain Fr. Martin of the province of Spain. [86] From the Order of the Hermits of St. Augustine there were Giles of Rome, known as an especially faithful disciple, and as "at once disciple, critic, and follower of Thomas Aquinas," [87] and also Augustine of Ancona, also called Trionfo. [88] Then there were Peter of Auvergne, a most devoted disciple, [89] and Peter Dubois, [90] the famous pamphleteer of King Philip "le Bel." It was Peter Dubois who used of Thomas the telling phrase "frater prudentissimus." Henry Bate, who studied in Paris between 1266 and 1270, [91] certainly attended some lectures of St. Thomas.

There are examples of laymen who came to Professor d'Aquino, as is shown by the answer to a question *De sortibus*, which was given to a man named James "de Burgo," [92] perhaps from a place called Bourg, and another on the problem *De occultis operibus naturae* for a gentleman from beyond the Alps. [93]

Thomas also received enquiries from more distant parts,

as from Fr. Gerard of Besançon, a lector, and from Fr. Bassanio of Lodi, lector in Venice. To the first Thomas gave his answers to the six questions submitted to him,[94] and his reply to the second exists in two recensions, the one divided into thirty articles and the other into thirty-six.[95] In both cases the holy Doctor concludes with a brotherly request for a remembrance in their prayers. During his sojourn in Paris he was also in frequent correspondence with William of Moerbeke, who was in Italy.[96]

On two occasions he was specially concerned with his distant Neapolitan homeland, when he intervened to obtain permission for his Order to make foundations in that area. Thus it was for the sake of Thomas d'Aquino, and Troiano, formerly Roman provincial and now the first procurator-general of the Order, that Abbot Bernard Ayglier on December 27, 1269, granted permission to the Dominicans to start a priory at San Germano;[97] and it was in March of the following year, 1270, that the Archbishop of Salerno, Matthew della Porta, through his friendship with Fr. Thomas d'Aquino, gave the Abbey of St. Paul at Palearia to the Dominicans for a new priory.[98]

The above-mentioned students and laymen, together with his companion Reginald of Priverno, were witnesses of St. Thomas' private life during his second period of teaching in Paris. To these we must add the secretaries to whom Thomas dictated his works. The presence of the last-mentioned surrounding Aquinas shows that the great professor was much more comfortably situated now than during his first period in Paris, when he had only just become a master in sacred theology. At that time, about 1259, he was writing his *Summa contra Gentiles* on bits of indifferent paper, for lack of anything better. Now not only did he have his special companion, as when he was in Italy, but he also made use of the services of secretaries.

The usual one was Evan Garnit, "scriptor suus."[99] Tocco says he was a Breton, and as he gives his diocese, it would seem that he was a cleric. But the manuscripts differ on the identity of the diocese. The Florentine and Vatican texts indicate Tréguier, while the London text gives "dioecesis Crocarensis."[100] This word "Crocarensis" must be a copyist's error either for Trecorensis, *i.e.*, Tréguier in Brittany, or else for Corcagiensis, *i.e.*, Cork in Ireland. In fact, the name Evan (Euan, Ewen, or Eaoin) is borne by an Irish saint of the sixth century whose feast is on December 22.[101] But the name is also that of a bishop of Tréguier in the fourteenth century,[102] and since Tocco is quite definite about the secretary's Breton nationality, and it appears that there was no diocese in Wales with a name resembling "Crocarensis," it may be fairly safely concluded that Evan Garnit belonged to, or at any rate came from, the diocese of Tréguier in Brittany. It is to Evan that we owe the information that "the holy Doctor was sometimes tired after a long spell of dictation to him and to two other secretaries, and would go and lie down to rest a little, but even while resting he would continue to dictate."[103] He is said to have sometimes made use of as many as four secretaries.[104] It is not surprising that Thomas had several secretaries when he was occupied with so many studies and had so many works that he wanted written down. The names of his writers during this second period in Paris include those of Reginald of Priverno and Peter of Auvergne.[105]

Exactly what is meant by Thomas dictating while resting—the Latin text says "dormiendo"—is not clear either from Evan Garnit or from William da Tocco. If the passage is not to be classed as mere legend, some explanation must be found. The most obvious is the practice current among masters of every age and civilization, according to which the master would sometimes give to the secretary or student a theme to work out, some notes to expand, or some material to complete. It may be that Garnit and Tocco meant no more than this: in which case their evidence not only presents no difficulty, but even helps to explain the problem of the authenticity of certain writings that go under the name of St. Thomas. In this matter western Scholasticism is easily outstripped by the practice of an Alexandrian sage: Origen is known to have made use of seven stenographers and as many copyists, as well as several special scribes.[106]

When we consider the amount of work that St. Thomas must have had in hand to require the services of so many secretaries, we can readily understand how intensely his mind must have been occupied to be able to deal with it all.

This surely explains to some extent his absent-mindedness at other times. One example we have already seen, on the occasion of the king's luncheon. A similar thing occurred in Paris, when his turn came for the usual cupping: for " before the doctor started work, he made certain that Thomas really was rapt in contemplation and oblivious of the outside world; he then proceeded to open the vein, feeling sure that the holy man's imagination would not be disturbed, for he had been found completely abstracted." Thus, although St. Thomas was quite exceptionally sensitive, in his case there occurred the exact contrary to what would be expected, " since in spite of the extreme sensitiveness of his body, sometimes he did not feel pain at all." [107]

It was only in virtue of this mental abstraction from external things and his profound application to study that Thomas was able to tolerate so easily the agitations and ever fresh complications which were constantly shaking the University of Paris. Yet we find him much saddened by these troubles that came over the *alma mater studiorum*.

After the condemnation in December, 1270, of the Averroist theses, many of the philosophers who had been reckoned among the followers of Siger returned to sounder principles. But there remained some confusion in matters of administration, so that at the end of March, 1272, not only did the Faculty of Arts split over the election of the rector and other officials, with the result that there arose two opposing faculties, but the whole university found itself at loggerheads with the Bishop of Paris, and all courses were suspended.[108]

In reality, however, not all the masters stopped their lectures and disputations, and it is known that round Easter Thomas held a *quodlibetalis* disputation.[109] But this general strike in the university was indeed a grave calamity, and hung over Paris from Lent until the feast of St. John the Baptist, June 24, in 1272.

It was not at all a favorable time for the holding of regular courses of lectures, and St. Thomas was recalled from Paris.

It was a moving scene when Thomas Aquinas was surrounded by his confrères and many of his colleagues as he took his leave. Above all there were the philosophers of the Faculty of Arts, who had taken up his teaching against Averroism, and who did not wish to let the eminent doctor depart without receiving his promise that he would grant the favor they were asking, of which we have already spoken.

His successor in the professorial chair in Paris was Fr. Romano of Rome, brother of Cardinal Matthew Rosso-Orsini, but he died in the course of the academic year 1272–3,[110] and was in turn probably succeeded by the Breton, William de Magno Saltu, or else by Fr. Ferrer from Aragon.[111]

Chapter Ten

Naples
1272–1274

HE PASSES THROUGH FLORENCE — HIS COMPANIONS
ON THE JOURNEY — VISIT TO THE CASTLE OF MOLARA
— HE IS APPOINTED REGENT OF THE " STUDIUM " AT
NAPLES — THE ROYAL SUBSIDY — HIS STUDENTS AND
ACQUAINTANCES — HIS SERMONS — HIS GRACES IN
PRAYER — RELATIONS WITH HIS FAMILY — PRE-
SENTIMENTS OF THE END — THE REMARKABLE OC-
CURRENCE OF DECEMBER 6, 1273 — HOLIDAY AT SAN
SEVERINO

IT was after Easter, and therefore after April 24, 1272, that
Thomas left Paris for his homeland, while the university was
in a state of turmoil and confusion.[1] As in 1269 he had arrived
in Paris after the academic year had already started, so now
he was leaving with the year unfinished. Such things are tiresome for a lecturer, but the venerable master d'Aquino put
up with them like the saint that he was.

It may have been the provincial of the Roman province
who requested or desired Thomas' return to Italy, though it
was more likely to have been the master-general of the Order,
since the general chapters of the period had placed exclusively
in his hands the provision of staff for the *studia generalia*.[2]
The general chapter of 1272 was to be in Florence, and opened
on the feast of Pentecost, June 12, while the Roman province
held its provincial chapter there at the same time, and St.

Thomas as a preacher-general had the right to take part in the latter assembly, and in all probability did so.[3]

Letters had already arrived from Paris addressed to the assembled Fathers of the general chapter in Florence by the rector of the university and the masters of the Faculty of Arts, with the earnest petition that Thomas d'Aquino should be permitted to remain in Paris.[4] The Order was, however, unable to grant this request.

The general chapters of the mendicants were often gatherings of great public importance. The illustrious Pope Gregory X, who was from Piacenza and had been recently elected, from the first days of his pontificate had thought of calling a general council. By this means, he hoped, a sound solution would be found to the problems of reform, discipline, and unity within the Church, and to the grave troubles in the Holy Land. One of his first acts was the translation of Thomas of Lentini from the archiepiscopal see of Cosenza to the patriarchal see of Jerusalem. But what was essential to the success of the council was the general peace of Christendom, and in particular of the Holy Land. John of Vercelli had, on behalf of Gregory X, successfully negotiated peace between the Papacy and the Republic of Genoa, and was now to do the same with Tuscany, but failed.[5] We read in Davidsohn's history of Florence the following passage relative to the Dominican general's mission and to Thomas' presence in Florence at the time: Gregory had sent John of Vercelli, the master-general of the Dominican Order, to Tuscany, to make peace between the factions who had started a fierce war. John began his mission in Florence, exhorted the citizens to unity, and at the general chapter of the Order in 1272, at Santa Maria Novella, addressed the assembled provincials whose provinces were in every country of Christendom. Among all the brethren of the white habit there was one who by his learning eclipsed all others, whose spirit still lives today and who is the most brilliant representative of the whole of Scholasticism—the " doctor angelicus," Thomas d'Aquino, who had just left the professorial chair in

Paris and stopped on his journey for a short time at Santa Maria Novella.

However, neither the edifying spectacle of the assembled reverend Fathers, nor their leader's appeal for reconciliation, made the slightest impression on the Guelfs who were in power and who were so fond of proclaiming their obedience to the Church.[6]

Then, of course, there was the gathering of the Fathers of the Roman province, where the question of placing the great master d'Aquino within their own province must have come under discussion. In fact, a conclusion on these lines was arrived at: "We entrust entirely to Fr. Thomas d'Aquino our *studium generale* of theology, both with regard to where it shall be, and as regards who and how many shall be sent there to study."[7] Such was the confidence that the Roman province had in its most illustrious son.

It is not known when Thomas replied to this instruction of the provincial chapter of Florence, or when he took steps to put it into effect. But the combination of circumstances, as he himself would have seen from previous recent declarations of the province and from the general state of studies at the time, rendered his task comparatively easy.

First of all, there was the explicit desire of the provincial chapter of 1269: "We order that there should be two *studia generalia* for theology, one at the priory of Naples, to which we assign . . . etc., and one at Orvieto, to which we assign . . . etc."[8] These decisions were made as a result of the project for the erection of a *studium generale* in the Roman province, already mooted at more than one general chapter. In fact, the multiplication of *studia generalia* at the time was connected with the process of dividing up the provinces, which had started at the general chapter of 1266.[9] Furthermore, the general chapter at Milan in 1270 had begun by ordering that the *studium generale* should be set up at Naples;[10] the order was repeated in 1272[11] and approved in 1273,[12] but it did not receive final confirmation at the next general chapter. For this

reason—and it is important to notice this—the *studium* at
Naples in the time of St. Thomas was not technically a *studium
generale* for the whole Order, but was merely a central study-
house for the Roman province. It was only later, in 1303, that
Naples was expressly recognized by the Order as a real
studium generale.[13] The order, which we have already noticed,
made at the provincial chapter of 1269, about the erection of
two so-called "general" houses of study, confirms our interpretation of events. And now in 1272, the capitular Fathers
of the Roman province appointed the priory of Pisa to be the
house of studies for philosophy,[14] while leaving to Thomas the
choice of place and priory for the *studium generale* for theology.

Naples suggested itself for several reasons as the most suitable city. Rome was in a state of decadence; Orvieto seemed
to have become nothing more than a refuge for the Popes, as
Avignon was later to become; while Naples was the residence
of the most powerful Italian ruler, and was the only one that
was able to offer some sort of university tradition, going back
to the time of Frederick II or at any rate to the attempted
restoration of Charles I.[15] Also the Bay of Naples provided
that natural beauty which appeals to youth.

King Charles had hopes of reaping some advantage for his
own kingdom out of the dispersion from Paris. With this object
he wrote a letter [16] on July 31, 1272, inviting both lecturers
and students of Paris to come to Naples and continue their
courses in peace. Thus did that cunning prince hope that the
university crisis in the capital of his nephew Philip III might
be turned to the profit of his own kingdom. It is possible that
he even asked Aquinas if he would move to Naples. Monti
thinks that the king made representations to Thomas' superiors
to have him recalled to Italy.[17]

St. Thomas, in obedience to the general and the provincial
chapters of Florence, and surely (we may permit ourselves
to suppose) not ignoring his own sentimental attraction, chose
Naples as the best place in which this study-house, which was

in some way to be " general," should be established for the furtherance of studies and the advantage of the students.

It may be that on his journey toward the Kingdom of Naples he passed through Pisa, and some are of the opinion that he spent some time at the priory there and taught. In this priory indeed there is still today shown a rostrum which is claimed as that of St. Thomas.[18] He certainly made a halt in Rome, where he was able to see Count Roger of San Severino, his sister Theodora's husband, who was King Charles' representative in Rome.[19]

The little company set off southwards, on foot. Thomas was accompanied by Fr. Reginald of Priverno and Fr. Ptolemy dei Fiadoni, of Lucca, the future historian of the Church and Bishop of Torcello,[20] a most intelligent and cultured man, who had probably just been assigned to Naples. When the party reached the Alban Hills, they turned aside to enable Thomas to pay a debt of friendship to Cardinal Richard degli Annibaldi at his castle of Molara. This easily located castle has been mentioned before. To identify it with the place called San Giorgio di Molaria in the diocese of Benevento, where the Order came into possession of a priory in the seventeenth century, as Mortier does when he alludes to this incident,[21] is quite out of the question. At the castle of Molara, to the south of Frascati and Rocca di Papa, Thomas and his companion Reginald both fell ill, the one of tertian fever, and the other of recurrent fever.[22] Thomas recovered quickly, but Reginald's high temperature continued. " And since all the critical symptoms [of fever] appeared, Cardinal Richard's own doctors declared his condition to be very serious. Whereupon the venerable Doctor took the relics of St. Agnes which he had brought with him from Rome and always wore about his person (round his neck or upon his breast) with tender devotion and told his friend to wear them and have faith in them. No sooner had Reginald taken them than he found himself cured from the illness that the doctors had diagnosed." " This was the reason why St. Thomas arranged for the feast [of St. Agnes] to be celebrated every year with special solemnity, and with a special dinner for the friars—a thing which he did the following year at Naples, but the year afterwards he went to his reward." [23] The special devotion to St. Agnes on the part of St. Thomas' disciple, Fr. Nicholas Brunacci, is probably to be attributed to his master's cult of the same virgin martyr. [24]

If we follow our travelers on the Via Latina toward Naples, we find that there are several places after the castle of Molara which they very probably passed through or visited. There was, for instance, the castle now known as Ceccano, [25] which belonged to Count Annibaldo, who had married one of Thomas' nieces called Frances; there was the family castle of Roccasecca, the small town of San Germano, and perhaps also the Abbey of Montecassino. Thomas would certainly have been glad of an opportunity of talking with Abbot Bernard, if only to thank him for the permission which he granted for the opening of the Dominican priory at San Germano. [26] Eventually, at the beginning or the middle of September, [27] Thomas arrived in Naples and was able to greet his brethren in the great and noble priory next to the spacious church of St. Dominic. [28] It was no doubt with special joy that he embraced the now venerable Fr. John of San Giuliano, who had been a father and friend to him during his first stay in Naples. [29] There were at the time in the community many excellent religious, in particular Eufranone della Porta, Troiano del Regno, James della Porta, Conrad of Sessa Aurunca, Peter of San Felice, John of Caiazzo, Hugh of Magdalano, Matthew of Castellammare, James of Manzano, John of Boiano, Ptolemy of Lucca, William da Tocco, who had so remarkable a veneration for St. Thomas both during the saint's lifetime and afterwards, [30] Leonard of Gaeta, [31] and others. William deserves a special note. He was born in the castle of Tocco in the province of Benevento (not that of the noble family of the Da Tocco of Capua), and entered the Dominican Order at Benevento. He had the good fortune when already a mature man to live in the same community with Thomas at Naples, to speak with him often, and to watch him teaching, preaching, and writing. He was later prior of Benevento, inquisitor for the Kingdom of Naples (in which office he came into conflict with King Charles II, the Lame), and eventually toward the end of his life he acquired special fame at the canonization of St. Thomas.

Although at this time the constitutions of the Order of Preachers had not yet granted any special privileges to masters in sacred theology,[32] we already find in the case of St. Thomas a concession, found later in other cases also, which was gradually acquiring the force of law. In virtue of this Thomas was given a more spacious cell, next to which there appears to have been a flat roof or open *terrazza*.[33] This was obviously a mark of special honor, as was also the fact that at Naples he had the services of Brother Bonfiglio Coppa,[34] and in 1274 of Brother James of Salerno as personal attendants.[35] The younger brother of Brother Bonfiglio, John Coppa, who at the time was often in and out of St. Dominic's Priory and used to come and see Fr. Thomas, has recorded a pleasing incident. Once, when St. Thomas was ill, young John was sitting up in the holy man's room in the place of his brother who was away, and suddenly saw a bright star come in by the window, move over to the sick man's bed, remain for a few moments, and then disappear.[36]

Thomas Aquinas, as regent of the Dominican house of studies at Naples, gave his lectures, disputations, and so forth, in the halls of the priory itself, which was adjacent to the University of Naples. The university precincts remained here until the seventeenth century, when they were transferred elsewhere.[37] And since the Dominican schools were of their nature public [38] and closely connected with the *studium* or university of Naples, it can be claimed that Thomas was in some way a professor of the *alma mater parthenopaea*. In any case, it is worth recording the observations of Monti, if we would understand Thomas' position at this time. During the Angevin period theology was not included in the curriculum of the royal university of Naples.[39] " It has been the general opinion until now, that this subject [*sc.* theology] was taught under Charles I and until 1302 by university lecturers appointed by the king, with St. Thomas among their number, and that from 1302 onwards, by decree of Charles II, the teaching of theology was entrusted to the Dominicans, Franciscans, and Augustinians of Naples, the sum of 12½ pounds (150 *once* or ounces) being paid annually to the three religious houses of St. Dominic, St. Laurence, and St. Augustine. This distinction, in the writer's opinion, is a false one; for already before 1302 there were members of the three orders teaching theology in their own houses and at the same time belonging to the *studium* of Naples. They represented, as we should say nowadays, independent faculties of the university, whose lecturers were not appointed by the king, nor came under the jurisdiction of the civil authorities, but were subject to their own ecclesiastical superiors and appointed by them, although they enjoyed the same privileges as the other lecturers. . . . The lectures in the religious houses were attended both by the members of the order in question and by students from outside, and of course the latter ' took part in the various scholastic exercises to which those were bound who were working for the degree of master in theology.' . . . Charles II indeed confirmed this arrangement, but he cannot be said to have initiated it: furthermore, St. Thomas, as the famous document of Charles I declares, was appointed to teach not in the university, but at the priory of St. Dominic, and the king paid a stipend of 12 ounces of gold, as to the other lecturers, not to him personally, but to his prior, ' to help with the expenses.' It was, moreover, natural enough that for the avoidance of unnecessary overlapping there should be no special chair of theology at the university, but that students should be invited to attend the courses in one of the three schools, the Dominican, Franciscan, or Augustinian."

The "most important of the three monastic *studia* of theology in Naples was that of the Dominicans, an importance easily attributable to the scholarly character of the Order, to the tradition of the priory of San Domenico Maggiore, whose greatest luminary was St. Thomas Aquinas, and to the fact that the king himself expressed his recognition of its importance by assigning to it over half the total subsidy." [40]

In fact, King Charles I, on October 15, 1272—after the meeting at Capua, of which more later, and in which Thomas' own desires can be discerned—granted a stipend to be reckoned from the beginning of the new academic year. The king ordered that the Reverend Father Thomas d'Aquino, his friend, " who was to teach theology at Naples, should receive a sum to cover his expenses, and for this purpose an ounce of gold according to the common weight was to be paid to him every month during what time he should remain there to teach." [41] This amounted to 12 ounces of gold a year, and we can tell its value from the fact, noted by Torraca, that King Conrad also paid 12 ounces of gold annually to a lecturer, and, as Monti observes, that King Charles II during the years 1302–6 disbursed annually 150 ounces of gold to the three houses of St. Dominic, St. Laurence, and St. Augustine, for the instruction given in sacred science. [42]

It is not certain when precisely Thomas began his teaching at Naples. The custom of Paris, in both the university and the conventual schools, was to hold lectures from the first half of September until the feast of SS. Peter and Paul, while in other houses of the Order the scholastic year was from September 29 to June 24. [43] Until the second half of September Thomas was obliged to occupy himself with certain family affairs, as we shall see presently.

The beginning of Thomas' lectures was most eagerly awaited, and from the first his hearers were overcome with admiration. A few names of the secular and regular clergy have come down to us, which enable us at least in part to reconstruct the audience that sat at the feet of St. Thomas during those years. Thus, apart from Ptolemy of Lucca [44] and William da Tocco, [45] who were both older men and advanced students, we find John of Caiazzo, [46] Tomasello of Perugia, [47]

Peter of Andria, the well-known stenographer who had already
been Thomas' student in Paris,[48] James del Mercato,[49] perhaps
a certain Gilbert, and others [50] among those who attended his
lectures. And let us not forget the faithful and well-beloved
Fr. Reginald of Priverno.[51] And then, in virtue of the ancient
law that governed studies in the Order, we may suppose that
all the brethren not actually occupied in the ministry also
attended St. Thomas' lectures on theology.[52] Taurisano and
Monti have indicated the presbyteries and offices of ecclesiastical administration in which were later to be found various
distinguished people who had been St. Thomas' students at
Naples.[53] Among the secular priests who came to listen to
him, we can reckon Marino of Eboli, Archbishop of Capua,
who had a great affection for the holy Doctor,[54] and Matthew
della Porta, Bishop of Salerno (†December 25, 1272).[55] In
addition to these ecclesiastics there were also various laymen
who can be considered Thomas' disciples at Naples. The most
eminent among these was a certain Bartholomew of Capua,
who in 1272 held a minor post at the court, but later received
promotion and became protonotary and *logotheta* of the Kingdom of Sicily. Although he was not in the strict sense Thomas'
student, he was in constant contact with him, studied his writings, and always held him in the greatest veneration, providing
the most valuable evidence at the process of canonization.[56]
Another gentleman who studied under Thomas was Nicholas
Fricia.[57]

These and many others whose names are not on record
formed the group before whom the holy Doctor delivered his
lectures and held his disputations. It was to this distinguished
audience that he lectured on the first part of the *Psalter* [58] and
perhaps completed his course on the *Epistles of St. Paul.*[59]
He also produced commentaries *In libros De caelo et mundo*
and *In libros De Generatione et corruptione* of Aristotle. The
latter was Aquinas' last philosophical writing.[60]

These lectures and commentaries he left in writing. One
of his chief preoccupations at the time was the continuation

of the *Summa theologiae*, but he also found time to go on answering problems put to him by various private individuals, to whom he always replied with kindness and promptitude, as for example to a certain Master Philip who consulted him on the problems *De mixtione elementorum* and *De motu cordis*.[61] And further, he did not forget the promise that he made to the lecturers in philosophy in Paris, to send them the works they asked for, as soon as they were ready.

Taurisano suggested that the "most dear John" to whom the holy man wrote a letter on how to study might perhaps be Fr. John of Caiazzo. But since the letter appears not to be written to a friar at all, it is more probable that John was a layman. And anyway, the authenticity of the letter is very questionable.[62]

As was his wont, St. Thomas continued zealously to preach the word of God in the pulpit. There is no doubt that in his instructions and sermons to the faithful he made ready use of the *volgare* or the Italian tongue, which was the only language other than Latin which he knew. His biographer writes: " He used to expound many and profitable things to the people, using his own native dialect, since his absent-mindedness prevented him ever learning any other." [63]

It was especially during the Lent of 1273 that Thomas dedicated himself to the instruction of the faithful from the pulpit of the priory church of St. Dominic. The sermons that we have on the *Apostles' Creed*, the *Our Father*, the *Ten Commandments* and the *Hail Mary*, represent this course preached day by day to the people.[64] It is probable that the series began on Sexagesima Sunday and continued till Easter, that is from February 12 to April 9.[65] And the people of Naples held him in such veneration and so esteemed his sanctity, that crowds came to his sermons every day. This is witnessed by Tocco, who was himself present.[66] It should be remembered that these popular sermons were attended not only by the common folk but also by many of the city's intelligentsia.

There were four laymen who gave evidence at the process

of canonization by recalling happy experiences of their youth: there was John Coppa, a notary of the city of Naples, brother of the Dominican Brother Bonfiglio, who remembered having heard the sermons on the *Pater Noster*.[67] The same was recounted by Peter Brancaccio, who was a soldier in Naples,[68] while Dr. John Zeccadenario, a doctor of law from Gaeta, claimed to have heard several of St. Thomas' sermons at Naples.[69] The fourth witness was John di Blasio, later " a judge in Naples, and a close friend of her Highness Queen Mary of Sicily," who stated that " during the whole of Lent he watched how the holy Doctor preached with his eyes either closed or ecstatically turned toward heaven, and that he was preaching during that Lent on the text *Ave Maria gratia plena, Dominus tecum*." [70]

Thomas indeed proclaimed the saving precepts of revelation in such a way that not only was his matter clear and profound, but so deeply did he enter into it and order his own life according to it, that he seemed to be entirely absorbed in a longing for heavenly things and to have already a certain foretaste thereof. His very appearance gave power to his words and persuasively impressed upon the minds of his hearers those eternal realities, which he himself so ardently desired. " The people listened reverently to his words as if they came from God himself." [71]

He was a perfect Friar Preacher, a spiritual man, beloved of God and men. Indeed " it seemed that men were overcome by the mere sight of his outward bearing, and whoever saw him or spoke with him even only once received the grace of remarkable consolation. Thus Fr. Eufranone of Salerno . . . used to say that when he looked devoutly upon the aforesaid Doctor, the mere sight of him and his words brought him a spiritual joy and comfort, which could only come from the presence of the Holy Spirit, the sole author of such graces." [72]

From the evidence at the canonization of St. Dominic [73] we know that it was his desire that his sons should speak either with God or of God. And St. Thomas' life was wholly recol-

lected in the presence of God, which accompanied and pro-
tected him wherever he might be. When he was obliged to
see people in the parlor or elsewhere and give help or consolation to his brethren or to others, " he would answer the
various questions which were put to him and then add a few
brief words of historical or moral import for general edification." [74] Furthermore, " if people turned the conversation away
from God or the things of God, he would withdraw from the
parlor or from the conversation, as if it were not his business
to speak of anything that was not edifying or even to talk of
God in any way that was unworthy." [75] Thus he kept himself
always in the presence of God, confident that this would give
him constant support. And when he had moments of fear, at
a sudden clap of thunder or such like, it is recorded that he
would protect himself with a sign of the cross and say, " God
became man for us; God died for us." [76]

He always tried to preserve this interior recollection, and
for fear that while his mind was engaged on high speculation
his devotion might flag, he imitated St. Dominic and " made
some spiritual reading every day from the *Collationes Patrum*," [77] thus seeing to the spiritual nourishment of his soul.

Other people could not help noticing how he seemed to be
favored with signal graces while at prayer, both at his private
prayer which he would make sometimes prostrated on the
floor of the church [78] and sometimes on his knees before the
altar,[79] as well as during the public prayer in choir. He was
so much given to prayer that it was to him like the air which
he breathed, amid his daily tasks of thought and speculation,
reading, writing, and preaching. " In fact, he made such profitable use of the time that was given him to gain merit during
his life, that apart from the brief moments that he gave to
sleeping and eating in fulfilment of his duty toward his health,
he devoted all the rest . . . to godly occupations." [80]

It was, after all, his life of prayer that stood out above
everything, so that when Fr. Reginald of Priverno, on his return
from the Abbey of Fossanova after his master's death, resumed

his lectures at the school in Naples, the one thing he insisted on, when mentioning the holy Doctor, was the learning that he acquired in answer to prayer. " For every time that he set about studying, disputing, reading, writing, or dictating, he began with silent prayer, begging with tears that it would be granted to him to discover the divine secrets of the truth, and so it often happened that before he had prayed he was puzzled by various problems, while after his prayer he saw the perfect solution." [81]

This interior recollection, which he maintained for his own intellectual and spiritual ends, was the cause also, in this period, of absent-mindedness and a remarkable oblivion of the world around him. An example was cited by Marino of Eboli, Archbishop of Capua, to Fr. Raymund Étienne, a Dominican of the province of Toulouse, who was sent to Armenia in 1318 and in 1322 became Archbishop of Ephesus: it appeared that Thomas had such an abstraction in the presence of a certain cardinal legate at Naples. [82]

St. Thomas had " a great devotion to the Blessed Sacrament of the altar. He who had the gift of writing so profoundly on this subject also had the gift of the greatest and devoutest veneration for this sacrament. Every day, unless prevented by illness, he celebrated Mass, and then assisted at another said by his companion or someone else, and this Mass he often served. Frequently he went into ecstasy during Mass, for he was so full of devotion, so immersed in the sacred mysteries, and so favored with heavenly gifts, that frequently his tears flowed." " And one day in the priory of Naples—it was Passion Sunday (March 26, 1273)—he was saying Mass with great devotion in the presence of many noble gentlemen, when in the course of the Holy Sacrifice he appeared to be so absorbed in the greatness of the sacrament that it was as if he had been admitted to the vision of the divine mysteries and permitted to share the sufferings of Christ. . . . For long he remained thus, until finally his brethren, full of wonder, approached him, shook him, and asked him to proceed with the sacred mysteries." [83] At the end of the service some of the brethren and some of his closer friends among the gentlemen who had been there besought him to tell them what had happened during that ecstasy. Thomas received them all in a kindly way, but preferred not to disclose anything.

This incident shows not only his devotion to the Holy Eucharist, but also his gentleness in dealing with others.

We have already seen how much Master Thomas' sermons were appreciated by the people, but at the same time he was "wonderfully compassionate towards the poor, and he regularly gave away quantities of his own clothes and other things, keeping nothing superfluous for himself, but rather trying to help" others.[84] Thus it was that he came to be known as "buon Fra Tommaso." [85]

But while on the one hand he was never forgetful of the needs of the poor, on the other hand he was mindful of the duties of his estate, the dignity of his position of Master, and the obligations of his noble birth. He had a quite particular affection and esteem for his relatives and friends. His relation with his companion Reginald was one of true intimate friendship. Other special friends of his whose names are known were, among his brethren in religion, Ptolemy of Lucca, whom he often chose as his confessor during the years at Naples,[86] and John of Caiazzo,[87] and among the gentry of Naples there was the judge John di Blasio, and others.[88]

Among the noble families of Naples the name of this truly illustrious and holy man Thomas d'Aquino was becoming a byword.[89] It is indeed a joy and a satisfaction to feel the warmhearted personality of the Angelic Doctor coming through the documents of his canonization, in spite of the arid legal style in which they are written. And how we treasure these glimpses into Thomas' loving soul.

What a delightful act of kindness on his part it was, to offer that festival luncheon at his expense in honor of St. Agnes in 1273! We can well imagine how pleased the brethren and

students were who attended it, and how grateful to this remarkable man.

And what of his relations with his family? His affection for
his own kinsfolk was deep, easy, faithful, and supernatural.
We know how he often prayed to God for his relatives, both
during their life and after their death, and how he prayed for
his nephews and other relatives who died, and asked for
prayers and Masses for them.[90] And this affection was mutual:
he was much beloved of them, and did what he could for
them while on this earth. As soon as he arrived in the Kingdom
of Naples he was called upon to put their affairs in order, a
task which appealed to his charity and patience, but which
must have gone against his passionate devotion to his studies.

Roger dell'Aquila, Count of Traetto and Fondi, the husband
of Adelasia d'Aquino, died at his castle on Friday, August 26,
1272.[91] The Count, knowing that his wife's brother was near
at hand (and perhaps he even had his assistance in his last
moments), had appointed him his executor. He had also hoped
to entrust the upbringing of his four small children to another
relative of his wife, Roger of San Severino near Salerno. But
King Charles, since the matter came under the jurisdiction of
the court of Naples, brought out a decree on September 1
"pro baliatu filiorum quondam comitis Rogerii de Aquila,"
appointing the procurator of the Terra di Lavoro to be responsible for these young children, provided that a near kins-
man of the count's was chosen to supervise the whole business.[92]

Now on September 10, after Thomas had put in a formal
request to the court, the king learned of the will of the late
Count Roger dell'Aquila, and that Thomas was his executor.[93]
On September 20 Thomas was at Traetto to fulfill his duty of
seeing to the disposal of the count's possessions according to
his will. In the long inventory we find a quantity of things
which were dispatched " by the hand of Fr. Thomas d'Aquino,"
and which included things like mules, trained and untrained

beasts of burden, saddles and other trappings, clothes, stores of grain, *etc*.[94]

It was no easy matter to carry out the many clauses of the will, but a particular problem arose with regard to justice in the disposal of certain immovable goods, which Count Roger had "incorrectly appropriated" from certain persons and places, and concerning which he had in his will ordered restitution. Thomas decided that a royal license was necessary for this transaction; and in spite of the difficulty of travel, he went on September 27 to see the king at Capua to obtain it. At this meeting Charles was so impressed with Master Thomas that henceforth he looked upon him as a dear friend, and on October 2 granted his request and issued an order which put straight the matter of the count's ill-gotten gains.[95] In addition to this, on September 27 Thomas asked the king to remove Richard, the count's eldest son, from the care of the royal procurator and to put him under the Count of San Severino; this favor was also granted.[96]

It was shortly after this that King Charles, in a document dated October 15, granted to his friend Fr. Thomas the stipend of which mention has already been made.

The royal favor which Thomas enjoyed was turned to good account by a niece of his, who tried to use her uncle's influence to gain entrance to the Kingdom of Naples. This was "my lady Frances, wife of my lord Annibaldo of Ceccano" and already known to us.[97] Her husband's political views had caused him to be reckoned by the Angevin government a traitor, an "enemy of the Holy Roman Church, and our own,"[98] with the result that it was not possible for her to set foot within the kingdom. But now, for reasons of health—she needed a cure at the baths of Pozzuoli—she sought and obtained through her uncle a safe-conduct. The lady herself, with her family and mounted attendants, was thus enabled freely to enter the territory of Naples and freely to leave again, permission having been obtained to remain from April 3 until June 3, 1273.[99] It is further known that Thomas stayed several times with this niece at the castle of Maenza near the Abbey of Fossanova, when he was passing that way.[100] These visits may have been connected with Thomas' journey to and from the provincial chapter appointed for September 29, 1273, in Rome, unless we are to place them earlier. At this chapter—according to an old record noted by Masetti—Thomas was one of the diffinitors.[101]

At the end of Paschaltide in 1273, Thomas, on account of the renown and sublimity of his doctrine, was invited by the Pope to take part in the General Council, which was to be held the following year at Lyons.[102] It was only right that Gregory X, having already summoned other eminent theologians, should also call upon Aquinas. From now onwards Thomas indeed merited to be considered by all to be " one of the most holy and most learned men of his time." [103] It may be said that from the time that he received the pontifical summons to Lyons, he had in the eyes of the world attained to the summit of authority, of honor, and of his scholarly career.

But now he was preparing for still higher flights, not indeed to any earthly heights, but toward the homeland of heaven.

His first reaction was to be greatly moved by both the words and the music [104] of that verse of the Psalms [105] which appears in the antiphon to the *Nunc dimittis* in the Lenten Compline: " Ne proicias nos in tempore senectutis, cum defecerit virtus nostra ne derelinquas nos." It almost seems that he had a presentiment of his approaching death, which no one can have thought was near to this man of not yet fifty years of age,[106] who was still in full vigor of both body [107] and mind.

In addition to this, he had a vision of Fr. Romano of Rome, his successor in the professorial chair in Paris, who had recently died (before May 28, 1273),[108] and who now revealed to him that before long he would have direct experience of the things of God. Romano also told him that he himself had reached salvation after having passed through Purgatory, which had been a punishment especially for some negligence on his part in carrying out some task entrusted to him by the

Bishop of Paris. Thomas immediately put to him a scholastic question: *utrum habitus scientiarum in hac vita acquisiti maneant in patria.* Romano did not reply exactly " in forma," but assured him of the fact of the Beatific Vision, whereupon Thomas immediately asked him how he saw God: *sine media vel mediante aliqua similitudine?* Romano answered in the words of the Psalmist: " As we have heard, so we have seen, in the city of the Lord of hosts," [109] leaving his interlocutor somewhat astonished, but also, because this was a thesis that was very dear to him,[110] not a little comforted. In fact, this vision brought to Thomas much joy and consolation, but he recognized in this also a premonition of his approaching death.

These premonitions, however, in no way slowed up Thomas' usual studies. He continued to work hard at the third part of the *Summa theologiae;* but when he had finished the questions on the most holy sacrament of the Eucharist, and had embarked on the treatise on the sacrament of Penance, he suddenly ceased writing.

With reference to his work on the *Tertia pars* of the *Summa,* and more particularly on the sections concerning the Passion and Resurrection of Christ, which he probably wrote during the first half of that year, we learn from Tocco, on the evidence of Brother Dominic of Caserta, who was sacristan at St. Dominic's Priory, Naples, that Thomas used to come down from his cell to the chapel of St. Nicholas, choosing a time when there would be no one in church, that is before matins, and there would pray before the crucifix. One day he was apparently raised up from the ground, and heard Our Lord on the Cross say to him: " Thoma, bene scripsisti de me; quam recipies a me pro tuo labore mercedem? " To which Thomas replied: " Lord, none other but thee." [111]

Certain modern critics, with Ubald of Alençon and Charles Balic, reject the authenticity of the " Bene scripsisti." [112]

On December 6, 1273, the feast of St. Nicholas, in whose chapel at San Domenico Maggiore he usually said his Mass, it happened that during Mass " he underwent a wonderful transformation." He seems to have had an ecstasy. After this Mass "he never wrote or dictated anything more, and even laid aside his writing materials in the middle of the treatise on Penance in the third part of the *Summa*." The exact words of the *logotheta* have a flavor that is quite their own: "Post ipsam missam nunquam scripsit neque dictavit aliquid, immo suspendit organa scriptionis in tertia parte *Summae*, in tractatu de paenitentia." [113]

This occurrence in the life of a man whose habit was, after his Mass and thanksgiving, to spend the whole day writing, dictating, or teaching, showed indeed a remarkable change. Fr. Reginald of Priverno, his friend and most faithful companion, noticed this unusual behavior on the part of Thomas, and said to him: "Why ever have you given up this great work, Father, which you began for the glory of God and the instruction of the world?" And Thomas replied: "I cannot go on." Reginald feared that the balance of the Master's mind had been upset by too much study and continued to insist on his going on writing. But Thomas always answered: "Reginald, I cannot." On one occasion he added: "Because all that I have written seems to me like so much straw compared to what I have seen and what has been revealed to me." [114] "I have reached the end of my writing . . . so I hope that the end of my life will come soon." [115]

These words are significant in more than one way. A scholar like St. Thomas would not have said what he did not mean. First of all, he wished to convey the fragmentary nature of his knowledge, as St. Paul did in I Corinthians 13:12 when he wrote: "Now I know partially; but then I shall know completely" (Spencer). Secondly, he felt that all that he had so far done had become out of date. Even the *Summa theologiae*, that unfinished masterpiece, seemed to him but a shadow compared to the flood of light that entered his mind on that December 6, 1273, at the end of his professorial career. We may well ask whether he could have thought out and put for-

ward a still more lucid and coherent system if he had remained longer upon this earth.

Beneath the aforementioned words, which show Aquinas'
soul so absorbed in God and yearning for heaven, we can also
see traces of the physical ailment that was attacking him. But
before we proceed, we must not omit to note the discrepancy
between the evidence of the *logotheta* Bartholomew of Capua
and that of Tocco concerning the place where the aforesaid
ecstasy occurred. Contrary to the *logotheta*, Tocco [116] indicates
that it happened while Thomas was staying with his sister
Theodora at the castle of San Severino, of which we shall
speak presently.

There was another occasion during Thomas' period in
Naples when he was unwell or actually ill in bed,[117] but this
time—in the December of 1273—it was more serious and urgent
measures had to be taken to safeguard his health.

He was therefore ordered, both on account of his general
state of health and in order to build up his strength again, to
take a holiday with his sister Theodora, Countess of Marsico.
He would have to go to the castle of San Severino, where she
usually spent the winter.[118] He set off with his companion,
Fr. Reginald,[119] taking the Via Popilia which runs through
Pompei, Nocera, and the little town formerly called Rota, but
now known as Mercato San Severino.[120] Eventually they arrived at the castle " which he [Thomas] reached with much
difficulty." [121] On the way he stopped at the priory of Salerno,
where there occurred a wonderful example of the heavenly
favors which he received in prayer. " For while the aforesaid
Doctor was at the priory of his Order at Salerno," writes his
biographer,[122] " he was praying before the high altar after
matins, and was seen by Brother James and by his companion
to be raised two cubits [three feet] from the ground, as if he
were sharing the agility of the blessed, or something of the
kind."

When at last he reached the castle, " the countess of San
Severino, his own sister whom he loved very much, came out

to meet him, but he hardly paused to greet her." It seemed as if Thomas had lost his old courtesy and charm of manner. The countess was saddened by this and anxiously asked Fr. Reginald: "What has happened to Fr. Thomas? He hardly spoke to me." Reginald answered that his beloved master had been like this since the feast of St. Nicholas and had not written anything more.

For some time the honored guests stayed in that lovely castle, but Thomas gained little from his stay.

Neither rest nor the most delicate attention was able to bring any improvement to the Master's broken health. They all felt, when he took his leave, that he was saying good-bye to them for the last time.

Countess Theodora was very upset when her brother left.[123] We can place, with Scandone, this final parting of brother and sister between the end of December, 1273, and the early days of January, 1274.[124] Thomas then took the road again, at dead of winter, back to Naples and to his priory of St. Dominic. Here he began preparations for a much longer journey, the journey to the Council of Lyons.

Chapter Eleven

The Last Journey
1274

HE IS SUMMONED TO THE COUNCIL OF LYONS — HE
FALLS ILL AT MAENZA — HE GOES TO THE CISTER-
CIAN ABBEY OF FOSSANOVA — HIS DEATH THERE AND
BURIAL — THE VENERATION OF THE FAITHFUL

THE time was rapidly approaching for the Master to set off
for the Council of Lyons, in obedience to the pope's command.
He had by no means regained his strength; his health was
very poor; and the journey was likely to cost him enormous
effort—yet obedience called, and he did not hesitate.

His departure northwards took place, we may easily suppose, after mid-January or at latest early in February.[1] He took
with him the *Libellus ad Urbanum (IV) papam,* which that
pontiff had ordered him to write against the errors of the
Greeks.[2] With him went his companion Fr. Reginald, and
Brother James of Salerno as an attendant.[3]

When they had got past the small town of Teano and were
going down toward Borgonuovo, it happened that either
through absent-mindedness or through some accident "he hit
his head against a tree that had fallen across the road."[4] The
others immediately ran to help him: Fr. Reginald, the Dean
of Teano, who was called William and later became bishop
of that city (✝1295), and the dean's nephew Roffredo. When
Fr. Reginald asked him if he had hurt himself, he answered,
"Not much."

Then Reginald thought he would cheer the Master up by conversation, and he talked about the object of their journey and how much good would be done at Lyons for the Church, for the Order, and for the Kingdom of Sicily, adding: " And of course you and Fr. Bonaventure will be made cardinals and so bring glory upon your two Orders." But Thomas answered: " I can be of much more use to the Order as I am." Reginald then said that he had meant the glory of the Order and not of the person of Thomas himself, whereupon Thomas told him plainly: " You may rest assured that I shall always remain as I am." [5]

It is not quite certain which road the party took after passing Teano and Borgonuovo: did they continue along the Via Latina through the Liri Valley, or did they follow the track of the old Via Appia through the Pontine Marshes along the sea? [6] Although it is more frequently stated that Thomas took the hilly road through the Campania [7] and wrote his famous letter to Abbot Ayglier from the foot of the hill of Montecassino itself, yet the bull of canonization indicates the coastwise route. [8]

It is possible to reconstruct the journey, which according to Toso was as follows: " Since we know that St. Thomas passed through Teano . . . and then went to Maenza . . . it is more likely that he took the road from Teano to Maenza by Minturno; for had he passed through Aquino on the way, his journey, trying enough already on muleback, would have been considerably lengthened." To explain Aquinas' halt below Montecassino, Toso thinks " that Thomas was taking the opportunity on this journey of revisiting the haunts of his childhood and youth, by passing through the valley of the Liri, which is dominated by the height of Montecassino, of Monte Cairo, and the neighboring hills. On one of these stood the castle of Roccasecca, which is visible from Aquino and from all the surrounding country." [9] However that may be, whether Thomas took the Via Latina or the Via Appia or one of the roads noted by Sthamer [10] linking the Via Appia and the Via

Latina, after Teano he touched San Germano-Cassino. On the hypothesis of a journey by the Via Latina he would have gone on from San Germano-Cassino to Aquino and Roccasecca to visit his relatives.

St. Thomas' letter to Abbot Bernard of Montecassino, which is authentic, though we do not possess the original, is regarded as the most intimate document of the holy Doctor. It elucidates certain passages in the book of the Moralia of St. Gregory the Great on the conversion of sinners and God's foreknowledge.[11]

But now we come to a fixed point on this journey: it is known that during the Lent of 1274,[12] Thomas was very exhausted and made a halt at the castle of Maenza in the diocese of Terracina. Maenza lies on the seaward slope of the hills called the Lepini, below Monte San Martino and the Colle Santo. The castle overlooks the deep valley of the Amaseno. Since Lent began in that year on February 14, it is supposed that Thomas arrived at Maenza in the second half of February. He was most cordially received by his niece Lady Frances, wife of Annibaldo, Count of Ceccano, whom, as we have seen, he used to visit from time to time.[13] When he was there he used regularly to visit the Abbey of Fossanova,[14] which is on the River Amaseno, three miles from Priverno. In this way he brought about very friendly relations between the counts of Ceccano and the monks of Fossanova: the counts were the patrons of the Cistercian abbey,[15] and just at that time, in 1274, the superior of Fossanova was Abbot Theobald, who was himself of the family of Ceccano.[16]

While at the castle of Maenza, Thomas was struck down by an illness, the nature of which is unknown to us, but which was shortly to bring him to the grave.[17] Let us bear in mind that already in Naples Thomas had been in bad health, and that after the vision on the feast of St. Nicholas a great physical change had come over him: yet we are not bound to consider that the events of the previous December were directly connected with the illness which attacked him in February. Nor need we pay any attention to the story [18] that St. Thomas' death occurred not from natural causes but by poisoning on the orders of Charles I of Anjou, of whom Dante wrote the famous line (*Purgatorio* XX 69): "Ripinse al ciel Tommaso, per ammenda" ("He sent back Thomas whence he came, to expiate"). His new illness did not stop his saying Mass: his great devotion, which showed itself during those days in the many tears he shed during Mass, is attested by the Cistercian monks from Fossanova who had come over to the castle to greet him, and for four or five days were witnesses of the holiness of his life under the test of illness. These monks were Dom James of Ferentino, the prior, Dom Peter who came from the castle of Montesangiovanni, Dom John of Piedemonte, and Brother Fidelis of Ferentino or of Tuscany.[19]

During this illness Thomas completely lost his appetite, and all food became distasteful to him. Fr. Reginald did his best to induce him to take some nourishment, and the doctor, John di Guido, used all his skill to propose something that might attract him.[20] Eventually Thomas thought that he might be able to manage some fresh herrings, which he remembered having had when he was away from Italy. At that very moment it happened that a fisherman from Terracina brought along a basket of herrings together with the usual sardines. This was a remarkable thing, because herrings were quite unknown in those parts, yet now by the arrangement of Providence they were offered to St. Thomas. At first he refused them, but then out of respect for his niece and the other people present, who included the Cistercians, some Franciscans, and his own companions, he joined them in eating them.[21] The episode of the herrings is attested to by Abbot Nicholas and Dom Peter, as well as by Tocco.

At the request of Dom James, the prior of Fossanova, St. Thomas consented during these days to tell them what had happened when he was preparing his inaugural lecture at the University of Paris. Reginald had always wanted to know this story, but had never dared to ask him, so this time he got the Cistercian Prior to ask him.[22]

Thomas only stayed a few days at the castle of Maenza.[23] In the " rocca " or stronghold of the castle a room is still shown, which is well identified as the holy man's sick-room.[24] St. Thomas was getting worse, and felt that the end was coming. His mighty spirit was completely calm. He entreated them to take him to the neighboring monastery, saying: " If the Lord is coming for me, I had better be found in a religious house than in a castle." [25]

His request could not be refused. He said good-bye to his relatives and hastened toward the house of God. They took every care, and he was borne upon a mule [26] to the abbey he knew so well. The Cistercian prior, the other monks, and his own companions rode with him. In the church at Fossanova there are still preserved as souvenirs of the Master's last journey a pair of stirrups and some mule's hoof-marks,[27] with the inscription: " Hoof-marks of St. Thomas Aquinas' mule." From the castle of Maenza to Fossanova is about six miles.[28]

The holy and learned Dominican was received by the Cistercians with true Benedictine hospitality, in an atmosphere of friendship and piety. It was still February.[29] As he crossed the threshold of the venerable abbey, he will have been received by Abbot Theobald of Ceccano, by the aged and half-blind subprior, Dom John of Ferentino, perhaps by the bursar, Dom John of Mola, and by the other monks, who had already been led by the Doctor's fame and glory to hold him in great veneration.[30] The whole of this impressive monastery is surrounded by walls, and the main entrance is through a turreted bastion. In the middle of the western façade the grand mosaic was still fresh, bearing the name of Frederick Barbarossa, in whose time the church was built. Thomas greeted the monks, went to visit the Blessed Sacrament in the church, entered the cloister, and then, in the presence of many of the monks and many friars of his own Order, including especially his companion Reginald,[31] in the abbey parlor or in the chapter-room near the choir,[32] gave utterance to these words of the Psalter: "This is my rest for ever and ever: here will I dwell, for I have chosen it." [33] He was then taken to the room they had got ready for him. William da Tocco says that the abbot had given him his own cell, but another tradition states that he was given the best room in the guest-quarters. It is worth noting what an able writer of today has to say about the room assigned to St. Thomas, which was to be the scene of his death.

Serafini observes: "Contrary to local tradition, which can be traced at least to the sixteenth century, the *Acta Sanctorum* quite illogically state that St. Thomas died in the abbot's cell and not in the guest-quarters. In the thirteenth century, however, the abbots of Fossanova preferred not to live within the abbey itself, but rather, in order to be freer for the duties of their office, in the new building which was over against the guest-quarters." "We have recently been able to examine, behind the main apse of the church of St. Mary at Fossanova, the remains of the old guest-quarters, in which is the small room—later turned into a chapel, and in the sixteenth century joined with the adjacent room by the Cardinal Commenda-tarius Aldobrandini—in which the Saint left this life for that of heaven." The altar erected in this room is adorned with a relief by the school of Bernini, and on one of the walls are inscribed these verses of a later humanist period:

> Occidit hic Thomas lux ut foret amplior orbi
> Et candelabrum sic Nova Fossa foret.
> Editus ardenti locus et non fossa lucerna
> Hanc igitur Fossam quis neget esse Novam? [34]

Thomas was already ill when he arrived; now he got rapidly worse and his strength was obviously failing.[35] During these critical days [36] not only did he give no trouble whatever to those who waited on him, but he gave "every example of admirable patience" [37] and edified the whole community by his conduct. They looked after him with wonderful kindness, for they held him in the greatest veneration for his renowned holiness.[38] " They vied with one another in carrying firewood on their own shoulders from the woods, and getting whatever was wanted for him, for they felt that it was more fitting that they themselves should carry the things he needed, than that so virtuous a man should be served by mere brute beasts." [39] But the monks afterwards remembered not only the great patience of St. Thomas, but also his gentleness and humility and unfailing goodness to them.[40]

All this kindness embarrassed Thomas,[41] and he wished to show his gratitude by doing something for his hosts. Some of the monks had besought him to leave them a last fruit of his wisdom, and so he agreed to give them a short commentary on the *Canticle of Canticles*.[42] In his explanation of the sacred text he poured out all the desire for union with God, which now filled his soul, and which was becoming every moment more ardent. He was anxious to prepare himself for eternity with all the means afforded by the Christian religion, and so in addition to his prayers he made a general confession to his usual confessor Fr. Reginald.[43]

He was now getting very weak, and asked for Viaticum, which was brought to him with full solemnity on March 4 or 5.[44] The abbot himself brought the Blessed Sacrament to the sick man.[45] The community knelt round the room, together with a number of Friars Minor,[46] who belonged chiefly to the household of the Bishop of Terracina, Francis, O.F.M.,[47] who was also present. Lastly there were many Dominicans, who on hearing of Thomas' illness, had come from the nearest priories,[48] which were at Anagni and Gaeta.

Thomas gathered all his strength and lifted himself from his bed, knelt and prostrated himself upon the floor, remaining a long time in adoration of the Blessed Sacrament,[49] and then, with tears of devotion, gave utterance to many expressions of surpassing beauty, among which were his profession of faith and the famous words recorded by Bartholomew of Capua, the monks of Fossanova, Tocco, and the bull of canonization:

" I am receiving thee, O price of my soul's redemption: all my studies, my vigils, and my labors have been for love of thee.[50] I have taught much and written much of the most sacred Body of Jesus Christ; I have taught and written in the faith of Jesus Christ and of the Holy Roman Church, to whose judgment I offer and submit everything." [51]

The next day he received Extreme Unction: he himself made the responses to the prayers.[52] On the third day following, the mighty spirit, serene, innocent, and angelic, of the Master, Thomas Aquinas, sped to the eternal embrace of God, to whom he had remained true during all his days upon earth, and whom he had loved with all his heart.

It was early in the morning on March 7, 1274,[53] which was a Wednesday.

> Lauda mater Ecclesia
> Thomae felicem exitum,
> Qui pervenit ad gaudia
> Per verbi vitae meritum.[54]

Thomas, who had spent his life doing good and performing wonders, did not cease from his good works after his death. While the venerable body was still lying upon the bed, the subprior Dom John of Ferentino, who was nearly blind, touched it and received his sight. This event was witnessed by Francis, Bishop of Terracina, by several of the Franciscans, and by nearly a hundred Cistercian monks.[55]

In addition to this, various other remarkable things happened after Thomas' death, which bore witness to his sanctity of life. A holy hermit of the Campania, at the moment of the Saint's death, saw a bright star over the Abbey of Fossanova, and then two other stars coming down towards it and escorting it to heaven.[56] It is also said that Albert the Great, at Cologne,[57] and Fr. Paul dell'Aquila, Dominican lector at Naples,[58] had special revelations at the passing of St. Thomas.

While his body was being carried in procession from the room where he had died to the church, a heart-rending occurrence interrupted the psalmody and chanting of the monks. His niece, Frances, who had not dared to enter the enclosure to visit the room of the dead man, came and begged the abbot to allow the procession to pass by the abbey entrance. Here she and other noble ladies with her manifested their love of him and their grief by their tears and sobs.[59]

Then everything was prepared in the abbey church for the solemn funeral of the Master. The service was attended by the Bishop of Terracina and the religious of St. Benedict, St. Francis, and St. Dominic, and also by many of the gentry of the Campania, " of whom many were drawn thither by their natural love, since the aforesaid Doctor had many relatives in the Campania, but many others were attracted by the fame of his wisdom, by the miraculous signs, and by the example of his holy life." [60]

At the end of the funeral service, the remains of St. Thomas were buried near the high altar in the abbey church.[61]

> Fossa nova tunc suscipit
> Thecam thesauri gratiae.[62]

After the burial, Fr. Reginald of Priverno, whose only consolation in his great grief was the thought of the happy death of his master, at the instance of one of the monks, rose, and with great emotion recalled the purity of heart and humility of him who had just died.[63] He did not speak in praise of his learning, but simply and in touching words told of the purity and humility of Thomas d'Aquino, who had been called from the uncertainties of earthly knowledge to the perfection of the vision of God. This was all he would say, or perhaps all he could say at that moment, of his own beloved " buon Fra Tommaso," the great master in sacred theology.

The following lines of the hymn at Lauds on the feast of St. Thomas make allusion to certain favors by which heavenly approval of Thomas' life and works was made manifest:

> Manens doctrinae veritas,
> Et funeris integritas,

Mira fragrans suavitas,
Aegris collata sanitas.[64]

Doctrinae veritas: in connexion with the truth of his teaching it is pleasant to record two specially significant witnesses: the first of Siger of Brabant (who died between 1281 and 1284), who after being Thomas' opponent became his admirer, and the other of a great prelate, the Archbishop of Naples, James of Viterbo (who died in 1307).

Van Steenberghen has proved from reliable sources that a remarkable change, from the philosophical standpoint, came over Siger of Brabant under the influence of St. Thomas and after his condemnation by the Bishop of Paris. It was owing to Aquinas' attack on the unorthodox theory of monopsychism in psychology that he abandoned this position, and in fact in his last psychological work, the *Quaestiones* on the *De Anima* of C.L.M.9559, he came close to the Thomist idea of the Aristotelian doctrine of the soul. It is possible that he was also influenced by one of his colleagues in the Faculty of Arts, Peter of Auvergne, who was known to be a " fidelissimus discipulus " of St. Thomas. Anyway, Siger came so highly to esteem Albert the Great and Thomas d'Aquino, that he spoke of them as " praecipui viri in philosophia Albertus et Thomas." A sign that Thomas was on good terms with the Faculty of Arts, whose head at the time was Siger, is the fact that at Aquinas' death it was this faculty that sent a moving letter of condolence to the general chapter of the Dominican Order assembled at Lyons, while the Paris Faculty of Theology, in which Thomas had twice been a professor, remained completely silent. . . .

The fact that Dante in the *Paradiso* places Siger in the circle of the twelve great doctors and puts his praise in the mouth of Thomas can no longer surprise us in the light of these new researches, for whatever were the philosophical preferences or opinions of the poet, Siger can no longer be considered the principal rival of St. Thomas. There was indeed at one time a keen dissension between the two teachers on the problem of the intellect, but the conflict was transitory: Siger and St. Thomas held almost the same philosophical ideas, and the former was strongly influenced by the latter.[65]

Blessed James of Viterbo, Archbishop of Naples, said: " The writings of many great and learned men have been attacked and pulled to pieces after their death, but even if the writings of Fr. Thomas have been attacked since his death, and assailed by sharp contradiction, yet his authority has never wavered, but on the contrary has become even more firm, and has spread throughout the world side by side with his cult and honor." [66]

Funeris integritas indicates that St. Thomas' body remained at least for a number of years incorrupt, a more remarkable thing when we consider that Aquinas had been a somewhat stout man, and that the place of his burial was rather damp.[67]

Mira fragrans suavitas: a wonderful fragrance issued from the tomb and from the sacred remains, when in the autumn of 1274, the tomb was opened already for the second time.[68]

For a certain period St. Thomas' body had been moved from its original place of burial, for fear that it might be stolen away from the monastery. When the relics were translated from the chapel of St. Stephen,[69] which stood not next to the church of St. Mary, but on the south side of the monastery,[70] and restored to their original position near the high altar, the monks noticed the wonderful fragrance that came from the relics and so they sang the Mass of a Confessor, feeling that it would be incorrect to sing the Mass of *Requiem,* as for anybody.

Aegris collata sanitas records the many miracles which God worked for the sick through the intercession of St. Thomas. These miracles occurred especially in the district of his death and burial, as is shown by the crowds who came to the abbey church of Fossanova to seek cures or help in trouble, and to offer their thanks for graces received.[71]

Chapter Twelve

The Holy Doctor

THOMAS D'AQUINO—as we have seen—was tall, stout, and of upright carriage. His complexion was of the color of corn, golden; his head was large and slightly bald.[1] Nicholas of Priverno says that he was " grossus et brunus." [2] His regular features, his steady eyes, his firm but gentle mouth—these things suggested a man who was spiritual, pure, and peaceful.

He had dedicated himself to the things of the spirit, and used the good things of this earth but sparingly, reducing them to bare necessities; he refused all honors, having no other ambition than to apply himself unceasingly to the duties of his vocation, fulfilling his obligations as a Christian, as a religious, as a priest, and as a teacher with brilliance, with patient and wholehearted perseverance and with utter gene-rosity. He avoided idle conversation and loved silence: he lived in the inner retreat of his own spirit. He liked to walk up and down the cloister or the garden, but even then his mind did not wander, but was engaged in meditation.[3] He was in every way a man of prayer: the various kinds of private prayer and liturgical prayer, so that he was described as " miro modo contemplativus." [4]

It is a significant fact that while in the lives of other doctors we read of supernatural phenomena of an affective nature, Thomas' visions are all concerned with the manifestation of

171

truth. He received from heaven the theme for his inaugural lecture *Rigans montes,* and from heaven he also received the elucidation of certain difficult passages in Isaias and St. Paul.[5] These divine illuminations came to him in answer to the ardent prayers and fasts by which he implored the grace of understanding in dark and difficult matters.

He lived his whole life in accordance with the faith of revelation, with a deep piety toward God and our Saviour, and with a remarkable recollection during Mass and a great devotion to the Saints. Toward others he showed a delicate Christian prudence,[6] he was always respectful, courteous,[7] and charitable, and his shining purity, his humility, and his charity caused him to be called " buon Fra Tommaso." [8] He had a great affection for his family, and a profound Christian piety.[9] He had few great friends, but to these he was always true and faithful. His personal life and his attitude toward others might be summed up in his own famous remark: " Sicut enim maius est illuminare quam lucere solum, ita maius est contemplata tradere aliis quam solum contemplari." [10]

Many facts about his life, both natural and supernatural, have been preserved for us by eyewitnesses such as Reginald of Priverno, William da Tocco, and others, but unhappily he never had a biographer who did for him what Eadmer did for St. Anselm. Nor can we look into his soul through his letters, as we can in the case of the Doctor of Canterbury, whose complete correspondence remains extant.

After Touron, various modern authors, such as De Groot, Maritain, Petitot, Deman,[11] Puccetti, and Taurisano, have given us a picture of St. Thomas' spiritual characteristics.

Msgr. Grabmann [12] considers the essential marks of Aquinas' spiritual life to be wisdom, charity, and peace. He also describes Thomas' approach to the knowledge of truth from the ethical standpoint.[13]

Finally, in his wonderful little book S. *Tommaso d'Aquino* [14] Msgr. Grabmann has given us a masterly portrait of St. Thomas the scholar. He describes his method of working, and shows how he united the qualities of the scholar and the saint, and looked with a single gaze towards the ultimate goal of life and that of scholastic attainment. This union was achieved, he says, by three things: first, a logical and methodical working-out of metaphysical and speculative thought, dominated by the single ideal of truth; secondly, by a careful combination of observation of fact with speculation, and of analysis with synthesis, so that he preserved a middle course between an exaggeration of reality to the detriment of thought on the one hand, and on the other hand an over-emphasis on thought which was out of touch with reality, thus avoiding both a positive empiricism and an exaggerated idealism; and thirdly, his fundamentally ethical and religious approach. In the work of St. Thomas, we stand as it were in a wonderful temple, and from the outer court of the world we pass into the Holy Place only to find ourselves face to face with the Holy of Holies—all is encompassed in a single divine harmony.

For St. Thomas' influence in the world of thought, and for his intellectual outlook, the works of Grabmann, Gilson, and Gagnebet may be consulted.[15]

Thomas was closely united to God, who is the ultimate end of all knowledge and of all culture, and his one desire was the search for truth. He had no subjective preoccupations, and all his labors were directed to arriving more easily and more surely at the truth in all its objectivity. Therefore, whenever he found the truth, he affirmed it without hesitation.

Starting from sound principles, his conclusions were clear and vigorous, and any personal attacks that were made on him he supported calmly, for he had no concern for himself, but only for the truth. Yet he felt a deep sorrow when he saw that noble minds were struggling to reach the truth and failing to do so.[16]

His method of study, as we have already observed, was always a combination of observation with speculation, and of analysis with synthesis.

As he proceeded, he penetrated problems more thoroughly,

and during his whole teaching career he made constant efforts to make both his own understanding and his teaching more coherent, more universal, and more lucid, expressing himself in terms that were sober, clear, precise, and objective, in a language that had grown out of his own thought—the "discreto latino," as Dante called it (*Paradiso* XII 144). Tocco notes how much Thomas' brief, clear, and easy manner of teaching was appreciated.[17] It was not only in logic and metaphysics that he was so outstanding, for he took the greatest care over the positive elements in his teaching.

He has also left us a few remarks which show his wide view of history.

He went back to sources, to the Scriptures and to the great authors, principally to Aristotle and to the Fathers,[18] especially the Latins. He assimilated them and interpreted difficult passages, either harmonizing them, or on rare occasions, indicating in a few precise words his disagreement. By this reverent use of the Fathers, St. Thomas—as Cajetan has observed in a famous passage [19]—has in some way captured the spirit of them all.

His prodigious memory was a great help to him in this use of positive documents.

He was very much *au courant* with the scholastic problems of his time, summed up exactly the positions of past and contemporary authorities, and had no fear of introducing innovations where principles were insufficiently understood, or where a new and better method of approach required them. He was not afraid of being dubbed an innovator [20] or a progressive: names which were given him because of his unhesitating tenacity in the application of scientific principles. " His prime innovation, which had been prepared by some of his predecessors, especially Albert the Great, but the fulfilment of which was reserved to him, was the integration of Aristotle into Catholic thought." [21]

He turned the Aristotle of history into something more Aristotelian than Aristotle himself had ever thought of. In this great work his own personal conviction was supported by his personal courage and humility.

St. Thomas was not, however, a mere disciple or interpreter of Aristotle: with the help of Platonic and Augustinian elements he placed his philosophical teaching on the plane of a higher synthesis altogether.[22]

Aquinas, the flower and glory of Scholasticism, had before him all the varied sources of previous philosophical thought, and the equally varied patristic and contemporary tendencies. With these in mind, he brought about as Grabmann rightly says,[23] the widest possible adoption of the Aristotelian philosophy of the Arabs, proving at the same time the error of their doctrines that ran counter to Christianity, and he created a Christian Aristotelianism in the sense of a synthesis of Augustine and Aristotle. In the field of philosophy there arose a Christian metaphysic, based upon Aristotle but with an Augustinian completion, a psychology and a theory of knowledge which remained substantially Aristotelian but included many Augustinian elements. In political and social ethics the Aristotelian political concepts were retained without prejudice to the Christian ideal. The construction of a system of speculative theology derived enormous help for its reasoned arguments and demonstrations from the Aristotelian doctrines of being, of act and potency, of matter and form, of movement, of causes, of the faculties of the soul, of the teaching on the virtues in the Nichomachean Ethics, and so forth. It was Albert the Great, who, with an extraordinary breadth of vision and intellectual generosity, was the first among the theologians to write commentaries on the "new Aristotle" and thus initiated Christian Aristotelianism; but it remained for his disciple Thomas d'Aquino to formulate an exact method. Aquinas' greatest achievement in the world of thought was the synthesis of Augustine and Aristotle.

The whole doctrinal organism which is called Thomism is not only a philosophy: it is rather the whole *ensemble* of philosophical and theological teaching which is derived from the system of Aquinas. There is a recent article on Thomism in the *Dictionnaire de Théologie Catholique* by Fr. Garrigou-Lagrange. Much has been written on the problems, both doctrinal and historical, of Thomism by many distinguished authors, among whom may be mentioned Baeumker, Bandas, Beltrán de Heredia, Billot, Browne, Buonpensiere, Cayré, Chenu, Commer, Cordovani, Dacik, D'Arcy, De Bruyne, De Groot, Del Prado, Deploige, De Raeymaker, De Wulf, Dezza, Diekamp, Dörholt, Dummermuth, Ehrle, Farrell, Gardeil, Garrigou-Lagrange, Gemelli, Geyer, Giacon, Gillet, Gilson, Glorieux, González, Grabmann, Gredt, Guinassi, v. Hertling, Horváth, Hugon, Janssens, Jolivet, Lepidi, Lorenzelli, Lumbreras, Mandonnet, Manser, Marin-Sola, Maritain, Masnovo, Mattiussi, McNabb, Mercier, Hans Meyer, Michelitsch, Nardi, Nys, Olgiati, Paquet, Pègues, Pelzer, Pieper, Prümmer, Ramírez, Reiser, Rickaby, Rolfes, Rolland-Gosselin, Satolli, Schultes, Sertillanges, Sheen, Stöckl, Szabó, de Tonquédec, Ueberweg, Vann, Van Steenberghen, Weiss, Zacchi, Zigliara, and others.

There are various periodicals devoted to the study of theoretical and historical problems of Thomism. Such are the *Divus Thomas* of Piacenza, and that of Fribourg, the *Acta academiae romanae S. Thomae*, the *Angelicum*, the *Revue Thomiste*, the *Revue des Sciences philosophiques*, the *Bulletin thomiste*, *La Ciencia Tomista*, *Sapientia* (La Plata), *The Thomist*, *Dominican Studies*, *Sapienza* (Bologna), the neoscholastic reviews of Louvain, Milan, and Washington, and others, the volumes of the *Bibliothèque thomiste* and of the *Biblioteca de los Tomistas Españoles*, a great part of the *Beiträge* of Baeumker and Grabmann, of the *Thomistische Studien* (Fribourg), and of the medieval studies of Toronto and Ottawa, and other writings of the kind. But let us return to St. Thomas.

The holy Doctor's conscientious and objective application to the search for truth and to its propagation is evident in the whole mass of his writings, the extent and clarity of which are so amazing. His *Summa theologiae* has enjoyed unparalleled esteem down to our own days, for this work shows the full might of his spirit and the nobility of his soul; it is conceived in the most perfect order and with a wonderful propriety of terms; it possesses that splendid simplicity which is the mark of classical genius; and its scientific expression betrays a rare pedagogic sense.

Thomas d'Aquino, with his limpid doctrine, at once so deep and so sure, has continued to instruct the generations that followed him, to enrich their studies and to inspire their spiritual life.

Chapter Thirteen

Aquinas' Writings

CLASSIFICATION OF HIS WORKS — A SYSTEMATIC LIST
OF HIS WRITINGS

ST. THOMAS' writings cover the greatest variety of subjects in the field of philosophy and theology.

His writings are partly the fruits of his lectures (*e.g.*, the *Commentaries* on the Bible and on the *Sentences*) and his scholastic disputations (*e.g.*, the *Quaestiones disputatae*), and partly the results of independent composition, either expressly systematic (as the *Summae*), or written in answer to some inquiry or to meet a particular case (as are most of the opuscula).[1]

Some of his works he either wrote himself or dictated, while others we have in the form of notes taken by his confrères or others.[2] Certain of his writings we possess in his original manuscript,[3] while others have only been preserved in copies.

On account of the various interruptions to his teaching career, both in Paris and in Italy, a grave problem has arisen with regard to his writings, with much debate about the authenticity or otherwise of certain of the works that go under his name.

Already the editors of the *Editio Piana* (Rome, 1570) noted that the authenticity of some works attributed to the holy Doctor was doubtful.

The most outstanding student of the transmission of the works of St. Thomas and of the vindication of their authenticity has been Fr. James Echard in his work *Scriptores Ordinis Praedicatorum*.[4] He has been followed, with varying degrees of precision, by Bernard de Rubeis, Thomas Soldati, Peter Anthony Uccelli, and others.[5] In the present century the names of two scholars stand out: Fr. Peter Mandonnet (✝1936) and Msgr. Martin Grabmann (✝1949), who have both greatly contributed in many publications to the solution of the problems of authenticity and of St. Thomas' literary output.

Mandonnet in his study *Des écrits authentiques de S. Thomas* brings under discussion the new criterion of the official catalogue,[6] a criterion or hypothesis which Grabmann in his *Die Werke des heiligen Thomas von Aquin* shows to be quite unreliable.[7]

Apart from the aforementioned scholars, others have entered the controversy on the authenticity and chronology of St. Thomas' writings. Among these are the learned editors of the Leonine Edition, and scholars such as Denifle, Gilson, De Bruyne, Destrez, Synave, Chenu, Dondaine, Motte, Lottin, Glorieux, Pelzer, Pelster, O'Rahilly, Beltrán de Heredia, Käppeli, Axters, and Castagnoli, chiefly in the following reviews: *Divus Thomas* (Piacenza), *Jahrbuch für Philosophie und spekulative Theologie* and *Divus Thomas* (Fribourg), *Revue Thomiste*, *Revue des Sciences philosophiques et théologiques*, *Bulletin thomiste*, *Angelicum*, *La Ciencia Tomista*, *Ephemerides theologicae Lovanienses*, *Recherches de Théologie ancienne et médiévale*.

The following researches should also be noted: Ambrose Bacic, *Introductio compendiosa in opera S. Thomae* (Rome, 1925); P. J. de Guibert, *Les doublets de S. Thomas* (Paris, 1926); J. Destrez, *Études critiques sur les oeuvres de Saint Thomas d'Aquin d'après la tradition manuscrite* (Paris, 1933); Palémon Glorieux in his *Répertoire des Maîtres en théologie à Paris au XIIIe siècle;* and Ferdinand Van Steenberghen in his *Siger*.[8]

Mandonnet[9] classifies St. Thomas' writings as follows: I. Philosophy: a) Commentaries on Aristotle (nos. 1–13), b) Various works (nos. 14–25); II. Scripture: a) Old Testament (nos. 26–31), b) New Testament (nos. 32–42); III. Theology: a) General theology (nos. 43–46), b) Dogmatic (nos. 47–49), c) Moral (nos. 50–62); IV. Apologetics (nos. 63–68); V. Canon Law (nos. 60–70); VI. Discourses (nos. 71–74 [a]); VII. Liturgy (no. 75).

In Grabmann's *Die Werke*, St. Thomas' works are listed according to their literary genus.[10]

An account of the editions and translations of the works of St. Thomas is given in the *Bulletin thomiste*, 1924–1936; Grabmann's *Tommaso d'Aquino* (1939), pp. 243–7; and in Bourke's *Thomistic Bibliography*, nn. 1350–1437.

A valuable piece of work could be done on the fortunes of Aquinas' writings and teaching among the Greeks.[11]

Mention should be made of the Pian and Leonine editions of the *Summa,* and that of Ottawa (1941–1945).

The *Summa Theologiae* has been translated into Spanish (Madrid, 1880 sq., and a new ed., 1947); into English (London, 1911 sq.—new ed., New York, 1947); into French (Paris, 1851 sq., 1857 sq., 1925 sq., Draguignan 1860 sq.); into Dutch (Antwerp, 1927 sq.); into Polish (I Pars, Cracow, 1927 sq.); into German (in the fourteenth century, and at Salzburg, 1933 sq., and in part at Leipzig, 1934 sq.); into Czech (Olomouc, 1932–42); into Portuguese (São Paulo, 1936 sq.); again into English ("Basic Writings of St. Thomas," New York, 1945); into Greek by Demetrius Cynodes in the fourteenth century and by Kamires at Athens in 1935 sq.; into Armenian in the fourteenth and seventeenth centuries; and into Chinese by Fr. Louis Buglio, S.J., in 1654 (with new editions at Peiping and Shanghai in 1930). An Italian translation is in preparation.

The following list of St. Thomas' writings is based on the work of Mandonnet, Grabmann, and others.

COMMENTARIES ON SCRIPTURE

1) *In Iob expositio* (1269–72, Ptolemy: 1261–64).

2) *In psalmos Davidis lectura* (as far as Ps. 51 inclusive, 1272–73, *notes taken* by Reginald of Priverno).

3) *In Isaiam prophetam expositio* (1256–59, Pelster 1252–53).

4) *In Ieremiam prophetam expositio* (1267–69, Pelster, 1252–53).

5) *In Threnos Ieremiae prophetae expositio* (1267–68, Pelster, 1252–53).

6) *In evangelium Matthaei lectura* (*notes taken* by Peter of Andria and Leger of Besançon, 1256–59).

7) *In evangelium Ioannis expositio* c. i–v, *lectura* c. vi–end (*notes taken* by Reginald, 1269–72).

8) *Catena aurea (Glossa continua) super quattuor evangelia: Super Matthaeum* (dedicated to Urban IV, 1261–64), *Super Marcum* (dedicated to Cardinal Annibaldo, 1265), *Super Lucam* (1266), *Super Ioannem* (1267).

9) *In S. Pauli epistulas expositio* Rom.–I Cor. 10 (1272–73) (the section on I Cor. 7.14–10.33 has been lost in the original, and in the printed editions it is replaced by a section from the commentary of Peter of Tarentaise), *lectura,* I Cor. 10 to the end of Heb. (*notes taken* by Reginald, 1259–65).

NB. The *In Cantica canticorum expositio,* if ever written (cf. p. 93), has been lost. The commentary which begins "Sonet vox tua" is by Giles of Rome, while that beginning "Salomon inspiratus" is by an author earlier than St. Thomas.

COMMENTARIES ON THE WORKS OF ARISTOTLE AND THE *LIBER DE CAUSIS*

1) *In libros Peri-Hermeneias expositio* (as far as Liber II lectio 2 inclusive, 1269–72, dedicated to the Provost of Louvain. The rest is supplied from various authors, generally from Cajetan).

2) *In libros Posteriorum Analyticorum expositio* (1269–72).

3) *In VIII libros Physicorum expositio* (after 1268).

4) *In libros De caelo et mundo expositio* (as far as Lib. III lect. 8, 1272. The remainder is by Peter of Auvergne).

5) *In libros De generatione et corruptione expositio* (as far as Lib. I lect. 17 inclusive, 1272–73. The remainder is by Thomas of Suthona).

6) *In IV libros Meteorologicorum* (as far as Lib. II lect. 10 inclusive, 1269–72. The rest of Lib. II, and Lib. III are by Peter

of Auvergne, and Lib. IV by yet another author, perhaps John Quidort).

7) *In libros De anima lectura in Lib. I* (*notes taken* by Reginald), *expositio in Lib. II et III* (1266 or after).

8) *In libros De sensu et sensato expositio* (1266–72).

9) *In libros De memoria et reminiscentia expositio* (1266–72).

10) *In XII libros Metaphysicorum expositio* (1268–72).

11) *In X libros Ethicorum expositio* (1269).

12) *In libros Politicorum expositio* (as far as Lib. III lect. 6 inclusive, 1272, Mandonnet c. 1269. The rest is by Peter of Auvergne).

13) *In librum De causis expositio* (1269–73).

SYSTEMATIC TREATISES

Scriptum (Commentum) in IV libros Sententiarum magistri Petri Lombardi (1254–56, Pelster 1253–55).

Summa contra gentiles Lib. I (1259), Lib. II, III, IV (1261–64).

Summa theologiae (as far as Part III, question 90 inclusive, the I Pars 1266–68, the I–II 1269–70, the II–II 1271–72, the III Pars 1272–73. The rest, the " Supplement," is taken from the Commentary on the *Sentences*).

Quaestiones disputatae (in connected series):

1) *De veritate* (1256–59).

2) *De potentia* (1265–67, Mandonnet 1269).

3) *De spiritualibus creaturis* (1266–68, Mandonnet 1269).

4) *De anima* (after 1265, Mandonnet 1269–70).

5) *De malo* (after 1269, Mandonnet 1263–68).

6) *De virtutibus* (in communi 1266–69; de virtutibus cardinalibus, 1269–72).

7) *De caritate* (1266–69, Mandonnet 1269–72).

8) *De correctione fraterna* (1269–72).

9) *De spe* (1269–72).

10) *De unione Verbi Incarnati* (1266–69, Mandonnet 1269–72).

(On isolated subjects):

De sensibus Sacrae Scripturae (1266).

De opere manuali religiosorum (1255–56).

De pueris in religionem admittendis (1271).

Quaestiones quodlibetales (de quolibet) 1–6 (1269–72), 7–11 (1265–67), 12 (1265–67), probably in the form of *notes taken down* by listeners.

OPUSCULA

(The numbers in brackets give the order of the *Editio Piana*. On the numbering of the Opuscula the reader should consult H. D. Simonin in the supplement to the *Revue thomiste* 35 (1930). The authenticity of the Opuscula marked with an asterisk is still under discussion.)

1 [1] *Contra errores Graecorum ad Urbanum IV pontificem maximum* (1261–64).

2 [2] *Compendium theologiae ad fratrem Reginaldum socium suum carissimum* (otherwise entitled: *De fide et spe; De fide, spe et caritate,* 1261–69).

3 [3] *De rationibus fidei contra Saracenos, Graecos et Armenos ad cantorem Antiochenum* (1261–64).

4 [4] (*Collationes*) *De duobus praeceptis caritatis et decem legis praeceptis* (Lent 1273, *from notes taken* by Peter of Andria.)

5 [5] *De articulis fidei et sacramentis ecclesiae ad archiepiscopum Panormitanum* (Leonard de Comitibus, 1261–68).

6 [6] *Expositio super Symbolum apostolorum* (called also *Collationes de Credo in Deum,* Lent 1273, *taken down* by Peter of Andria).

7 [7] *Expositio orationis dominicae* (called also *Collationes de Pater noster,* Lent 1273, *taken down* by Peter of Andria).

8 [8] *Expositio super salutationem angelicam* (called also *Collationes de Ave Maria,* Lent 1273, *taken down* by Peter of Andria).

9 [9] *Responsio ad fratrem Ioannem Vercellensem generalem magistrum Ordinis Praedicatorum de articulis CVIII sumptis ex opere Petri de Tarantasia* (called also *Declarationes dubiorum,* etc., 1265–66).

10 [10] *Responsio ad fratrem Ioannem Vercellensem generalem magistrum Ordinis Praedicatorum de articulis XLII* (called also *Declaratio 42 quaestionum,* 1271).

11 [11] *Responsio ad lectorem Venetum de articulis XXXVI* (called also *Declaratio 36 quaestionum,* to Bassiano of Lodi, 1269–71).

12 [12] *Responsio ad lectorem Bisuntinum de articulis VI* (called also *Declaratio 6 quaestionum,* to Gerard of Besançon, 1271).

* 13 [13] *De differentia verbi divini et humani.*

* 14 [14] *De Verbo* (called also *De natura verbi intellectus*).

15 [15] *De substantiis separatis seu de angelorum natura ad fratrem Reginaldum socium suum carissimum* (incomplete, 1261-69).

16 [16] *De unitate intellectus contra Averroistas* (1270).

17 [17] *Contra pestiferam doctrinam retrahentium homines a religionis ingressu* (1270).

18 [18] *De perfectione vitae spiritualis* (1269).

19 [19] *Contra impugnantes Dei cultum et religionem* (1256).

20 [20] *De regimine principum ad regem Cypri* (as far as Lib. II cap. 4 inclusive, the remainder being by Ptolemy of Lucca. To Hugh II or III, 1265-66).

21 [21] *De regimine iudaeorum ad ducissam Brabantiae* (Aleide. Otherwise entitled *Ad comitissam Flandriae Margaritam*, 1261-72).

22 [22] *De forma absolutionis ad generalem magistrum Ordinis* (1269-72).

23 [23] *Expositio Iae Decretalis ad archidiaconum Tudertinum* (1259-68).

24 [24] *Expositio IIae Decretalis ad eundem* (1259-68).

25 [25] *De sortibus ad dominum Iacobum de Burgo* (1269-72).

26 [26] *De iudiciis astrorum ad fratrem Reginaldum socium suum carissimum* (1269-72).

27 [27] *De aeternitate mundi contra murmurantes* (1270).

28 [29] *De principio individuationis.*

29 [30] *De ente et essentia* (1250-56).

30 [31] *De principio naturae ad fratrem Silvestrum* (1255).

31 [32] *De natura materiae et dimensionibus interminatis* (1252-56).

32 [33] *De mixtione elementorum ad magistrum Philippum* (1273).

33 [34] *De occultis operibus naturae ad quendam militem* (1269-72).

34 [35] *De motu cordis ad magistrum Philippum* (1273).

* 35 [36] *De instantibus.*

* 36 [37] *De quattuor oppositis.*

* 37 [38] *De demonstratione.*

38 [39] *De fallaciis ad quosdam nobiles artistas* (1272-73?).

39 [40] *De propositionibus modalibus.*

* 40 [41] *De natura accidentis.*

* 41 [42] *De natura generis.*

42 [43] *Officium de festo Corporis Christi ad mandatum Urbani IV papae* (1264).

43 [67] *De emptione et venditione ad tempus* (to James of Viterbo, lector in Florence, 1262).

* 44 [68] *De modo acquirendi divinam sapientiam ad quendam Ioannem* (also called *Epistula de modo studendi*).

45 [69] *Expositio in librum Boethii De hebdomadibus* (1257–58).

46 [70] *Expositio super librum Boethii De trinitate* (1257-58).

47 *Expositio in Dionysium De divinis nominibus* (1261).

48 *De secreto* (1269).

49 *Responsio ad Bernardum Casinensem* (Ayglier, Lent 1274).

SERMONS

Sermones (collationes) dominicales et festivi (1254–64, see GRAB-MANN, *Die Werke,* 329–342. KÄPPELI in *AFP* 13 [1943] 59–94).

DISCOURSES

Principium (in S. Scripturam) "Hic est liber" (1252).

Principium (doctoratus) "Rigans montes de superioribus" (1256).
  Both to be found in the editions of F. Salvatore (Rome, 1912), and of Mandonnet, Op. IV (Paris, 1927), 481 sq., 491 sq.

For other works which are more or less authentic, or certainly spurious, see MANDONNET, *Écrits,* 147–156, BACIC, *Introductio,* 118–122, and GRABMANN, *Die Werke,* 345–360 (3rd ed. 465-467).

Chapter Fourteen

The Church's Honor

HIS CANONIZATION — SAINT THOMAS IN THE LITURGY
AND IN ART — HIS POSITION IN THE CHURCH AS A
THEOLOGIAN — " DOCTOR ANGELICUS " — THE PRAISE
OF ST. THOMAS IN PAPAL PRONOUNCEMENTS

THE whole life of St. Thomas was spent in so noble and so spiritual a way that already many of his contemporaries had conceived the greatest admiration and veneration for him. It was natural that after his death his cult should begin. Many people received graces through his intercession, and there were several visions, notably that granted to Brother Ranieri Maturo at the priory of Anagni.[1] These things stimulated devotion to him. Some of his brethren in religion were especially faithful to his memory, and preserved and recorded many details of his life. Notable among these were Fr. Reginald of Priverno, Fr. John del Giudice, Fr. William da Tocco, Fr. Albert of Brescia, and learned men like Fr. Ptolemy of Lucca and Fr. Bernard Gui.

The Cistercians, as guardians of his relics, examined the venerable body no less than three times: in 1274, 1281, and 1288.

The new province of Naples (Provincia Regni), detached from the Roman province in 1294, held its provincial chapter in 1317, and here the matter was raised of the canonization of their great compatriot.[2] Fr. Robert of San Valentino and Fr.

186

William da Tocco, fully provided with the necessary documents and postulatory letters, went to Avignon where they had an audience with John XXII. The pope's support for this cause from the Kingdom of Naples was now assured, both from the ecclesiastical and political angle. The arrangements for the canonization of Thomas d'Aquino were able to proceed in favorable and providential circumstances which are of the greatest interest to both the ecclesiastical and the profane historian.

A preliminary investigation of the life and miracles was made by a commission of cardinals. On September 18, 1318, a commission of inquiry was set up at Naples, where on July 21, 1319, the tribunal was held which during the next few days examined 42 witnesses drawn from the Dominicans and Cistercians, and from other clergy and laity.

The " processus verbalis " was sent to Avignon by order of the pope, being brought before the judges by William da Tocco,[3] while a further inquiry was held at Fossanova in November, 1321.[4]

With regard to the examination of Aquinas' doctrine, there was the evidence of the decisions arrived at after the academic struggles of the preceding decades, and it is likely that use was made of the *Concordantiae dictorum fratris Thomae* drawn up by Benedict of Asiago († 1339).[5]

When the evidence contained in the " processus " had been duly examined and discussed, John XXII held a consistory on July 14, 1323, in which the final requests for canonization were presented by the Dominican Order, by certain prelates, and by King Robert of Naples.

The canonization itself took place with full solemnity on July 18, 1323, in the presence of the King and Queen of Naples, a great number of the clergy both secular and regular, many of the nobility, including Thomas of San Severino, the Saint's nephew, and a crowd of the faithful.[6] The memorable occasion was marked by the bull of canonization *Redemptionem misit.*[7]

The feast was fixed on March 7, and indulgences were attached to devotion to the Saint. In 1368, at the command of Urban V, his body was taken to Toulouse, where at first it rested with his own brethren, who in 1629 placed it in a new and beautiful sarcophagus, enclosed in a magnificent shrine. This was, however, destroyed in 1799; since then the relics have been kept in the cathedral of Toulouse, which is dedicated to St. Saturninus.[8]

Christian art was not slow to occupy itself with the portrayal of the holy Doctor, and there are several well-known examples of the " triumph " of St. Thomas in various conventual churches, notably those at Pisa (by Traini) and Florence (by Bonaiuto). The many and varied painted panels and canvases [9] glorifying Thomas Aquinas form a series of inspired works of art reaching down the centuries into our own times.

Thomas' spiritual heirs were his own faithful disciples and admirers, both within and without the Order, who preserved his teaching, spread it, and defended it, so that it was not long before a flourishing Thomistic school arose.[10] The general chapters of the Friars Preachers held at Milan (1278), Paris (1279, 1286), Perugia (1308), Saragossa (1309), Metz (1313), London (1314), and Bologna (1315) made special recommendations of the teaching of St. Thomas.[11] It was no less a theologian than Godfrey of Fontaines who in 1295, in a celebrated *Quodlibet*, put forward the contention that the ban, which in 1277 Stephen Tempier, Bishop of Paris, had placed on a certain theory of Aquinas, should be lifted.[12]

On May 14, 1324, Stephen of Bourret, Bishop of Paris, withdrew the condemnation of the articles proscribed in 1277, in so far as they concerned, or seemed to concern, the teaching of Aquinas.[13] The position of the Thomist school had grown stronger since their patron was declared a Saint of the universal Church.

Since 1317, St. Thomas had been given the title of " Doctor communis "; [14] in the fifteenth century he began to be called " Doctor angelicus "; [15] on April 11, 1567, St. Pius V proclaimed

SAINT THOMAS OFFERING HIS WRITINGS TO THE CHURCH

(Rome, Vatican)

by LUDWIG SEITZ

(late nineteenth century German School)

him a Doctor of the Church; [16] and on August 4, 1879, Leo XIII in his encyclical *Aeterni Patris* gave the highest praise to his teaching, declaring him, on August 4, 1880, to be the heavenly patron of all Catholic schools.[17]

Important witnesses to his unique position in the Church are canons 589 and 1366 in the new Code of Canon Law, Pius XI's encyclical *Studiorum Ducem* of June 29, 1923,[18] and the apostolic constitution *Deus scientiarum Dominus* on ecclesiastical studies of May 24, 1931, art. 29.[19]

John of St. Thomas († 1644) has very truly said: " Maius aliquid in Thoma quam Thomas suscipitur et defenditur," [20] for indeed what we receive from Thomas, and what in Thomas we defend, is more than merely Thomas himself. Pius XI's great encyclical *Studiorum ducem* points out to men of our own times the vital importance of the Angelic Doctor's holy life and the outstanding nature of his teaching, and Pius XII has repeatedly given encouragement to the study of Aquinas. It is in the name of the Church that the pope calls unceasingly to all students and to the faithful in general: " Ite ad Thomam." [21]

The strength and serenity of the life of Thomas Aquinas, and the clarity and sureness of his teaching, will remain for ever an example and a guide to all who draw near to him and receive of his life-giving light.

Footnotes

p. 1]

¹ TOCCO, c. 1: de domo Aquinorum, de regno Siciliae genitus. *An. Boll.* 42 (1923) 340. *XTh* III 174.

² *Enc. Ital.* III 810–812x. *DHGE* III 1150 sq. Ph.FERRARIUS-M. A. BAUDRAND, *Lexicon Geographicum* II (Paris 1670) 254: " Terra laboris, *terra di lavoro*, provincia regni Neapolitani, in ora maris Tyrrheni, ubi alias Campania felix cum parte Latii novi. Irrigatur Liri et Volturno fluviis et terminatur a septentrione Aprutio ab oriente Comitatu Molisino et Principatu ulteriori, a meridie Principatu citeriori et ab occasu mari Tyrrheno et Campania Romana. Tota admodum fertilis est et rigua. Provinciae urbs primaria est Neapolis, *Napoli*, totius regni caput et amplissima."

³ TOCCO, c. 3.

⁴ *Acta SS. Martii* (Paris-Rome 1865) I 659. EUBEL, *Hierarchia* I 99.

⁵ This diocese belongs to the conciliar region of lower Latium (Lazio inferiore), and is still immediately subject to the Holy See. After the fusion of the dioceses in 1818 it has been known as the diocese of Aquino (Vth cent.), Sora (IIIrd cent.) and Pontecorvo (23. 6. 1725). Cf. *Annuario Pontificio* 1944, 88. F. LANZONI, *Le origini delle diocesi antiche d'Italia* (Studi e Testi 35 [Rome 1923]) 120.

⁶ PELSTER, *La giovinezza di S. Tommaso d'Aquino* 399 sq. SCANDONE, *La vita, la famiglia e la patria* 103 sq.—It should be observed that SCANDONE, op. cit., 108 sq., in order to prove that Roccasecca was the home of St. Thomas quotes certain passages from the process of canonization, which passages, however, indicate Roccasecca dei Volsci near Fossanova, and not Roccasecca near Aquino.—R. BONANNI, *Uomini illustri di Aquino e diocesi* (Alatri 1923) 24 considers Roccasecca to be the castle of the town of Aquino. The same BONANNI, *Aquino patria di S. Tommaso* (Alatri 1923) 34, however, bases his assertion that Aquino was the birthplace of St. Thomas upon a text that is ill-preserved and interpolated.

⁷ SCANDONE, *La vita, la famiglia* 41 sq. 65 n. 1. PELSTER, *La famiglia di San Tommaso* 402. *Enc. Ital.* III 812. KANTOROWICZ, *Friedrich* II 277: "Die Aquinos lebten nach langobardischem Recht." P. HARTIG, *Albert der Grosse und Thomas von Aquin,* Untersuchung zur Bedeutung volksheitlicher Verwurzelung im Mittelalter, *Deutsche Vierteljahrsschrift für Literaturwissenschaft u. Geistesgeschichte* 5 (1927) 25–36.

⁸ SCANDONE, *La vita la famiglia* 42.—Scandone made two genealogical tables of the house of Aquino, the earlier and perhaps better one in the mono-

[pp. 1–3

graph *Per la controversia sul luogo di nascita di S. Tommaso d'Aquino* (Naples 1903), and the other in his article *La vita, la famiglia* (Rome 1924).

[9] F. SCANDONE, *Il Gastaldato di Aquino dalla metà del secolo IX alla fine del secolo X,* Arch. stor. per le prov. Napoletane 37 (1909) 53. DU CANGE-HENSCHEL, *Glossarium mediae et infimae latinitatis* IV (Niort 1885) 40 sq; G. POCCHETTINO, *I langobardi nell' Italia meridoinale, 570–1080* (Caserta 1930) 335, cf. 508.

[10] SCANDONE, *La vita, la famiglia* 42 sq.

[11] MARTINORI, *Lazio turrito* II 217. The castle is 78 miles from Rome, 25 from Frosinone, and 20 from Sora.

[12] LECCISOTTI, *Il Dottore Angelico* 533 n. 3. SCANDONE, *La vita, la famiglia* 43.

[13] SCANDONE, *La vita, la famiglia* 43. POCCHETTINO, I *langobardi* 376.

[14] SCANDONE, *La vita, la famiglia* 45.

[15] KANTOROWICZ, *Friedrich II* 45, 282. SCANDONE, *La vita, la famiglia* 46, 60. PELSTER, *La famiglia* 402. This is perhaps the explanation of the relation that some historians, until ENDRES, *Thomas v. Aquin* 16, claimed for St. Thomas with the Swabian house.

[16] KANTOROWICZ, *Friedrich II,* Erg. 45, 138: the most important families, politically, were the d'Aquino, Eboli, Fasanella, Filangieri, Francisci, Montefuscolo, Ruffo, Tocco, &c. 299: these favoured families became related to one another by intermarriage carefully arranged by the Emperor. An example is the marriage of William da Tocco (299, 123), the court notary from 1225 to 1248, with Sigilgaita d'Aquino. Cf. W. HOLTZMANN, *Unbekannte Staufer-urkunden u. Reichssachen, Quellen u. Forschungen aus ital. Bibliotheken u. Archiven* 18 (1926) 171–190.

[17] SCANDONE, *La vita, la famiglia* 46.

[18] R. BONANNI, *Ricerche per la storia di Aquino* (Alatri 1922) 18, 37 sq. MARTINORI, *Lazio turrito* I 56.

[19] Cf. SCANDONE, *La vita, la famiglia* 42.

[20] SCANDONE, op. cit., 46.

[21] SCANDONE, op. cit., 47.

[22] *Doc.* 1 (Fontes 531 sq), SCANDONE, l. c. 47, 105. *Acta imp. inedita* (ed. E. Winkelmann, Innsbruck 1880) I 769: " Nomina castrorum imperialis iusticiariatus Terre Laboris . . . et nomina terrarum iusticiariatus eiusdem, per quas castra ipsi possunt et debent reparari . . . Aquinum, villa de Canta-lupo et Rocca sicca sunt sibi vicine qui possunt ire ibidem."

[23] SCANDONE, *La vita, la famiglia* 47, DAVIDSOHN, *Geschichte von Florenz* II 1,200: Thomas d'Aquino, the Marquess Manfred Lancia, Pier della Vigna, and others, gave sentence in 1232 against Florence.

[24] Cf. PELSTER, *La famiglia* 406.

[25] LECCISOTTI, *Il Dottore Angelico* 533 n. 2.

[26] SCANDONE, *La vita, la famiglia* 48. TOSO, *Tommaso d'Aquino* 78–82.

[27] TAURISANO, *S. Tommaso* 48.

[28] Cf. CALO, c. 1: de Neapoli. Cf. PELSTER, *La famiglia* 403.

[29] TOCCO, c. 1, CALO, c. 1.

pp. 3–4]

[30] *Acta SS. Martii* I 655.

[31] Cf. SCANDONE, *La vita, la famiglia* 51–55, against those who hold that he was descended from the family of Count Caracciolo. This also disposes of the view noted by PIZAMANO, *Opuscula* S. *Thomae* (Venice 1497), and others as far as ENDRES, *Thomas v. Aquin* 16, that St. Thomas' mother was the sister or relative of the queens of Sicily and Aragon. PELSTER, *La famiglia* 404. TOSO, *Tommaso d'Aquino* 82 sq.

[32] MANDONNET, *Date de naissance de* S. *Thomas d'Aquin* 652, gives a list of ten sons of this marriage, and the same writer in the *Revue des Jeunes* 9 (1919) 148 enumerates twelve, while SCANDONE in the genealogical table in *La vita, la famiglia* also gives twelve. TOSO, *Tommaso*, 83 sq and his table. HOLTZMANN, *Unbekannte Stauferurkunden* 180, states that many genealogical assertions about the d'Aquino are exaggerated, but claims at the same time that sources for this study have not yet been exhausted.

[33] PELSTER, *I parenti prossimi* 299. SCANDONE, *La vita, la famiglia* 76 sq. *Doc.* 35 *(Fontes* 592 sq).

[34] TOCCO, c. 44. PTOLEMY, *Historia eccl.* XXII 20. *Proc. Neap.* n. 78. PELSTER, *I parenti* 300 sq.; SCANDONE, *La vita, la famiglia* 79 sq. Mandonnet calls him a poet, SCANDONE a " master." KANTOROWICZ, *Friedrich II* Erg. 279 identifies this Ronald, a valet at the court, with St. Thomas' brother and the poet (146), the martyr of imperial tyranny, includes him in 1244 " inter maiores in curia Friderici " and claims that he was still alive in 1266 as a supporter of Charles of Anjou.

[35] SCANDONE, *La vita, la famiglia* 79, says that Landulf died about 1261. PELSTER, *I parenti prossimi* 306, notes that it is TOCCO c. 44 alone that gives the name of Thomas' third brother, and supposes it is given in error for Adenulf *Doc.* 35 *(Fontes* 592 sq).

[36] SCANDONE, *La vita, la famiglia* 79. *Doc.* 2–3 *(Fontes* 532–535). *Doc.* 6 *(Fontes* 536). *Doc.* 8 *(Fontes* 539). Scandone is supported by Mandonnet, Taurisano and Toso in admitting the existence of these three brothers. PELSTER, *I parenti prossimi* 303–305, maintains that this sense can only be arrived at by the arbitrary placing of a comma. Therefore, as for example in the *Proc. Neap.* n. 62 " coram ipso deponente, iudice et notario publico et testibus iuratis," this document must be interpreted in the sense of *Doc.* 8 *(Fontes* 540): " coram domino de Aquino fratre eius (domino Adenulfo), magistro Raynaldo (indice et advocato) et quampluribus aliis."—BÖHMER-FICKER-WINKELMANN, *Regesten des Kaiserreichs 1198–1212,* V 33 2208, give fourteen names of d'Aquino, contemporaries of St. Thomas. Were they all his brothers or relatives?

[37] SCANDONE, op. cit. 51, 77. KANTOROWICZ, *Friedrich II* Erg. 276, 282.

[38] SCANDONE, op. cit. 28, 80 sq. children Pandulf, Ronald, Frances.

[39] Ibidem 51, 77.

[40] Ibidem 81 sq.

[41] PELSTER, *I parenti prossimi* 308. SCANDONE, op. cit. 56 sq., 79. TOCCO, c. 44.

[pp. 4–9

42 PELSTER, op. cit. 309. SCANDONE, op. cit. 57–60. TOCCO, c. 37.

43 PELSTER, op. cit. 310. SCANDONE, op. cit. 61–67, 55. Proc. Neap. n. 62. Fontes 350.

44 TOCCO, c. 2. PELSTER, op. cit. 312. SCANDONE, op. cit. 34, 55.

45 PELSTER, op. cit. 311. SCANDONE, op. cit. 67–69.

46 TOCCO, c. 65.

47 Denifle in notes left by him. DE GROOT, Het leven van den H. Thomas 5. MANDONNET, Date de naissance 657. CASTAGNOLI, Regesta (1927) 710. SCANDONE, La vita, la famiglia 9: 1225; 110: "towards the end of 1224."

48 DE RUBEIS, Dissertationes 1a c. 9, II: 1226 "probabilior fert chronographia." PRÜMMER, De chronologia vitae S. Thomae Aquinatis 2–3. PELSTER, Kritische Studien z. Leben u. zu den Schriften Alberts d. Gr. 76. Cf. Scholastik 2 (1927) 454.

49 QUÉTIF-ECHARD, Scriptores Ord. Praed. I 271 sq. BERTHIER, S. Thomas "Doctor communis" Proc. Neap., n. 62. Recently J. ABATE, Miscellanea Franciscana 50 (1950), 231–274.

50 TOSO, Tommaso d'Aquino 87–132. SCANDONE, op. cit. 101–129.

51 SCANDONE, op. cit. 85–103.

52 Ibidem, 80.

53 Cf. EUBEL, Hierarchia I 99.

54 Ibidem, 47.

55 TOCCO, c. 3. Cf. PRÜMMER in Fontes 60.

56 TOCCO, c. 3. CALO, c. 2. GUI, c. 2.

57 TOCCO, c. 2.

58 TAURISANO, S. Tommaso 41.

59 BONANNI, Ricerche per la storia di Aquino 5,208.

60 SCANDONE, op. cit. 107.

61 BONANNI, op. cit. 42–45. A few years ago this ancient church, which had so long lain derelict, once more received attention. Thanks to the Royal Superintendence of the Monuments of the Campania, the apse and the central nave have been roofed in harmony with original twelfth century style. Cf. the Osservatore Romano for 10. 6. 1933. During military operations in 1944 the church was unhappily damaged, as was also the whole district and diocese of Aquino.

FOOTNOTES FOR CHAPTER II

1 Doc. 2–3 (Fontes 533–535).

2 Cf. supra p. 4.

3 TOCCO, c. 4. CASTAGNOLI, Regesta (1927) 711.

4 TOCCO, c. 4.

5 U. BERLIÈRE, Les écoles claustrales au moyen âge, Académie Royale de Belgique, Bulletin de la classe des Lettres (1921) 553 sq., 566. LECCISOTTI, Il Dottore Angelico 529–532.

6 DE RUBEIS, Dissertationes 1a c. 3 I. TOSTI, Storia della Badia di Montecassino II 195.

pp. 9–12]

[7] DE RUBEIS, *Dissertationes* 1a c. 3 II, 7 II.

[8] LECCISOTTI, op. cit. 519–547. Cf. *Studia Anselmiana* 18–19 (1947) 195–225, esp. 208.

[9] TOCCO, c. 4. LECCISOTTI, op. cit. 522.

[10] *Proc. Neap.* n. 76.

[11] MANDONNET, *Date de naissance* 658, 660. Cf. GRABMANN, *Das Seelenleben des hl. Thomas von Aquin* 76. G. G. COULTON, *Five centuries of religion* (Cambridge 1923) I 224 sq.

[12] LECCISOTTI, *Il Dottore Angelico* 537.

[13] LECCISOTTI, op. cit. 533–535. TOCCO, c. 1: "habentes spem ad magnos ipsius monasterii reditus pervenire per ipsius promotionem ad apicem praelaturae."

[14] Cap. 59. LECCISOTTI, op. cit. 523 sq.

[15] TOCCO, c. 4. Cf. MANDONNET, *Date de naissance* 658.

[16] LECCISOTTI, op. cit. 534, 529. INGUANEZ, *Cronologia degli abati cassinesi del sec. XIII* 421. TOSTI, *Storia della Badia* II 284, 203. WINKEL-MANN, *Kaiser Friedrich II* (Leipzig 1897) II 49, holds that this abbot was the nephew of Thomas d'Aquino, Count of Acerra.

[17] TOSTI, op. cit. II 184.

[18] As can be seen in BÖHMER-FICKER-WINKELMANN, *Die Regesten des Kaiserreichs* V 1, 357 sq., Frederick II was at Aquino on September 21st and from the 11th to 27th November 1229, i. e. before and after the destruction of the town of Sora.

[19] TOSTI, op. cit. II 185 sq.

[20] LECCISOTTI, op. cit. 519 sq. EUBEL, *Hierarchia* I 35.

[21] KANTOROWICZ, *Friedrich II* 192 sq., Erg. 75. BÖHMER-FICKER-WINKELMANN, *Die Regesten* V 1, 363 sq. I. KUCZYNSKI, *Le bx. Guala de Bergame de l'Ordre des Frères Prêcheurs* (Estavayer 1916) 73. LEC-CISOTTI, *Il Dottore Angelico* 520. The town which in medieval times was called San Germano after a holy bishop of the place was called Casinum by the old Romans, and is now again known as Cassino.

[22] MANDONNET, *Date de naissance* 660 sq.

[23] On the meaning of an "oblate," see M. P. DEROUX, *Les origines de l'oblature bénédictine* (Ligugé 1927). MANDONNET, l. c. 660.

[24] TOCCO, c. 4.

[25] MANDONNET, loc. cit. 660 sq.

[26] MANDONNET, loc. cit. 663. Ib. 662: "Vingt onces d'or à puissance relative vaudraient de nos jours une dizaine de mille francs. C'était là une somme considérable pour l'époque . . . On comprend donc sans peine que les largesses de Landolphe d'Aquin envers le Mont Cassin n'ont pu être provoquées que par un évènement qui les justifient et les expliquent, telle l'entrée du jeune Thomas d'Aquin dans la milice bénédictine du Mont Cassin." SCANDONE, *La vita, la famiglia* 47 sq.: 1200 lire.

[27] BERLIÈRE, *Les écoles claustrales* 557 sq.

[28] LECCISOTTI, *Il Dottore Angelico* 529.

[29] SABA, *Bernardo I Ayglerio* 137 sq. Idem, *Bernardo I abate di Monte-*

cassino, Bollettino Istit. stor. ital. n. 47 (1932) 217–226. *DHGE* V 1281–1283. INGUANEZ, *Cronologia degli abati* 433–438.

[30] LECCISOTTI, op. cit. 531.

[31] MANDONNET in the *Revue des Jeunes* 9 (1919) 283. COULTON, *Five centuries* I 224 sq., 225: a master for each boy.

[32] LECCISOTTI, op. cit. 531 n. 2.

[33] Cf. E. MICHAEL, *Geschichte des deutschen Volkes* (Freiburg i. B. 1899) II 356 sq.

[34] LECCISOTTI, op. cit. 530, with the quotation from Alfanus.

[35] P. RENAUDIN, S. Thomas et S. Benoît, *RTh* 17 (1909) 513–537. GRABMANN, *Das Seelenleben* 77. G. DIAMARE, S. *Tommaso d'Aquino nella badia di Montecassino, Rivista storica benedittina* 15 (1924) 138 sq. A. STEHLE, *St. Thomas at Monte Cassino, The Cath. Educ. Ass. Bull.* 21 (1924) Nov., 658–665. M. CORDOVANI, S. *Benedetto e S. Tommaso, Casinensia* (Montecassino 1929) 17–21.

[36] G. BATELLI, *Lezioni di Paleografia,* 2nd ed., (Vatican City 1939) 113–130, cf. 130–132, 194–198. On music, LECCISOTTI, op. cit. 539.

[37] LECCISOTTI, op. cit. 529.

[38] LECCISOTTI, op. cit. 530.

[39] A. M. WEISS, *Apologie des Christentums,* 2–3 ed. (Freiburg i. B. 1898) V, 14th lecture.

[40] Ps. 83. 6.

[41] St. Thomas, *Summa Theologiae* II-II 180 3 ad 2: "videre autem aliquid per speculum est videre causam per effectum in quo eius similitudo elucet. Unde speculatio ad meditationem reduci videtur."

[42] TOCCO, c. 4.

[43] Ibidem.

[44] Ibidem.

[45] LECCISOTTI, *Il Dottore Angelico* 540.

[46] TOCCO, c. 5. GUI, c. 4. DE RUBEIS, *Dissertationes* la c. 9: 1235 aut 1236 ineunte.

[47] TOSTI, *Storia della Badia* II 202. DE RUBEIS, *Dissertationes* 1a c. 4, 9. DE GROOT, *Het leven* 17.

[48] II-II 189 8.

[49] INGUANEZ, *Cronologia degli abati* 424–425.

[50] KANTOROWICZ, *Friedrich II* 437, Erg. 190.

[51] LECCISOTTI, op. cit. 542. KANTOROWICZ, op. cit. 436: a garrison of 100 soldiers. CASTAGNOLI, *Regesta* (1927) 711 sq.

FOOTNOTES FOR CHAPTER III

[1] A. HUILLARD-BRÉHOLLES, *Historia diplomatica Friderici II* (Paris 1852–1861) passim: "Dei gratia Romanorum imperator semper Augustus, Ierusalem et Siciliae rex."

[2] DENIFLE, *Die Entstehung der Universitäten* 453–455. TORRACA, *Le origini. L'età sveva, Storia della Università di Napoli,* 1–16. D'IRSAY, Histoire

pp. 19–21]
des Universités I 134 sq., 109. KANTOROWICZ, *Kaiser Friedrich II* 124 sq., 160 sq. Erg. 51 sq., 119 sq.

3 DENIFLE, *Die Entstehung* 14. Cf. the article *Il VII Centenario dell'-Università di Napoli*, in *La Civiltà Cattolica* 45 (1925) II 204. RASHDALL, The Universities II 21 sq. MORGHEN, *Il tramonto della potenza sveva* 87 sq., 160 sq.

4 DENIFLE, op. cit. 12 sq. D'IRSAY, op. cit. I 134.

5 DENIFLE, op. cit. 13. MONTI, *Storia dell'Università di Napoli* 26 sq.

6 DENIFLE, op. cit. 454 sq. D'IRSAY, op. cit. I 135, 109, 119.

7 DENIFLE, op. cit. 454–456.

8 HEFELE-LECLERCQ, *Histoire des Conciles* V 1587.

9 DENIFLE, op. cit. 456.

10 ibid. K. HAMPE, *Zur Gründungsgeschichte der Universität Neapel* (Heidelberg 1924).

11 DENIFLE, op. cit. 457–459. D'IRSAY, op. cit. I 135.

12 MONTI, op. cit. 26 sq., 88 sq., 130 sq.

13 TOCCO, c. 5. CASTAGNOLI, *Regesta* (1927) 712. M. L. RICCIO, S. *Tommaso e l'Università di Napoli, Studium* 20 (1924) 237–244. A. BELLUCCI, *L'Università di Napoli e S. Tommaso d'Aq., Ricerche e Documenti, Studium* 20 (1924) 251–269. G. S. LAMPO, *Tommaso e l'Università di Napoli, MD* 41 (1924) 113–122.

14 LECCISOTTI, *Il Dottore Angelico* 543. Cf. TOSTI, *Storia della Badia* II 196.

15 DENIFLE, *Die Entstehung* 98 sq. D'IRSAY, *Histoire des Universités* I 165 sq.

16 Cf. KOPERSKA, *Die Stellung der religiösen Orden zu den Profanwissenschaften im 12. und im 13. Jahrhundert* 6, 36. Here on p. 112 it is observed that in general even in the Order of Preachers no more was required for the acceptance of a postulant than a knowledge of the principal matters of the trivium (grammar, dialectic, rhetoric), while in the early days of the Order the postulants were not required to know the matter of the quadrivium, i. e. geometry, arithmetic, music and astronomy (cf. M. GRABMANN, *Geschichte der scholastischen*•*Methode* (Freiburg i. B. 1911) II 40 sq., 123, and PARÉ-BRUNET-TREMBLAY, *La Renaissance du XIIe siècle* 97 sq.; indeed, only literature and grammar were required, cf. WALZ, *Compendium historiae Ord. Praed.* 92 sq. (2nd ed. 114 sq.).

17 A. GIRY, *Manuel de diplomatique* (Paris 1925) 454 sq.

18 GIRY, *Manuel* 682. *LThK* X 125.

19 GEYER, *Die patrist. n. scholast. Philosophie* 143, 353 sq.

20 GRABMANN, *Mittelalterliches Geistesleben* II 103–137: Kaiser Friedrich II u. sein Verhältnis zur aristotelischen u. arabischen Philosophie 620. M. SCHIPA in *The Cambridge Medieval History* VI (1929) 143, 874. A. DE STEFANO, *La cultura alla corte di Federico II Imperatore* (Palermo 1938).

21 KANTOROWICZ, *Kaiser Friedrich II* Erg. 266–269.

22 *LThK* VII 167 sq. KANTOROWICZ, op. cit. 313, Erg. 149 sq., 153.

[pp. 22–25

C. H. HASKINS, *Michael Scot and Frederick II, Isis* 4 (1922) 250–275.

²³ TOCCO, c. 5. MONTI, *Storia dell'Università di Napoli* 88. CASTAG-NOLI, *Regesta* (1927) 713. KANTOROWICZ, op. cit. Erg 268, 152. RASH-DALL, *The Universities* II 24.

²⁴ *Petrus von Hibernia der Jugendlehrer des Thomas von Aquin, und seine Disputation vor König Manfred.* Sitzungsber. d. Bayer. Akad. d. Wissenschaften, Philos.–Philol. u. hist. Klasse 1920, 8. Abhdlg 33 sq.

²⁵ *Le cours inédit d'Albert le Grand sur la Morale à Nicomaque receuilli et rédigé par s. Thomas d'Aquin* 23–25.

²⁶ *Mittelalterliches Geistesleben* I 249–265.

²⁷ KANTOROWICZ, *Kaiser Friedrich II*, Erg. 268. GRABMANN, *Mittelalterliches Geistesleben* I 251 sq.

²⁸ TOCCO, c. 5.

²⁹ *Proc. Neap.* n. 76. DE GROOT, *Het leven* 19.

³⁰ "Cui [Deo] non appropinquatur passibus corporis sed affectibus mentis" St. Thomas *Sum. theol.* II–II 24 4, from St. Augustine's *Tract. in Ioannem* 32.

³¹ I Kings 2. 3.

³² KANTOROWICZ, op. cit. Erg. 270–273.

³³ MANDONNET, *S. Dominique* I. WALZ, *Compendium* 10–25 (2nd ed. § 2–3).

³⁴ ALTANER, *Die Briefe Jordans von Sachsen* 111 sq. SCHEEBEN, *Beiträge zur Geschichte Jordans von Sachsen* 96–126.

³⁵ LECCISOTTI, *Il Dottore Angelico* 543 sq.

³⁶ ALTANER, *Die Briefe Jordans* 111 sq. BERLIÈRE, *Les écoles claustrales* 568: " au XIII siècle les ordres mendiants qui s'efforcent de dominer le mouvement scientifique, attirent à eux la jeunesse studieuse. Le général des Frères-Prêcheurs, Humbert de Romans, fait remarquer que les moines noirs forment bien leurs oblats à l'office divin, mais il regrette que ces jeunes gens ne reçoivent pas de formation scientifique, et que leur manque d'instruction devient pour eux une cause de ruine religieuse. Quoi d'étonnant qu'à une époque où la science était si appréciée, les esprits d'élite soient allés vers les nouveaux ordres, qui avaient le culte de la science? "

³⁷ WALZ, *Compendium* 14 sq. (2nd ed. 16).

³⁸ Cf. *MOPH* III 15.

³⁹ SCHEEBEN, *Beiträge zur Geschichte Jordans*. MORTIER, *Histoire des Maîtres Généraux* I 137–253. WALZ, *Compendium* 26–28 (2nd ed. 28–31). SCHEEBEN, *Jordan der Sachse* (Vechta 1937).

⁴⁰ *MOPH* I 327. KOPERSKA, *Die Stellung der religiösen Orden* 113.

⁴¹ ALTANER, *Die Briefe* 140, 116 sq. SCHEEBEN, *Beiträge* 172. WALZ, *B. Jord. Ep.* ix–xi.

⁴² ALTANER, op. cit. 138, 116 sq. SCHEEBEN, op. cit. 171.

⁴³ ALTANER, op. cit. 139, 117. SCHEEBEN, op. cit. 172.

⁴⁴ ALTANER, op. cit. 101, 103. SCHEEBEN, op. cit. 66.

⁴⁵ ALTANER, op. cit. 140, 117. SCHEEBEN, op. cit. 172.

⁴⁶ ALTANER, op. cit. 139, 117 sq. SCHEEBEN, op. cit. 173.

⁴⁷ ALTANER, op. cit. 139, 118. SCHEEBEN, op. cit., 32–78.

⁴⁸ *MOPH* I 125. LECCISOTTI, *Il Dottore Angelico* 545.

198   SAINT THOMAS AQUINAS

pp. 26-34]

⁴⁹ ALTANER, op. cit. 119, 112. According to Altaner, Jordan embarked at Marseilles for his journey to the East.

⁵⁰ SCHEEBEN, op. cit. 81 sq.

⁵¹ TOCCO, c. 6. *Proc. Neap.* n. 76. MANDONNET, *Thomas d'Aquin novice prêcheur* 26. CASTAGNOLI, *Regesta* (1927) 713.

⁵² TOCCO, c. 1.

⁵³ TOCCO, c. 6.

⁵⁴ TOCCO, c. 6. San Giuliano is near Priverno, called in medieval times Piperno. TAURISANO, *I discepoli* 121.

⁵⁵ *Proc. Neap.* n. 76.

⁵⁶ *AOP* 3 (1895) 61.

⁵⁷ W. HOTZELT, *Kirchengeschichte Palästinas im Zeitalter der Kreuzzügen 1099-1291* (Cologne 1940) 220-226. ALTANER, *Die Dominikanermissionen des 13. Jahrhunderts* (Habelschwerdt 1924) 36. *DHGE* I 991 (Coulon). M. A. CONIGLIONE, *La provincia domenicana di Sicilia* (Catania 1937) 4, 149, 291, 400. EUBEL, *Hierarchia* I 135, 220, 275. *AFP* 4 (1934) 129.

⁵⁸ GUI, c. 5. Cf. PRÜMMER *in Fontes* 171 n. 2. MANDONNET, *Thomas d'Aquin novice* 28, 31. CASTAGNOLI, *Regesta* (1927) 714.

⁵⁹ TOCCO, c. 6. Cf. DE GROOT, *Het leven* 28.

⁶⁰ *Sum. theol.* II-II 188 6. WALZ, *Compendium* 23 sq. (2nd ed. 26).

FOOTNOTES FOR CHAPTER IV

¹ *Processionarium Ordinis Praedicatorum* (Rome 1930) 149 sq.

² WALZ, *Compendium historiae Ord. Praed.* 213-216 (2nd ed. 139-142).

³ PRÜMMER, *De Chronologia* 5 sq. De RUBEIS, *Dissertationes* 1a c. 6, 9. MANDONNET, *Thomas d'Aquin novice* 3, 14. PELSTER, *Kritische Studien* 70 sq. Cf. DENIFLE, *Die Entstehung* 456.

⁴ *AFP* 4 (1934) 127.

⁵ GUI, c. 5. Note PRÜMMER'S wise remark (*Fontes* 171 n. 2), rejecting the supposition of Mandonnet, according to which Thomas received the habit from John the Teutonic.

⁶ "Nullus recipiatur infra octodecim annos." H. C. SCHEEBEN, *Die Konstitutionen des Predigerordens unter Jordan von Sachsen*, QF 38, 57 n. XIV, 2; cf. AOP 3 (1896) 628 sq., 5 (1898) 54.

⁷ WALZ, *Compendium* 92 (2nd ed. 114 sq.).

⁸ MANDONNET, *Thomas d'Aquin novice* 42. BOP I 74.

⁹ TOCCO, c. 6.

¹⁰ TOCCO, c. 7.

¹¹ SCHEEBEN, *Die Konstitutionen* 56 n. XIII. MANDONNET, loc. cit. 180 sq.

¹² TOCCO, c. 7. Cf. CALO, c. 4, GUI, c. 5. MANDONNET, loc. cit. 52 sq. CASTAGNOLI, *Regesta* (1927) 715.

¹³ BOP I, 15 n. 29. SCHEEBEN, *Der hl. Dominikus* 293, 448.

¹⁴ BERTHIER, *Le couvent de Sainte Sabine à Rome* 162, 23, 283-289. A. MUÑOZ, *Il restauro della basilica di Santa Sabina* (Rome 1938).

[pp. 34–38

¹⁵ MANDONNET, loc. cit. 7, thinks it is possible to assign to this period John's journey to Naples and residence in Rome. Later in the same article, pp. 14, 31, without adducing any further proof, he gives the above conjecture as a certain and indisputable fact.

¹⁶ MANDONNET, loc. cit. 6, 15.

¹⁷ Bonum universale de apibus I 20. Cf. MANDONNET, loc. cit. 14 sq.

¹⁸ MOPH I 201.

¹⁹ TOCCO, c. 8. Cf. MANDONNET, loc. cit. 60 sq.

²⁰ TOCCO, c. 8. SCANDONE, La vita, la famiglia 54 sq.

²¹ MOPH I 201. PTOLEMY, Hist. eccl. XXII 20.

²² MANDONNET, loc. cit. 13. CASTAGNOLI, Regesta (1927) 717 sq.

²³ TOCCO, c. 8. MANDONNET, loc. cit. 87 sq.

²⁴ T. MANCINI, S. Tommaso d'Aquino nel castello paterno di Montesangiovanni Campano (Pistoia 1934) 15, 26.

²⁵ MANCINI, op. cit. 16–24. Idem, S. Tommaso d'Aquino e Montesangiovanni Campano (Frosinone 1943) 12–16. GUI, c. 6.

²⁶ TOCCO, c. 8. Endorsed by PRÜMMER, De Chronologia 5.

²⁷ MARTINORI, Lazio turrito II 77 sq.

²⁸ TOCCO, c. 8. MANDONNET, Thomas d'Aquin novice 7–9, 54 sq., 75 sq. PELSTER, Kritische Studien 78 sq.

²⁹ TOCCO, c. 8. MANDONNET, loc. cit. 32. PELSTER, op. cit. 78 sq. PRÜMMER, De Chronologia 5.

³⁰ MOPH I. MANDONNET, loc. cit. 93–99.

³¹ Bonum universale I 20.

³² TOCCO, c. 9.

³³ TOCCO, c. 9. The mention of a firebrand indicates a cold season when a fire was necessary. Pelster holds this, against Mandonnet. Cf. MANDONNET, loc. cit. 97. CASTAGNOLI, Regesta (1927) 718 sq.

³⁴ ENDRES, Thomas von Aquin 20. Cf. MANDONNET, loc. cit. 92 sq.

³⁵ TOCCO, c. 37, 44. PTOLEMY, Hist. eccl. XXII 20.

³⁶ PRÜMMER in Fontes 23.

³⁷ TOCCO, c. 10. C. PERA, Il sacro cingolo di S. Tommaso d'Aquino XTh III 459–515, esp. 484 sq.

³⁸ MANDONNET, loc. cit. 99 sq.

³⁹ SCANDONE, La vita, la famiglia 107. TOSO, Tommaso d'Aquino 145–153.

⁴⁰ MANDONNET, loc. cit. 89, 96. MANCINI, S. Tommaso d'Aquino nel castello paterno 25.

⁴¹ MANCINI, op. cit. 27–34.

⁴² TOCCO, c. 9, who only mentions one of them by name.

⁴³ TOCCO, c. 11. Proc. Neap. n. 76. Cf. MANDONNET, loc. cit. 42, 137.

⁴⁴ TOCCO, c. 9. MANDONNET, Thomas d'Aquin novice 124 sq., 171.

⁴⁵ GRABMANN, Die Werke 228–232, 307; BACIC, Introductio 111 sq.: De fallaciis. GRABMANN, Die Werke 229 sq., 307; BACIC, Introductio 112: De modalibus propositionibus. Cf. CASTAGNOLI, Regesta (1927) 720 sq. I. M.

pp. 38–44]
BOCHENSKI, S. *Thomae Aquinatis De modalibus opusculum et doctrina,*
Angelicum 17 (1940) 180–218.
[46] GRABMANN, op. cit. 360. SCANDONE, *La vita, la famiglia* 2. MAN-
DONNET, loc. cit. 100–109, considers it authentic.
[47] TOCCO, c. 11. MANDONNET, loc. cit. 114 sq.
[48] TOCCO, c. 11. CASTAGNOLI, op. cit. 721.
[49] *MOPH* I 201. THOMAS CANTIPRATANUS, *Bonum universale* I 20.
PTOLEMY, *Hist. eccl.* XXIII 21. Cf. Acts 9. 25.
[50] TOCCO, c. 11. Cf. II Cor 11. 33. MANDONNET, loc. cit. 134–137.
[51] DE GROOT, *Het leven* 43. TOSO, *Tommaso d'Aquino* 152 sq.
[52] *Proc. Neap.* n. 76. SCANDONE, op. cit. 50.
[53] *Fontes* 520.
[54] MANDONNET, loc. cit. 43 sq. LECCISOTTI, *Il Dottore Angelico* 545:
Landulf died probably on the 24th December 1243, cf. 533.
[55] Cf. HEFELE-LECLERCQ, *Histoire des Conciles* V 1642, 1678 sq.
[56] SCANDONE, op. cit. 64. KANTOROWICZ, *Kaiser Friedrich II* 575 sq.,
Erg. 235 sq., 298–302.
[57] SCANDONE, op. cit. 64, 57. TOSO, *Tommaso d'Aquino* 60 n. 1.
[58] *Proc. Neap.* n. 78. Cf. TOCCO, c. 44. SCANDONE, op. cit. 80.
[59] MANDONNET, *Thomas d'Aquin novice* 114, 171. CASTAGNOLI, op.
cit. 722.
[60] TOCCO, c. 11.
[61] TOCCO, c. 12.

FOOTNOTES FOR CHAPTER V

[1] *Zum Kölner Studienaufenthalt des Aquinaten* 46 sq. Cf. *RHS* 22 (1926)
906.
[2] *Zum Kölner Studienaufenthalt* 54.
[3] SCHEEBEN, *Die Konstitutionen* 75: "Conventus . . . sine priore et
doctore non mittatur."
[4] HUMBERT DE ROMANS *Opera de vita regulari* II 262 sq.
[5] ALTANER, *Die Briefe Jordans* 51. *MOPH* III 4, 47, 65, 99. WALZ, *B.
Jord. Ep.* 57.
[6] PELSTER in *Theol. Revue* 25 (1926) 436.
[7] *Contra* MANDONNET, *Thomas d'Aquin novice* 141 sq. The novitiate is
not a *profectus.*
[8] WALZ, *Studi domenicani* 51–58.
[9] GRABMANN, *Storia della Teologia* 40.
[10] K. BIHLMEYER, *Kirchengeschichte* (10th & 11th ed. Paderborn 1940)
§ 121. D'IRSAY, *Histoire des Universités* I 55–56 (France), 121 sq. (Oxford);
RASHDALL, *The Universities,* passim. GRABMANN, op. cit. 50–67. PARÉ-
BRUNET-TREMBLAY, *La Renaissance,* passim.
[11] *LThK* VI 91.
[12] TOCCO, c. 12. Cf. MORTIER, *Histoire des Maîtres Généraux* I 317,
406–408, 368. TAURISANO, *I discepoli* 121 n. 3.
[13] *MOPH* I 201. Cf. PELSTER, *Kritische Studien* 63.

14 TOCCO, c. 12. GUI, c. 9. CALO, c. 4.

15 *Bonum universale* I 20. Cf. PELSTER, op. cit. 66.

16 *Hist. eccl.* XXIII 20–21.

17 *Proc. Neap.* n. 62. Cf. *XTh* III 124 sq.

18 GUI, c. 9.

19 CALO, c. 8.

20 *Vitae Patrum inclyti Ord. Praed.* (Bologna 1529) f. cxxvii.

21 *Vitae sanctorum Patrum Ord. Praed.* (Louvain 1575) f. 134.

22 DE RUBEIS, *Dissertationes* 2a c. 1.

23 *Liber de memorabilibus sive chronicon* (POTTHAST [Göttingen 1859]) 201.

24 Cf. PELSTER, *Kritische Studien* 79 sq. The same idea as DENIFLE, *Zum Kölner Studienaufenthalt* 52.

25 *Hist. eccl.* XXIII 21. The text given by TAURISANO, *I discepoli* 183 does not include the word *primum*.

26 TOCCO, c. 38. MANDONNET, *Thomas d'Aquin novice* 170. CASTAGNOLI, *Regesta* (1927) 723 sq.

27 ALTANER, *Die Briefe* 118. SCHEEBEN, *Beiträge* 60. WALZ, *B. Jord. Ep.* 56.

28 SCHEEBEN, *Albert der Grosse* 24–35. DENIFLE, *Die Entstehung* 388 (705).

29 *MOPH* III 34, 38, 41; 36: cum domus Parisiensis multum sit gravata.

30 *Legenda B. Alberti Magni* (Cologne 1928) c. 4, 6.

31 *Opuscula S. Thomae* (Venice 1497) fol. a. a. 3.

32 Fol. 171 v.

33 *Vita ex pluribus auctoribus recenter collecta* I (Rome 1570).

34 *Historia general de Santo Domingo* I (Madrid 1584) 388a, 389a.

35 *Vita de' Santi, Beati e Venerabili del S. Ord. dei Predicatori* (Florence 1588) 124.

36 *Regula S. Augustini et Constitutiones FF. Ord. Praed.* (Rome 1690).

37 *Scriptores Ord. Praed.* I 275 sq.

38 PUCCETTI, *S. Alberto Magno* I 131 n. 1.

39 DE GROOT, *Het leven* 45–57. Cf. PRÜMMER, *XTh* III 6. TOSO, 152 sq.

40 PELSTER, *Kritische Studien* 79–81. In the Dominican church at Cologne, an altar was erected in 1401 in honour of St. Thomas who had prayed there, cf. G. LÖHR, *Beiträge zur Geschichte des Kölner Dominikanerklosters im Mittelalter* I, QF 15 (Leipzig 1920) 4 sq. F. STEILL, *Ephemerides dominicano-sacrae* (Dillingen 1692) I 401, notes that many souvenirs of the Saint's residence at Cologne were lost in the fire of 1659, as for example the board on which St. Thomas used to pray.

41 DENIFLE, *Zum Kölner Studienaufenthalt* 49, 52. Idem, *Die Entstehung* 388 sq.: Thomas came to Cologne about 1248.

42 *LThK* I 214.

43 *Thomas d'Aquin novice* 169.

44 *S. Tommaso d'Aquino* 4 sq.

45 *Regesta* (1927) 722, (1928) 110–112.

pp. 47–53]

46 *Répertoire* I 85.

47 SCHEEBEN, *Albert der Grosse* 24–35. LÖHR, *Beiträge* I 9, 57–60.

48 P. DE LOE, *De vita et scriptis B. Alberti Magni* 277. PELSTER in *LThK* I 214. SCHEEBEN, *Albert d. Gr.* 21, is not in agreement.

49 M. GRABMANN, *Der Einfluss Alberts d. Gr. auf das mittelalterliche Geistesleben* 348, 336.

50 GRABMANN, op. cit. 345–360. RASHDALL, *The Universities* II 254 sq.

51 *BOP* I 387.

52 *Opus minus* (BREWER, London 1859), 14, 30 sq., 327.

53 *Summa de bono* l. 4, tr. 3, c. 9.

54 SCHEEBEN, *De Alberti Magni discipulis* 200 sq.

55 PTOLEMY, *Hist. eccl.* XXIII 18.

56 Cf. PUCCETTI, S. *Alberto Magno;* J. WILMS, *Albert der Grosse* (Munich 1930, Eng. Tr. P. HEREFORD 1933); SCHEEBEN, *Albertus Magnus* (Bonn 1932), passim. *Serta Albertina* in honorem caelestis patroni a S.P. Pio PP. XII rerum naturalium indagatoribus recens dati, *Angelicum* 21 (1944) passim.

57 Cf. UEBERWEG-GEYER, GRABMANN, MANDONNET, GORCE.

58 WALZ-SCHEEBEN, *Iconographia albertina* (Freiburg i. B. 1932) p. 39, n. 7.

59 In *Aeterni Patris* Thomas, Bonaventure and Albert are mentioned by name.

60 *Nella luce di S. Alberto Magno, Angelicum* 9 (1932) 143.

61 LÖHR, *Beiträge* II 13.

62 A. WALZ, *Albert der Grosse als lector Coloniensis, Angelicum* 9 (1932) 147–167.

63 TOCCO, c. 9.

64 *Hist. eccl.* XXIII 21.

65 TOCCO, c. 9. CALO, c. 8.

66 MEERSSEMAN, *Introductio* 103–104. GRABMANN, *Die Autographe* 529–532.

67 H. C. SCHEEBEN, *Albert der Grosse und Thomas von Aquino in Köln,* DTF 9 (1931) 28–34, esp. 32 sq.

68 TOCCO, c. 12. GRABMANN, *Die Werke* 267. BACIC, *Introductio* 25. MANDONNET, *Des écrits* 31, 104.

69 M. GRABMANN, *Drei ungedruckte Teile der Summa de creaturis Alberts des Grossen,* QF 13 (Leipzig 1919) 83.

70 PELZER, *Le cours inédit d'Albert le Grand sur la Morale à Nicomaque,* passim. MEERSSEMAN, *Introductio* 72. Idem, *Les manuscrits du cours inédit d'Albert le Grand sur la Morale à Nicomaque, RNSP* 38 (1935) 64–83. VAN STEENBERGHEN, *Siger* II 468. LOTTIN, *Psychologie et Morale* I 126 sq. Cf. *Scholastik* 12 (1937) 124 sq. (Pelster).

71 T. S. CENTI, *La spiritualità dell'anima in S. Tommaso d'Aquino* (Dissertation, in typescript, Angelicum, Rome 1943) 31 sq., 191.

72 GRABMANN, *Die Werke* 302 sq. Idem, *Mittelalterliches Geistesleben* I 667 sq. Cf. idem, *De commentariis in opusculum S. Thomae Aquinatis De ente et essentia, Acta Pont. Acad. Romanae S. Thomae Aq. et Religionis Cath.,*

[pp. 53–58

N.S. V (1938; Turin-Rome 1939) 7–20 (Eng. tr. of *De Ente et Essentia* C. C. RIEDL, Toronto 1934. Cf. Bourke n. 14422). BACIC, *Introductio* 95. Roland-Gosselin made his edition without using the excellent manuscripts used by Baur. Cf. *Ephemerides Theol. Lovan.* 3 (1926) 530 (Teetaert).

[73] *Het leven* 65.

[74] *Le couvent de S. Sabine* 304.

[75] *Kritische Studien* 81.

[76] *La vita, la famiglia* 16.

[77] *Albert d. Gr. u. Thomas von Aquino* 34.

[78] *Zum Kölner Studienaufenthalt* 55.

[79] *Fontes* 520.

[80] KANTOROWICZ, *Kaiser Friedrich II* 627, Erg. 243, 249.

[81] Ibidem, and Erg. 249, 158. D'IRSAY, *Histoire des Universités* I 96.

[82] KANTOROWICZ, op. cit. 564, Erg. 232.

[83] CANTIMPRÉ, *Bonum universale* I 20. PTOLEMY, *Hist. eccl.* XXIII 21. LECCISOTTI, *Il Dottore Angelico* 546. CASTAGNOLI, *Regesta* (1928) 115.

[84] INGUANEZ, *La cronologia degli abati* 424 sq.

[85] Op. cit. 425 sq.

[86] Op. cit. 427.

[87] Op. cit. 429.

[88] Cf. TOCCO, c. 42. MANDONNET, *Thomas d'Aquin novice* 172–180. On the rebellion cf. KANTOROWICZ, op. cit. 577–581, Erg. 235 sq., 298 sq.

[89] *Doc.* 10 (*Fontes* 541 sq.).

[90] TOCCO, c. 32, 63. *Proc. Neap.* n. 78.

[91] POTTHAST, *Regesta Romanorum pontificum* II 1089 n. 12939.

[92] R. KNIPPING, *Die Regesten der Erzbischöfe von Köln im Mittelalter* III 1 (Bonn 1909) 199, 201.

[93] SCHEEBEN, *Albert der Grosse* 24.

FOOTNOTES FOR CHAPTER VI

[1] *Chartularium* I 252–258 n. 230. DENIFLE, *Archiv* I 67 sq.

[2] *MOPH* XVI 50. MANDONNET, *S. Dominique* I 62. SCHEEBEN, *Der hl. Dominikus* 265 sq. F. Cardinal EHRLE, *San Domenico, le origine del primo studio del suo Ordine a Parigi e la somma teologica del primo Maestro, Rolando di Cremona.* Extract from the *Miscellanea Domenicana* (Rome 1923) 5.

[3] EHRLE, *San Domenico* 6 sq.

[4] *Chartularium* I 253.

[5] EHRLE, loc. cit. 8. E. FILTHAUT, *Roland von Cremona, O.P. und die Anfänge der Scholastik im Predigerorden* (Vechta 1936). GLORIEUX, *Répertoire* I 42 n. 1. A. MASNOVO, *Guglielmo d'Auvergne e l'università di Parigi dal 1229 al 1231, Mélanges Mandonnet* II 191–232. VAN STEENBERGHEN, *Siger* II 404–438.

[6] GLORIEUX, *Répertoire* I 43 n. 2. EHRLE, loc. cit. 9.

pp. 58–63]

[7] GLORIEUX, op. cit. I 42. SCHEEBEN, *Beiträge zur Geschichte Jordans* 115 sq., 120 sq.

[8] EHRLE, loc. cit. 9 sq. MANDONNET, *Thomas d'Aquin novice* 154.

[9] *Chartularium* I 79 n. 20. GLORIEUX, op. cit. I 23. M. and C. DICKSON, *Le cardinal Robert de Courson, Archives d'Histoire doctrinale et litteraire di Moyen Age* 9 (1934) 53–142.

[10] DENIFLE, *Die Entstehung* 100 sq. GLORIEUX, op. cit. I 21 sq.

[11] D'IRSAY, *Histoire des Universités* 151, quotes John of Salisbury, *Metal.* I 25: " Hesterni pueri, Magistri hodierni."

[12] *Chartularium* I 137 sq.

[13] SCHEEBEN, *Beiträge* 55. ALTANER, *Die Briefe* 36 (Paris), *diotelarii* is a lapsus calami for *baccalaurei*, 50 (Vercelli), WALZ, B. *Jordani Ep.* 39, 57.

[14] FELDER, *Storia degli studi scientifici* 510, 537.

[15] *Chartularium* I 79: "Nullus sit scolaris Parisius, qui certum magistrum non haberet," cf. also I 137. GLORIEUX, op. cit. I 21.

[16] GLORIEUX, op. cit. I 22 mentions a student appearing before seven masters.

[17] L. LEMMENS, S. *Bonaventura* 305. GLORIEUX, op. cit. II 37–51 n. 305.

[18] TOCCO, c. 14. A. WALZ, De Alberti Magni et S. Thomae de Aquino personali ad invicem relatione, *Angelicum* 2 (1925) 305.

[19] *Chartularium* I 79. CASTAGNOLI, *Regesta* (1928) 115.

[20] TOCCO, c. 14. SCHEEBEN, *Albert der Grosse* 28.

[21] J. H. H. SASSEN, *Hugo von St. Cher*, seine Tätigkeit als Kardinal (Bonn 1908) 5. WALZ, I *cardinali domenicani* p. 15 n. 1.

[22] SASSEN, op. cit. 26–38.

[23] SASSEN, op. cit. 62.

[24] TOCCO, c. 14.

[25] DE GROOT, *Het leven* 95, and the other authors there quoted.

[26] CASTAGNOLI, *Regesta* (1928) 116 sq. GRABMANN, *Die Werke* 342-344. BACIC, *Introductio* 104. GLORIEUX, *Répertoire* I 22.

[27] Cf. the bibliography in CLASEN, *Der hl. Bonaventura und das Mendikantentum*, and P. GLORIEUX, *Le " Contra Geraldinos," RTAM* 7 (1935) 129. VAN STEENBERGHEN, *Siger* II 465. G. MEERSSEMAN, *Giovanni di Montenero O. P., difensore dei Mendicanti* (Rome 1938) 11–15.

[28] *Zum Kölner Studienaufenthalt* 49.

[29] Cf. *RSPT* 23 (1934) 483. HALPHEN, *L'essor* 326, 331, 540. COULTON, *Five centuries* II xv, 195.

[30] D'IRSAY, *Histoire des Universités* I 69 sq., 95, 118, 126.

[31] HOTZELT, *Kirchengeschichte Palästinas* 210–212.

[32] *Chartularium* I 226 n. 200, cf. p. 254. P. GLORIEUX, *Le " Contra impugnantes" de S. Thomas, Mélanges Mandonnet* I 55 sq. Idem, *Répertoire* I 343 n. 160.

[33] *Chartularium* I 242 sq. n. 319. HALPHEN, *L'essor* 540–549.

[34] *Chartularium* I 247–251 n. 222–228. CASTAGNOLI, *Regesta* (1928) 251 sq.

[35] GLORIEUX, *Répertoire* I 343 n. 160.

[36] H. DENIFLE, *Das Evangelium aeternum u. die Commission zu Anagni,* *ALKM* I 49–142, esp. 70: 31 errors. *LThK* IV 416.

[37] *LThK* X 888.

[38] *Chartularium* I 267–270 n. 240, cf. 263 n. 236.

[39] *Chartularium* I 279–285 n. 247.

[40] GLORIEUX, *Répertoire* I 343–345.

[41] *Chartularium* I 292 n. 256. CASTAGNOLI, op. cit. 252, 262.

[42] Cf. *Chartularium* I 297. *LThK* V 448 sq. (Joachim), IV 416 (Gerhard von Borgo S. Donnino).

[43] *Chartularium* I 309 n. 272.

[44] GLORIEUX, *Le "Contra impugnantes"* 75. *Mon. Germ. Script.* XXVIII 363, 365.

[45] *MOPH* V 32–38.

[46] GRABMANN, *Die Werke* 293 sq. BACIC, *Introductio* 86 sq. CASTAGNOLI, *Regesta* (1928) 260.

[47] GLORIEUX, *Répertoire* I 84 n. 12.

[48] D'IRSAY, *Histoire des Universités* I 70. GLORIEUX, op. cit. I 22.

[49] CASTAGNOLI, op. cit. 123–125. GRABMANN, *Die Werke* 268–270. In his 3rd edition (226–228, 462) he gives the dates 1254–1256. BACIC, op. cit. 30 sq. PELSTER, in *Scholastik* 15 (1940) 109, proposes 1253–1255. LEMMENS, *S. Bonaventura* 53, holds that he lectured on the *Sentences* in Paris from 1252, having already given a course on the Scriptures at Cologne.

[50] PELSTER, ibidem, and orally on Isaias (cf. AXTERS in *Angelicum* 11 (1935) 502–517), Jeremias and the Lamentations.

[51] BACIC, op. cit. 95 sq.

[52] *Storia della Teologia* 109, *Die Werke* (3rd ed.) 428–434.

[53] TOCCO, c. 14. S. Thomas Opera XIII 5. A. MASNOVO, *La novità di S. Tommaso d'Aquino,* in S. *Tommaso d'Aquino* (Milan 1923) 41–51.

[54] D'IRSAY, op. cit. I 70.

[55] Cf. *Chartularium* I 136–137 n. 79.

[56] GLORIEUX, op. cit. I 21–23.

[57] GLORIEUX, op. cit. I 332 n. 149.

[58] *Chartularium* I 307 n. 270.

[59] GLORIEUX, op. cit. I 22.

[60] GLORIEUX, op. cit. I 19. M. D. CHENU, *Maîtres et bacheliers de l'Université de Paris vers 1240, Études d'hist. litt. et doctrinale au XIIIe siècle* I (Paris-Ottawa 1932) 28–30. D'IRSAY, op. cit. I 151.

[61] TOCCO, c. 16.

[62] *Chartularium* I 321 n. 280.

FOOTNOTES FOR CHAPTER VII

[1] Cf. supra p. 83 FELDER, *Storia degli studi scientifici nell'Ordine francescano* 218, 235, 531.

[2] TOCCO, c. 16. *XTh* III 175. CASTAGNOLI, *Regesta* (1928) 249.

[3] *Proc. Neap.* n. 49.

[4] *Proc. Neap.* n. 92.

pp. 71–75]

5 F. SALVATORE, *Due sermoni inediti di* S. *Tommaso d'Aquino* (Rome 1912). CASTAGNOLI, op. cit. 250 sq. GRABMANN, *Die Werke* 342–344. BACIC, *Introductio* 103 sq.

6 TOCCO, c. 16. *Proc. Neap.* n. 49: quidam frater predicator canus et antiquus, n. 60: frater quidam de Caputio senex.

7 *MOPH* I 216: quidam dabat ei librum.

8 *Proc. Neap.* n. 92. On Capotto *MOPH* XX 87, 101, 107.

9 *Proc. Neap.* n. 49.

10 FELDER, *Storia* 235, 533 sq.

11 LEMMENS, S. *Bonaventura* 85, 226. *Chartularium* I 187. GLORIEUX, *Répertoire* I 37 n. 305.

12 *Chartularium* I 338–340 n. 293.

13 GLORIEUX, op. cit. I 348 n. 163: *Chrétien de Beauvais, originaire de Verdun.*

14 EUBEL, *Hierarchia* I 391.

15 *Chartularium* I 360 n. 312, 366 n. 317. LEMMENS, op. cit. 85.

16 FELDER, op. cit. 234 sq.

17 *Doc.* 31 (*Fontes* 585). *Chartularium* I 504.

18 *Zum Kölner Studienaufenthalt* 52.

19 *La Ciencia Tomista* a. 18 t. 34 (1926) 359 sq.

20 Cf. *Bulla Can. XTh* III 175. For the phrase " in sacra pagina " see H. DENIFLE, *Quel livre servait de base à l'enseignement des Maîtres en Théologie dans l'université de Paris*, RTh 2 (1892) 152. FELDER, *Storia* 218, 489–495, 527. GLORIEUX, op. cit. I 15. VOSTÉ, S. *Thomas Aquinas epistularum* S. *Pauli interpres* 258–260. J. DE GHELLINCK in *Mélanges A. Pelzer* (Louvain 1947) 23–59.

21 MASETTI, *Monumenta* I 224.

22 (P. MOTHON) *Vie du bx Innocent V* 18. MANDONNET, S. *Thomas d'Aquin lecteur* 21.

23 GLORIEUX, op. cit. I 15–20.

24 GLORIEUX, op. cit. I 21 (1. 9–29. 6). D'IRSAY, *Histoire des Universités* I 150 (9. 10–29. 6).

25 *Chronologie des écrits scripturaires de* S. *Thomas d'Aquin*, RTh 33 (1928) 116–130, 130–134. VOSTÉ, op. cit. 261–263. GRABMANN, *Die Werke* 50 n. 1, 247–249, 251–253. CASTAGNOLI, *Regesta* (1928) 329; (1929) 57–61. BACIC, op. cit. 57, 59 sq. According to TOCCO, c. 31, and *Proc. Neap.* n. 59, the commentary on Isaias was dictated to Reginald, and dates consequently from after 1259.

26 BACIC, *Introductio* 5. CHENU, *Maîtres et bacheliers* 24–27. VOSTÉ, op. cit. 261.

27 GRABMANN, *Die Werke* 252.

28 GLORIEUX, *Répertoire* I 17–19. GRABMANN, *Storia* 109–111. BACIC *Introductio* 31–33. CASTAGNOLI, *Regesta* (1928) 256–260.

29 GRABMANN, *Storia* 80.

30 CASTAGNOLI, op. cit. 253 sq.

31 GRABMANN, *Storia* 109–111.

32 Ibidem 80. BACIC, op. cit. 40 sq., 32.

³³ R. JANSSEN, *Die Quodlibeta des hl. Thomas von Aquin* (Bonn 1912) 13–77.

³⁴ GRABMANN, *Die Werke* 282–284. BACIC, op. cit. 40–48. To Grabmann's bibliography should be added E. AXTERS, *Où en est l'état des manuscrits des questions quodlibétiques de S. Thomas d'Aquin*, RTh 41 (1936) 505–530. DTP 41 (1938) 293–301 (Axters) and 42 (1939) 61, 93 (Glorieux).

³⁵ TOCCO, c. 17.

³⁶ *Proc. Neap.* n. 66, 67. Cf. *S. Thomae Opera* XIII viii b.

³⁷ Cf. supra p. 73.

³⁸ TOCCO, c. 27.

³⁹ *Proc. Neap.* n. 92. *Fontes* 398. C. DOUAIS, *Acta cap. prov. Ord. Frat. Praed.* (Toulouse 1894) 434, 124, 479. DOUAIS, *Essai sur l'organisation des études dans l'Ordre des Frères Prêcheurs* (Toulouse 1884) 225, 230, 234. G. R. GALBRAITH, *The Constitution of the Dominican Order* (Manchester 1925) 267, esp. 123 n. 3: Raymund Sycredi.

⁴⁰ GLORIEUX, *Répertoire* I 117 n. 19. DE GROOT, *Het leven* 115, proposes Romano de Rossi.

⁴¹ GLORIEUX, op. cit. I 84 n. 13, 104 n. 15, 105 n. 16.

⁴² GLORIEUX, op. cit. 107–112 n. 17, 113–116, n. 18, 117 n. 19. LAURENT, *Le bx Innocent* V 39 sq. RUSSELL, *Dictionary of Writers* 180 sq.

⁴³ (MOTHON), *Vie du bx Innocent* V 7. *LThK* X 629 sq.

⁴⁴ *MOPH* XVIII 17. (MOTHON), op. cit. 37.

⁴⁵ *MOPH* V 253 sq.

⁴⁶ LEMMENS, *S. Bonaventura* 85 sq., 267. GRABMANN, *Die persönlichen Beziehungen* 315. E. GILSON, *La philosophie de St. Bonaventure* (Paris 1924) 30. *AFH* 18 (1925) 387. In 1257 the Seraphic Doctor was promoted to be general of his Order and was relieved of his duties as professor. LEMMENS, op. cit. 161 sq.

⁴⁷ *Die persönlichen Beziehungen* 315.

⁴⁸ ALTANER, *Die Briefe Jordans* 36, cf. 117. WALZ, *B. Jord. Ep.* 39.

⁴⁹ TOCCO, c. 35. DE GROOT, *Het leven* 390.

⁵⁰ e. g. DIACCINI, *Vita di S. Tommaso d'Aquino* (Rome 1934) 133.

⁵¹ *MOPH* I 215 sq. TOCCO, c. 44. CASTAGNOLI, *Regesta* (1929) 64.

⁵² GLORIEUX, *Le "Contra impugnantes"* 51–81. BACIC, *Introductio* 86, follows Mandonnet and assigns it to 1257.

⁵³ KOPERSKA, *Die Stellung der religiösen Orden* 145.

⁵⁴ *MOPH* V 31.

⁵⁵ *MOPH* I 45.

⁵⁶ *MOPH* III 82 sq. MORTIER, *Histoire* I 465.

⁵⁷ *Revelationes Gertrudianae ac Mechtildianae* II (Poitiers-Paris 1877), 528. J. ANCELET-HUSTACHE, *Mechtilde de Magdebourg* (Paris 1926) 272–282.

⁵⁸ *Chartularium* I 319–323 n. 280.

⁵⁹ Ibidem, I 331–333 n. 288.

⁶⁰ KOPERSKA, *Die Stellung* 152–172.

⁶¹ DENIFLE, *Chartularium* I 333, bases himself on Tocco. DE GROOT, *Het leven* 101.

pp. 81–87]

62 Cf. DE LOË in *An. Boll.* 20 (1901) 285. SEPPELT, *Der Kampf der Bettelorden* 127, is uncertain, but 112 supposes that Thomas had been at Anagni. SCHEEBEN, *Albert der Grosse* 44, says Thomas was not there. MORTIER, *Histoire* I 471 sq., says he was.

63 *MOPH* I 215.

64 TOCCO, c. 19.

65 *Proc. Neap.* n. 47.

66 SCHEEBEN, *Albert der Grosse* 43–47. PUCCETTI, S. *Alberto Magno* I 182, 188. KOPERSKA, op. cit. 149.

67 DENIFLE, *Zum Kölner Studienaufenthalt* 50.

68 SCHEEBEN, op. cit. 46 sq.

69 *Chartularium* I 358 sq. n. 311. *MOPH* V 43 sq.

70 *MOPH* V 46 sq.

71 *Chartularium* I 391 sq. n. 342. CASTAGNOLI, *Regesta* (1929) 64.

72 GRABMANN, *Storia* 117. Idem, *Die theol. Erkenntnis- u. Einleitungslehre des hl. Thomas v. Aquin auf Grund seiner Schrift " In Boethium de trinitate "* (Fribourg [Switz.] 1948). P. WYSER, in *DTF* 25 (1948) 437 sqq., between 1255 and 1259. BACIC, *Introductio* 99 sq. CASTAGNOLI, *Regesta* (1928) 263–265. *Bull. thom.* 11 (1934) 46. *DTP* 42 (1939) 397–399 (Degl'Innocenti).

73 GRABMANN, Die werke (3rd ed.) 428–434. G. F. ROSSI, *Gli autografi di S. Tommaso della Biblioteca Vaticana*, *DTP* 37 (1934) 594–600.

74 *Note sur la date du Contra Gentiles*, *RTh* 44 (1938) 806–809.

75 *La lutte " Contra Gentiles " à Paris au XIIIe siècle*, *Mélanges Mandonnet* I 223–243.

76 VAN STEENBERGHEN, *Siger* II 487–489, 707. D. SALMAN, *Sur la lutte " Contra Gentiles " de s. Thomas*, *DTP* 40 (1937) 488, 509.

77 *Storia* 111–113. *Die Werke* 270–272. CASTAGNOLI, op. cit. 265–268, 488–492. T. OHM, *Thomas von Aquin u. die Heiden u. Mohammedaner, Aus der Geisteswelt des Mittelalters* II 735–748, esp. 737 sq.

78 SUERMONDT, *Tabulae Summae Theologiae et Summae Contra Gentiles* 41–50.

79 QUÉTIF-ECHARD, *Scriptores* I 280.

80 *MOPH* III 99 sq., 174 sq. CASTAGNOLI, *Regesta* (1929) 65. SCHEEBEN, *Albert der Grosse* 48, 56. B. *Innocentius* V 84. LAURENT, *Le bx Innocent* V 46–51. For Bonhomme, see GLORIEUX, *Répertoire* I 83 n. 11.

81 KOPERSKA, *Die Stellung* 128, 183.

82 GLORIEUX, op. cit. I 113, n. 18.

83 GLORIEUX, op. cit. I 117, n. 19. SIMONIN, *Les écrits* 192 sq.

FOOTNOTES FOR CHAPTER VIII

1 *Hist. eccl.* XXIII 24.

2 Op. cit. XXIII 21. MANDONNET, *Thomas d'Aquin lecteur à la Curie Romaine* 9–10.

3 *Chartularium* I 505.

4 MANDONNET, *Thomas d'Aquin lecteur* 10. CASTAGNOLI, *Regesta* (1929) 65 sq.

5 Cf. *Chartularium* I 404.

6 *Monumenta* I 173.

7 Cf. SASSEN, *Kardinal Hugo von St Cher* 128 sq. CASTAGNOLI, op. cit. 444 sq., considers Thomas' candidature for the cardinalate unlikely.

8 MANDONNET, loc. cit. 24 sq.

9 TOCCO, c. 64. MANDONNET, *Thomas d'Aquin novice* 30.

10 TAURISANO, *I discepoli* 125 n. 3. *MOPH* XX 43.

11 *Die persönlichen Beziehungen* 310. TAURISANO, op. cit. 126 sq.

12 MASETTI, *Monumenta* II 268. This nomination is not to be found in *MOPH* XX 24 sq.

13 SCHEEBEN, *Die Konstitutionen* 67, 77. WALZ, *Compendium historiae Ord. Praed.* 86 sq., 155 sq. (2nd ed. 106 sq., 252 sq.).

14 GALBRAITH, *The Constitution of the Dominican Order* 63. *MOPH* III 310 n. 3.

15 *Proc. Neap.* n. 75. *MOPH* XX 43.

16 MASETTI, *Monumenta* I 40. *MOPH* XX 23 sq.

17 *MOPH* XX 25–35. *Doc.* 30 (*Fontes* 582 sq.).

18 *Proc. Neap.* n. 47.

19 TOCCO, c. 25.

20 MASETTI, *Monumenta* I 224–230.

21 *MOPH* XX 32. CASTAGNOLI, *Regesta* (1929) 449.

22 DENIFLE, *Die Entstehung* 300. CASTAGNOLI, op. cit. 450.

23 Cf. infra p. 94.

24 *MOPH* II 100. MORTIER, *Histoire des Maîtres Généraux* II 46. T. ALFONSI, *Probabile cronologia della vita di S. Tommaso d'Aquino, MD* 40 (1923) 496. CASTAGNOLI, op. cit. 452. Perhaps it was then that he gave the example of humility, rather than in December 1269. See under n. 140 in CASTAGNOLI, op. cit. 456.

25 Cf. *MOPH* XX 33.

26 *Doc.* 21 (*Fontes* 570). CASTAGNOLI, op. cit. 452.

27 CASTAGNOLI, op. cit. 453 sq. ENDRES, *Thomas von Aquin* 54.

28 *MOPH* III 138.

29 QUÉTIF-ECHARD, *Scriptores* I 272. DE RUBEIS, *Dissertationes* 11a c. 2.

30 *Monumenta* I 137, 151.

31 DENIFLE, *Die Entstehung* 301–311. RASHDALL, *The Universities* II 28–31: Roman Court; 38 sq.: Studium Urbis.

32 R. CREYTENS, *Le "Studium Romanae Curiae" et le Maître du Sacré Palais, AFP* 12 (1942) 5–83, esp. 16 sq., 49 sq.

33 GRABMANN, *Die Werke* 249 sq. BACIC, *Introductio* 58 sq.

34 VOSTÉ, *S. Thomas Aquinas epistularum S. Pauli interpres* 262–276. GRABMANN, *Die Werke* 255–260. BACIC, *Introductio* 63–69.

35 GRABMANN, op. cit. 244–247. BACIC, op. cit. 57.

pp. 93–97]

36 A. DONDAINE, S. *Thomas et la dispute des attributs divins (I Sent. d. a.2, 3)*, AFP 8 (1938) 253–262. Cf. *RTAM* 9 (1937) 219–236 (Hayen).

37 GRABMANN, *Die Werke* 275–281. Idem, *Storia* 110 sq. BACIC, op. cit. 33–37.

38 P. MANDONNET, *Chronologie des Questions disputées de S. Thomas d'Aquin*, RTh 23 (1918) 334 sq., esp. 366–371. Cf. GRABMANN, *Die Werke* 344.

39 A. DONDAINE, *Le problème de l'attribution du " Tractatus de Beatitudine " du Manuscrit 784 de la Bibliothèque Vaticane latine, Notes et communications du Bulletin Thomiste* N. 6 (Avril-Juin 1932) 109 *–118 *.

40 GRABMANN, *Die Werke* 282–284, *Storia* 111. F. PELSTER, *Gregorianum* 28 (1947) 78–100.

41 GRABMANN, *Die Werke* 312–317. BACIC, *Introductio* 101 sq.

42 DE GROOT, *Het leven* 244.

43 Ibidem, 136.

44 *Proc. Neap.* n. 75. TOCCO, c. 53. CASTAGNOLI, *Regesta* (1929) 450 sq. TAURISANO, *I discepoli* 125.

45 TOCCO, c. 53.

46 GRABMANN, *Die Werke* 250. BACIC, op. cit. 61 sq.

47 Ibidem. Ibidem. WALZ, *I cardinali domenicani* 16 n. 2.

48 TOCCO, c. 17.

49 BACIC, op. cit. 62.

50 S. *Thomae Opera* XIII vi sq.

51 HEFELE-LECLERCQ, *Histoire des Conciles* VI 153 sq., 1457–1471. A. FLICHE, *Le problème oriental au second concile oecuménique de Lyon* (1274), *Orientalia christ. period.* 13 (1947) 475–485.

52 S. *Thomae Aquinatis in Isaiam prophetam expositiones. Accedit anonymi liber De fide sanctae Trinitatis a S. Thoma examinatus in opusculo Contra errores graecorum una cum ipso opusculo* (Rome 1880) 365 sq.

53 R. LOENERTZ, *Autour du Traité de Fr. Barthélemy de Constantinople contre les Grecs*, AFP 6 (1936) 361–371. A. DONDAINE *in DTC* 28 (1950) 313–340.

54 EUBEL, *Hierarchia* I 213.

55 TOCCO, c. 22. GRABMANN, *Die Werke* 285. BACIC, op. cit. 111. Cf. B. ALTANER, *Die Kenntnis des Griechischen in den Missionsorden des 13. Jahrhunderts, Zeitschrift für Kirchengeschichte* 53 (1934) 470–472, and R. LOENERTZ in *AFP* 5 (1935) 389 sq.

56 According to a manuscript note on p. 375 of the copy of this work in the library of the Angelicum in Rome.

57 M. GRABMANN, *Die Schrift De rationibus fidei contra Saracenos, Graecos et Armenos ad cantorem Antiochenum, Scholastik* 17 (1942) 187–216. Idem, *Die Werke* 286. BACIC, *Introductio* 73. EUBEL, *Hierarchia* I 93. ALTANER, *Die Dominikanermissionen* 28, 37.

58 GRABMANN, *Die Werke* 289 sq. BACIC, op. cit. 75 sq. EUBEL, op. cit. I 388.

59 GRABMANN, op. cit. 311 sq. BACIC, op. cit. 99.

60 GRABMANN, op. cit. 300. BACIC, op. cit. 90 sq. HEFELE-LECLERCQ, *Histoire des Conciles* V 1324–1327.

61 GRABMANN, op. cit. 317–324. BACIC, op. cit. 98. O. HUF, *De Sacramentshymnen van den h. Thomas van Aquino* (Maestricht 1924). *Deutsche Thomasausgabe* 30 (Salzburg 1938) [8]–[15]. E. STAKEMEIER, *Fronleichnam, Theologie und Glaube* 34 (1924) 133–145. M. GRABMANN, *La filosofia della cultura secondo Tommaso d'Aquino* (It. tr. Bologna 1931) 136.—On the *Pange lingua, Verbum supernum,* and *Lauda Sion,* see *LThK* VII 915, X 539. VI 410.

62 *Auteurs spirituels et textes dévots du moyen âge* (Paris 1932) 360–414. Cf. *AFP* 2 (1932) 37. Cf. *Studia eucharistica,* ed. S. Axters (Bussum-Antwerp 1946) 269–303, 440 sq.

63 MANDONNET-DESTREZ, *Bibliographie thomiste* 28 sq., n. 592–606. For Maison cf. R. COULON, *Scriptores Ord. Praed.* (Rome 1909) 51. *Bulletin thomiste* 2 (1935) Nov. 22–26; 7 (1930) 22–27. Cf. GALBRAITH, *The Constitution* 193. A monograph on the liturgical office of Corpus Christi is awaited from Alphonsus Schönherr, of the Roman Oratory. On the recent studies of Lambot, Baix and Fransens, see *RHE* 41 (1946) 381 sq.

64 MICHAEL, *Geschichte des deutschen Volkes* IV 337. The melody of the Lauda Sion is in the prototype of the Dominican liturgy in the General Archives of the Order in Rome, f. 364 sq.

65 According to the tradition of Orvieto. P. PERALI, *Orvieto* (Orvieto 1919) 72.

66 POTTHAST, *Regesta* p. 1538, n. 18998, 18999.

67 SASSEN, *Kardinal Hugo von St Cher* 41–45. HUF, *De Sacramentshymnen* 8–14, 49.

68 *Acta Ap. Sedis* 15 (1923) 320.

69 GRABMANN, *Storia* 116, *Die Werke* 286. BACIC, *Introductio* 72. A. R. MOTTE, *Un chapitre inauthentique dans le Compendium theologiae de S. Thomas, RTh* 45 (1939) 749–753. Cf. *Scholastik* 16 (1942) 442 (Pelster).

70 GRABMANN, *Die Werke* 292. BACIC, op. cit. 81 sq.

71 MORTIER, *Histoire des Maîtres Généraux* II 21, 15.

72 SIMONIN, *Les écrits de Pierre de Tarentaise* 164, 178, 192 sq. GRABMANN, *Die Werke* 325 sq. BACIC, op. cit. 106. B. M. SMERALDO, *Intorno all'Opuscolo IX di S. Tommaso d'Aquino,* Pietro da Tarantasia ha errato in teologia? (Rome 1945). LAURENT, *Le bx Innocent V* 54–56. R. MARTIN, in *Mélanges Pelzer* 303–323.

73 CREYTENS, *Pierre de Tarentaise professeur à Paris* 91 sq.

74 GRABMANN, *Die Werke* 296 sq. BACIC, *Introductio* 87 sq.

75 GRABMANN, op. cit. 299 sq. BACIC, op. cit. 88 sq. *DTP* 39 (1936) 153–160 (Glorieux): about 1270.

76 H. FINKE, *Ungedruckte Dominikanerbriefe des 13. Jahrhunderts* (Paderborn 1891) 58 n. 12.

77 GRABMANN, op. cit. 272–275. BACIC, op. cit. 51–54. A. WALZ, *De genuino titulo " Summa theologiae," Angelicum* 18 (1941) 142–151.

78 GRABMANN, *Storia* 113 sq.

pp. 101–106]

[79] Ibidem, 80 sq.

[80] Ibidem, 114 sq.

[81] *Le plan de la Somme théologique de S. Thomas, RTh* 45 (1939) 93–107.

[82] *Tabulae schematicae* 23–31, (41).

[83] TOCCO, c. 17.

[84] POTTHAST, *Regesta* p. 1429 n. 18471. VAN STEENBERGHEN, Siger II 430–490 sq. M. GRABMANN, *I divieti ecclesiastici di Aristotile sotto Innocenzo III e Gregorio IX* (Rome 1941) 133.

[85] S. MERKLE, *Antonio Uccelli u. Thomas Contra errores Graecorum, Römische Quartalschrift* 35 (1927) 223 sq.

[86] Cf. S. *Thomae Opera* IX xiv a.

[87] GLORIEUX, *Répertoire* I 119–122 n. 21. *LThK* X 902 sq. CASTAGNOLI, *Regesta* (1929) 447 sq. ALTANER, *Die Kenntnis des Griechischen* 455, 478–481. GRABMANN, *Mitteralterliches Geistesleben* II 413–423. DE WULF, *Histoire de la Philosophie* 267–269. VAN STEENBERGHEN, Siger II passim. M. GRABMANN, *Guglielmo di Moerbeke, O. P., il traduttore di Aristotile,* (Rome 1946).

[88] GRABMANN, *Methoden und Hilfsmittel des Aristotelesstudium im Mittelalter* (Munich 1939), esp. 9–49.

[89] GRABMANN, *Die Werke* 262 sq.

[90] Ibidem, 265 sq. BACIC, *Introductio* 22 sq. G. VERBEKE (*Rev. de Philos. de Louvain* 1947, 314–318) places Lib. I in 1268/9, in Italy.

[91] GRABMANN, op. cit. 266. BACIC, op. cit. 23 sq.

[92] PTOLEMY, *Hist. eccl.* XXIII 24.

[93] TOCCO, c. 42. CASTAGNOLI, *Regesta* (1929) 451. G. SCHERILLO, *Della venuta di S. Pietro Apostolo nella città di Napoli* (Naples 1859) 384. This church was, since the XIIth century, served by canons regular under an abbot. At the time of Napoleon they were replaced by Franciscans. The church marks the spot were St. Peter on arrival offered Mass. The ample revenues of this monastery are attested by many papers preserved in the Vatican secret Archives.

[94] TOCCO, c. 42. PETITOT, *S. Thomas d'Aquin* 43.

[95] GREGOROVIUS, *Storia della città di Roma nel medio evo* II 2, 483. Cf. SALVATORELLI, *L'Italia comunale* 611–655.

[96] K. HAMPE, *Urban IV und Manfred* (1261–1264) (Heidelberg 1905) 17 sq., 23, 29.

[97] GREGOROVIUS, ibidem, and 483–494.

[98] Ibidem, 491.

[99] HEFELE-LECLERCQ, *Histoire des Conciles* VI 46 sq.

[100] POTTHAST, *Regesta* p. 1551 n. 19149. MORGHEN, *Il tramonto della potenza sveva* 232 sq.

[101] POTTHAST, op. cit. p. 1557 n. 19234.

[102] GREGOROVIUS, op. cit. II 2, 499. POTTHAST, op. cit. p. 1571 n. 19434.

[103] POTTHAST, *Regesta* p. 1569 n. 19408, 1570 n. 19421, 1577 n. 195515. TOSO, Tommaso d'Aquino 75–77.

[104] *MOPH* III 142, XX 32–34.

[105] MORGHEN, op. cit. 242.

[106] GREGOROVIUS, op. cit. III 13–23, 39 sq., 51 sq. For the Sanseverino cf. *Enc. Ital.* XXX 754, SCANDONE, *La vita, la famiglia* 57, *The Cambridge Medieval History* VI 183–189 (C. W. Previté-Orton).

[107] *Doc.* 19 (*Fontes* 566), cf. *Doc.* 20 (*Fontes* 569 sq.). TOSO, *Tommaso d'Aquino* 70.

[108] TOCCO, c. 37, 42.

[109] SCANDONE, *La vita, la famiglia* 82.

[110] TOSO, op. cit. 84, 76 sq. SCANDONE, op. cit. 81.

[111] TOCCO, c. 44. CASTAGNOLI, *Regesta* (1929) 445.

[112] TOCCO, c. 44. Cf. SCANDONE, op. cit. 79 sq.

[113] *MOPH* I 215 sq.

[114] *Proc. Neap.* n. 49. MARTINORI, *Lazio turrito* II 6, places the visit in 1250, which is of course much too early.

[115] I. FONTANINUS, *Codex canonizationum* (Rome 1719) 97 sq., 102 sq.

[116] WALZ, *I cardinali domenicani* 15 n. 1.

[117] GLORIEUX, *Répertoire* I 304–311 n. 137.

[118] *AFH* 19 (1926) 156, 165, 168.

[119] SCHEEBEN, *Albert der Grosse* 63–72.

[120] *LThK* X 944. GLORIEUX, op. cit. I 119.

[121] INGUANEZ, *Cronologia degli abati* 431–433 for Theodinus, and 433–438 for Bernard I. Cf. SABA, *Bernardo I Ayglerio* 134–137.

[122] EUBEL, *Hierarchia* I 359: † 1281.

[123] MORTIER, *Histoire des Maîtres Généraux* II 18.

[124] POTTHAST, *Regesta* p. 1558 n. 19252.

[125] *Proc. Neap.* n. 47, 6. TOCCO, c. 27, 53, 65.

[126] QUÉTIF-ECHARD, *Scriptores* I 382.

[127] HUMBERTUS DE ROMANIS, *Opera* II 255.

[128] SCHEEBEN, *Albert der Grosse* 163.

[129] TOCCO, c. 63. A. D'ACHILLE, *Una fervida amicizia nella vita di S. Tommaso d'Aquino*, MD 41 (1924) 97–113. CASTAGNOLI, *Regesta* (1929) 445.

[130] On the compiler of the Supplement, see S. *Thomae Opera* XII, praef. in suppl. § 7. GRABMANN, *Die Werke* 274 sq. BACIC, *Introductio* 53.

[131] DE GROOT, *Het leven* 229 sq. BERTHIER, *Le couvent de S. Sabine* 304, 311. G. TOMASETTI, *Della Campagna Romana*, Archivio Storico della R. Soc. di Storia Patria 29 (1906) 303.

[132] MARTINORI, *Lazio turrito* II 45. GREGOROVIUS, *Storia della Città di Roma* II 1, 400.

[133] Bartholomew of Capua, in *Proc. Neap.* n. 86, is more exact than TOCCO, c. 22.

[134] MANDONNET, *Thomas d'Aquin lecteur* 26.

[135] GLORIEUX, *Répertoire* I 107, 113. In 1287 William of Hothun was recalled for a second period, but in point of fact did not go, ibidem 144.

[136] *Thomas d'Aquin lecteur* 33 sq.

[137] GLORIEUX, op. cit. I 123 n. 23.

pp. 113–117]

[138] Ibidem, I 118 n. 20.

[139] SCHEEBEN, *Albert der Grosse* 90–92.

[140] MANDONNET, loc. cit. 31. CASTAGNOLI, *Regesta* (1929) 454.

[141] MANDONNET, loc. cit. 38 sq. CASTAGNOLI, op. cit. 455. On Brunacci, see TAURISANO, *I discepoli* 134–139, 176. *MOPH* III 322 (Bramasii), XX 57, 388.

[142] MANDONNET, loc. cit. 29–31. P. A. UCCELLI, *Due sermoni inediti di S. Tommaso d'Aquino, Genio Cattolico* (Reggio Emilia 1875) 55, 57. A. SABA, *Un discorso di S. Tommaso a Milano, La Scuola Cattolica* 62 (1934) 345. Mandonnet fixed the Sundays according to the present arrangement of the Epistles and Gospels, but from the manuscript of Dominican liturgy approved in 1267, which is preserved in the General Archives in Rome, it becomes evident that the sermon at Bologna is on the Epistle of the 1st Sunday of Advent (f. 422), and that at Milan on the Gospel of the 3rd Sunday (f. 436).

[143] TOCCO, c. 29. CASTAGNOLI, op. cit. 456.

[144] CASTAGNOLI, ibidem. DE GROOT, *Het leven* 259, is inclined to reject the visit to the tomb of St. Peter Martyr.

[145] MORTIER, *Histoire des Maîtres Généraux* II 15. SEBASTIANO D'OL-MEDA (*Fontes* 582 [4]), SOMMER-SECKENDORFF, *Studies in the Life of Robert Kilwardby* 36, and others claim that Thomas was present at the general chapter in London. LAURENT, *Le bx Innocent V* 67 sq.

[146] MORTIER, op. cit. III 151 sq.

[147] MANDONNET, *Thomas d'Aquin lecteur* 26–33.

FOOTNOTES FOR CHAPTER IX

[1] CREYTENS, *Pierre de Tarentaise* 96–100: 1269–72.

[2] QUÉTIF-ECHARD, *Scriptores Ord. Praed.* 407. For Peter of Dacia cf. J. GALLÉN in *AFP* 5 (1935) 314–316, 318.

[3] MANDONNET, *Siger* I 89.

[4] La Baronne de WEDEL-JARLSBERG, *Une page de l'histoire des Frères Prêcheurs, La province de Dacie* (Rome-Tournai 1899) 223. WALZ in *Angelicum* 5 (1928) 385 sq. J. GALLÉN, *La province de Dacie* (Helsingfors 1946) 240 sq., 264.

[5] TOCCO, c. 38 Cf. *Proc. Neap.* n. 15.

[6] Job 7. 1.

[7] MANDONNET, *Siger* I 81. On the "nationes" see DENIFLE, *Die Entstehung der Universitäten* 106. D'IRSAY, *Histoire des Universités* I 71, 146. RASHDALL, *The Universities* I 122 sq. WALZ, *Studi domenicani* 40.

[8] MANDONNET, *Thomas d'Aquin lecteur* 31 sq. L. B. GILLON in *DThC*, art. Thomas d'Aquin.

[9] GLORIEUX, *Répertoire* I 356 n. 174.

[10] Ibidem, I 354 n. 172.

[11] L. OLIGER, *Die theologische Quästion des Johannes Peckham über die vollkommene Armut, Franziskanische Studien* 4 (1917) 134–137. *LThK* VIII 58. GLORIEUX, op. cit. II 87 n. 316. RUSSELL, *Dictionary* 70 sq.

[pp. 117–122

12 CLASEN, *Der hl. Bonaventura* 14–17, 23 sq.

13 Ibidem, 17, 19.

14 GRABMANN, *Die Werke* 293. BACIC, *Introductio* 85 sq.

15 GRABMANN, ibidem. BACIC, op. cit. 84 sq.

16 GLORIEUX, *Les polémiques*, *RTAM* 6 (1934) 6–41. KÄPPELLI, *Una raccolta* 67 sq.

17 KÄPPELI, op. cit. 64.

18 Ibidem, 65 sq.

19 GLORIEUX, *Répertoire* I 355.

20 BIERBAUM, *Bettelorden* 255. GLORIEUX, "*Contra Geraldinos*" 129–155. CLASEN, *Der hl. Bonaventura* 12–23. Cf. *Chartularium* I 270 sq.

21 HEFELE-LECLERCQ, *Histoire des Conciles* VI 202.

22 MANDONNET, *Siger* I 98. St. Bonaventure, *Opera* V (Quaracchi 1891) 440b.

23 *Proc. Neap.* n. 77. MANDONNET, op. cit. I 99–102.

24 MANDONNET, op. cit. I 59 sq., 103 sq. VAN STEENBERGHEN, *Siger* II 490 sq.: first appeared in 1266. C. KRZANIC, *Grandi lottatori contro l'Averroismo*, RFNS 22 (1930) 161, 206.

25 VAN STEENBERGHEN, *Siger* II, deuxième partie, chap. II.

26 Ibidem, I 1–5, II 360 sq.

27 P. DELHAYE, *Siger de Brabant, Questions sur la Physique d'Aristote* (Louvain 1941) 9 n. 28, 13. VAN STEENBERGHEN, op. cit. II 541–543, 565, 577, 642 sq., 644 n. 4, 683 (habituels, préjugés). Cf. LOTTIN, *Psychologie et Morale* I 262 n. 1.

28 VAN STEENBERGHEN, op. cit. I 5. M. GRABMANN, *Neu aufgefundene Werke des Siger von Brabant und Boethius von Dacien* (Munich 1924). Idem, *Der lateinische Averroismus des 13. Jahrhunderts und seine Stellung zur christlichen Weltanschauung* (Munich 1931) 5 sq.

29 List in *Siger* II 745.

30 List in *Siger* II 742.

31 GILSON, *La philosophie de saint Bonaventure* 29–34.

32 MANDONNET, *Siger* I 108. M. GRABMANN, *Sigieri di Brabante e Dante*. *RFNS* 32 (1940) 126. VAN STEENBERGHEN, *Siger* II 90–97.

33 GLORIEUX, *Répertoire* I 127 n. 27. MANDONNET, *Siger* I 105 sq., II 29 sq. GRABMANN, *Mittelalterliches Geistesleben* II 512–530. LOTTIN, *Psychologie et Morale* I 251 n. 2. VAN STEENBERGHEN in *Mélanges Pelzer* 415–439.

34 *Chartularium* I 487 n. 432. GRABMANN, *Sigieri* 127, 137. VAN STEENBERGHEN, *Siger* II 719–722.

35 L. W. KEELER, S. *Thomae Aquinatis tractatus de unitate intellectus contra averroistas* ed. *critica* (Rome 1936). KEELER, *History of the Editions of St. Thomas' " De unitate intellectus,"* *Gregorianum* 17 (1936) 58–81. VAN STEENBERGHEN, op. cit. II 629, 633–642, 649 n. 1. GRABMANN, *Die Werke*, 292 sq. BACIC, *Introductio* 82 sq.

36 VAN STEENBERGHEN, op. cit. II 641, 546, 633.

37 GRABMANN, *Die Werke* 301. BACIC, op. cit. 64. VAN STEEN-

pp. 123–128]
BERGHEN, op. cit. II 458 sq., 717. GLORIEUX, *Répertoire* I 96: early in 1271.

[38] GRABMANN, S. *Tommaso d'Aquino* 134 sq. Cf. H. MEYER, *Thomas von Aquin* (Bonn 1938) 305–307.

[39] VAN STEENBERGHEN, op. cit. II 509, 551 sq., 642–661.

[40] GLORIEUX, op. cit. I 94–97: 1271.

[41] KÄPPELI, *Una raccolta* 71 sq.

[42] GRABMANN, *Die Werke* 241–243. BACIC, *Introductio* 55 sq.

[43] Ibidem, 253–255. Ibidem, 60 sq. GLORIEUX, op. cit. I 376 n. 186. GRABMANN, *Die persönlichen Beziehungen* 312, 315.

[44] GRABMANN, *Die Werke* 278–282. BACIC, op. cit. 34–39. LOTTIN, op. cit. I 252–258: La question VI du " De malo." GLORIEUX, *Les polémiques,* passim.

[45] GRABMANN, op. cit. 284. BACIC, op. cit. 42–48.

[46] A. M. JACQUIN, *Un exercise scolaire au moyen âge, A travers l'histoire de France* (Lille-Paris 1925) 67–84.

[47] *Psychologie et Morale* I 258–262: 1370.

[48] GRABMANN, *Die persönlichen Beziehungen* 317.

[49] GRABMANN, *Die Werke* 260–268. BACIC, op. cit. 15–26. Cf. c. 8 n. 85–87. A. MANSION, *Le commentaire de s. Thomas sur le De sensu et sensato d'Aristote, utilisation d'Alexandre d'Aphrodise, Mélanges Mandonnet* I 83–102: 1270–1272. F. PELSTER in *Scholastik* 25 (1950) 154–155, in disagreement with Verbeke.

[50] *Proc. Neap.* n. 58. GRABMANN, *Die Werke* 267 sq. Idem, *Die mittelalterlichen Kommentare zur Politik des Aristoteles* (Munich 1941) 14–17. BACIC, op. cit. 26–82.

[51] GRABMANN, *Die Werke* 268. BACIC, op. cit. 28 sq.

[52] *Histoire des Universités* I 166–171. Cf. DE WULF, *Histoire de la Philosophie* II 184 sq.

[53] *Die persönlichen Beziehungen* 316. GRABMANN, *Die Werke* 307, 228–232.

[54] GRABMANN, *Die persönlichen Beziehungen* 315.

[55] *Doc.* 31 (*Fontes* 583–586).

[56] GRABMANN, *Die persönlichen Beziehungen* 316.

[57] GRABMANN, *Die Werke* 324 sq. BACIC, *Introductio* 102 sq. MORTIER, *Histoire des Maîtres Généraux* II 120–123. MANDONNET, *Des Écrits authentiques* 139–142. MANDONNET, *Siger* I 88. D. PLANZER in *AFP* 5 (1935) 35. CREYTENS, *Pierre de Tarentaise* 95. LAURENT, *Le bx Innocent V* 64 sq. GLORIEUX, *Répertoire* I 83, 105, 107, 123, 118.

[58] MORTIER, op. cit. II 123 sq. MANDONNET, *Siger* I 83 sq.

[59] MANDONNET, *Siger* I 87 sq. SOMMER-SECKENDORFF, *Studies in the Life of Robert Kilwardby* 36. RUSSELL, *Dictionary* 138 sq. *MOPH* III 155. *Doc.* 23 (*Fontes* 572 sq.). On Kilwardby see WALZ, *I cardinali domenicani* 18 n. 5, and on Latino see ibidem 17 n. 4.

[60] GRABMANN, *Die Werke* 300. BACIC, op. cit. 89 sq. GLORIEUX,

[pp. 128–133
Répertoire I 95. See CASTAGNOLI's edition (Piacenza 1933). *Bull. thom.* 11 (1934) 13–20.

[61] GRABMANN, op. cit. 290. BACIC, op. cit. 78 sq. M. D. CHENU, *Les réponses de s. Thomas et de Kilwardby à la consultation de Jean de Verceil (1271), Mélanges Mandonnet* I 191–222. *MOPH* III 156 (Milan 1270). Chenu places the praise of Kilwardby at the chapter of Montpellier and not at that of Milan. Cf. *MOPH* III 156.

[62] Cf. MORTIER, *Histoire* I 212, 399, 632. CREYTENS, *Pierre de Tarentaise* 98 sq.

[63] TOCCO, c. 43. Cf. GUI, c. 25 and CALO, c. 24.

[64] A. VON RUVILLE, *Die Kreuzzüge* (Bonn-Leipzig 1920) 331 sq.

[65] DE RUBEIS, *Dissertationes* 12a, c. l. DE GROOT, *Het leven* 323.

[66] S. *Thomae opera* XIII xvib-xviia, cf. XIV App. 7*.

[67] M. D. CHAPOTIN, *Histoire des Dominicains de France* (Rouen 1898) 661. VON RUVILLE, *Die Kreuzzüge* 337 sq. ALTANER, *Die Dominikanermissionen* 96, 103 sq., 109. P. ANDRIEU-GUITRANCOURT, *L'archevêque Eudes Rigaud et la vie de l'église au XIIIe siècle d'après le "Registrum visitationum"* (Paris 1938) 436 sq.

[68] *MOPH* III 161.

[69] *MOPH* III 165, 170. WALZ, *I cardinali domenicani* 16 n. 2.

[70] ENDRES, *Thomas von Aquin* 60.

[71] *Quaestiones de anima intellectiva*, III. MANDONNET, *Siger* II 152. VAN STEENBERGHEN, *Siger* II 554–559.

[72] *AFH* 18 (1925) 447.

[73] TOCCO, c. 52.

[74] GLORIEUX, *Répertoire* I 125, 126, 133–135.

[75] TOCCO, c. 26. *Fontes* 99.

[76] TOCCO, c. 42. *Proc. Neap.* n. 66.

[77] Cf. H. AYMÈS, *De S. Thomae ad studentes sui temporis habitudine, Unio tomistica (Angelicum)* 1 (1924) 13, 20.

[78] *Quelques aperçus nouveaux sur l'opus imperfectum in Matthaeum, Revue Bénédictine* 37 (1925) 239.

[79] GLORIEUX, *Répertoire* I 129 n. 28. PTOLEMY, *Hist. eccl.* XXIII 16. M. GRABMANN in *DTF* 19 (1941) 166–184. R. MORGHEN, *Il cardinale Matteo Rossi Orsini, Archivio della R. Soc. Romana di Storia Patria* 46 (1923) 273 sq.

[80] Cf. supra p. 115.

[81] GRABMANN, *Die persönlichen Beziehungen* 311. *LThK* VIII 625. GLORIEUX, op. cit. I 170 sq. n. 51.

[82] TAURISANO, *I discepoli* 133 sq. GRABMANN, *Die Werke* 77 sq., 251 sq., 287. BACIC, *Introductio* 60. GRABMANN, *Mittelalterliches Geistesleben* I 336.

[83] *Proc. Neap.* n. 76. TAURISANO, op. cit. 124. MASETTI, *Monumenta* I 234 sq.

[84] TAURISANO, op. cit. 139–143. *LThK* VIII 816 sq. GRABMANN, *Mit-*

pp. 133–137]

telalterliches Geistesleben II 530–547, *Die persönlichen Beziehungen* 310 sq.

[85] MANDONNET, *Thomas d'Aquin lecteur* 137. TAURISANO, op. cit. 134–139. GRABMANN, *Mittelalterliches Geistesleben* I 335 sq.

[86] TOCCO, c. 52.

[87] G. BRUNI, *Di alcune opere inedite e dubbie die Egidio Romano*, RTAM 7 (1935) 174. E. HOCEDEZ, *Gilles de Rome et s. Thomas, Mélanges Mandonnet* I 385–409. GLORIEUX, *Répertoire* II 293–308 n. 400. F. PELSTER, *Thomistische Streitschriften gegen Aegidius Romanus und ihre Verfasser: Thomas von Sutton und Robert von Oxford*, Gregorianum 24 (1943) 135–170. TOCCO, c. 40 and CALO, c. 22 incorrectly prolong Giles' period as student to thirteen years in place of three.

[88] GLORIEUX, op. cit. II 321–327 n. 409. GEYER, *Die patrist, u. scholast. Philosophie* 547, 722, 794.

[89] VAN STEENBERGHEN, *Siger* II 559 sq. DE WULF, *Histoire* 303–305. GLORIEUX, op. cit. I 412–417 n. 210.

[90] GRABMANN, *Die persönlichen Beziehungen* 316 sq.

[91] G. WALLERAND, *Henri Bate de Malines et s. Thomas d'Aquin*, RNSP 36 (1934) 387–411. GLORIEUX, op. cit. I 409–411 n. 209. DE WULF, *Histoire* 305–308.

[92] GRABMANN, *Die Werke* 300 sq. BACIC, *Introductio* 92 sq.

[93] Ibidem 306. Ibidem 97.

[94] Ibidem 291. Ibidem 80 sq. Cf. KÄPPELI in *AFP* 13 (1943) 181 sq.

[95] Ibidem 290 sq. Ibidem 79 sq. Cf. KÄPPELI, loc. cit.

[96] Cf. BIRKENMAJER, *Vermischte Untersuchungen* 10.

[97] *Doc.* 22 (*Fontes* 571 sq.). TAURISANO, *I discepoli* 122. The friars did not come until 1562. See *AOP* 3 (1895) 104.

[98] *Doc.* 34 (*Fontes* 573 sq.).

[99] TOCCO, c. 17, cf. 43.

[100] *Fontes* 89.

[101] I am indebted to Fr M. H. Laurent, O. P., for the identification of St Evan, and for a reference to W. SMITH and H. WACE, *Dictionary of Christian Biography* II (London 1880) 63 sq.

[102] EUBEL, *Hierarchia* I 494: E. de Begaynon 1362/71.

[103] TOCCO, c. 17. Cf. A. WALZ, *Vom Buchwesen im Predigerorden, Aus der Geisteswelt des Mittelalters* I 111–127.

[104] DE GROOT, *Het leven* 335.

[105] GRABMANN, *Die Werke* 254, 265, 268. BACIC, *Introductio* 60, 21, 27.

[106] B. ALTANER, *Patrologia* (3rd Italian ed., Turin 1944) 129 (2nd German ed. *Patrologie*, Freiburg i. B., 1950, 167).

[107] TOCCO, c. 47.

[108] MANDONNET, *Siger* I 197 sq.

[109] GLORIEUX, *Répertoire* I 97.

[110] Ibidem I 129 n. 28.

[111] Ibidem I 138 n. 33, 135 n. 31.

FOOTNOTES FOR CHAPTER X

[1] MANDONNET, *Bibliographie thomiste* xi. Idem, *Siger* 203.

[2] e. g. *MOPH* III 126, 155, 161.

[3] MANDONNET, *Bibliographie thomiste* xi. *MOPH* XX 39-41.

[4] *Doc.* 31 (*Fontes* 585). BIRKENMAJER, *Vermischte Untersuchungen* 2 sq.

[5] MORTIER, *Histoire des Maîtres Généraux* II 82-84.

[6] DAVIDSOHN, *Geschichte von Florenz* II 2, 84.

[7] *MOPH* XX 39. *Doc.* 30 (*Fontes* 583).

[8] *MOPH* XX 36.

[9] *MOPH* III 135, 143, 167, 179. WALZ, *Compendium Historiae Ord. Praed.* 198 sq. (2nd ed. 124 sq.). MORTIER, op. cit. II 42 sq.

[10] *MOPH* III 153.

[11] *MOPH* III 164.

[12] *MOPH* III 167.

[13] *MOPH* III 325. WALZ, *Compendium* 133, (2nd ed. 221).

[14] *MOPH* XX 39. *Doc.* 30 (*Fontes* 583).

[15] DENIFLE, *Die Entstehung* 360. D'IRSAY, *Histoire des Universités* I 135.

[16] DENIFLE, *Chartularium* I 501 sq., n. 443.

[17] *Storia dell'Università di Napoli* 88.

[18] MD 44 (1927) 201. About the year 1665 " St Thomas' rostrum " at Pisa was bought by the Dominicans of Lima in Peru. See the Archives of the Order in Rome IV 111, p. 343 sq., IV 122, 125. But it was never removed and is still at Pisa.

[19] G. PORTANOVA, *Il Castello di S. Severino nel secolo XIII e S. Tommaso* (Badia di Cava 1926) 57 sq. On Theodora and Roger of San Severino, cf. SCANDONE, *La vita, la famiglia* 57 sq.

[20] *Proc. Neap.* n. 60. TAURISANO, *I discepoli* 185. Cf. *DThC* IX 1062-1067 (Rivière). *LThK* X 108 sq. BOCK, *Kaisertum, Kurie* 119 sq., 171, 203.

[21] MORTIER, *Histoire* I 644.

[22] PTOLEMY, *Hist. eccl.* XXIII 10. TOCCO, c. 50, gives a different version, but Tocco in the *Proc. Neap.* n. 60 follows Ptolemy. MARTINORI, *Lazio turrito* II 46 mentions Fr. Raymund and not Fr. Reginald as his companion.

[23] PTOLEMY, ibidem.

[24] MANDONNET, *Thomas d'Aquin lecteur* 40.

[25] MILLER, *Itineraria* 329 sq. TOSO, *Tommaso d'Aquino* 124.

[26] Cf. supra p. 134.

[27] SCANDONE, *La vita, la famiglia* 21, says that Thomas left Rome at the end of August or the beginning of September.

[28] In 1269 the concession of this church to the Dominicans was reconfirmed. See R. M. VALLE, *Descrizione di S. Domenico Maggiore* (Naples 1854) 34. L. RUGGIERO, *La chiesa di S. Domenico Maggiore a Napoli,* Cenno storico (Naples 1887).

[29] Supra pp. 26, 31.

[30] *Proc. Neap.* n. 76. Cf. n. 42 (Caiazzo), 45 (Peter of S. Felice), 47 (Conrad), 58 (Tocco), 89 (Boiano). T. VALLE, *Compendio degli più illustri*

pp. 143–147]

Padri della Provincia del Regno di Napoli (Naples 1651) 32–34, TAURISANO, *I discepoli* 126 n. 1, and MONTI, *Da Carlo I a Roberto d'Angiò* 249, all speak of Matthew of Castellammare (Castromaris), while *Proc. Neap.* 76, probably through a scribe's error, gives Matthew of Castro-Maioris. TAURISANO, *I discepoli* 120–126, 132, 149. For Tocco, see TOCCO, c. 28 and A. WALZ, *Historia canonizationis* 122 sq. *MOPH* XX 377. For Eufranone, Boiano, Caiazzo, Troiano, see *MOPH* XX 373, 381, 398.

[31] *Proc. Neap.* n. 75.

[32] Cf. *MOPH* III 322 n. 1, 310 n. 3. MORTIER, *Histoire* II 183 sq.

[33] *Proc. Neap.* n. 70.

[34] TOCCO, c. 54. Cf. *Proc. Neap.* n. 87.

[35] TOCCO, c. 33. For these attendants see MORTIER, *Histoire* II 273 sq.

[36] *Proc. Neap.* n. 87. TOCCO, c. 54.

[37] SCANDONE, *La vita, la famiglia* 27. TAURISANO, *I discepoli* 148. V. SPAMPANATO, *Vita di Giordano Bruno* (Messina 1921) 106.

[38] FELDER, *Storia* 335.

[39] G. M. MONTI, *Nuovi studi angioini* (Trani 1937) 229.

[40] MONTI, *Storia della Università di Napoli* 26–29. Idem, *Da Carlo I a Roberto d'Angiò* 232. Idem. *Nuovi studi angioini* 61.

[41] *Doc.* 28 (*Fontes* 579 sq.). MONTI, *Storia* 89. SCANDONE, *La vita, la famiglia* 26, 83.

[42] MONTI, *Nuovi studi* 229. D'IRSAY, *Histoire des universités* I 152. TORRACA in *Storia della Università di Napoli* 10.

[43] *Chartularium* II 692.

[44] TAURISANO, *I discepoli* 163–166. GRABMANN, *Mittelalterliches Geistesleben* 354.

[45] *Proc. Neap.* n. 58. GRABMANN, op. cit. 337.

[46] TAURISANO, op. cit. 124–126.

[47] Ibidem 126 sq.

[48] Ibidem 133 sq.

[49] *MD* 44 (1927) 201. James was a Preacher-General in 1270.

[50] TAURISANO, op. cit. 129. MONTI in *Storia della Università di Napoli* 130.

[51] TAURISANO, op. cit. 118–120.

[52] *MOPH* III 99, 251.

[53] TAURISANO, op. cit. 118–155. MONTI, *Da Carlo I a Roberto d'Angiò* 249.

[54] TOCCO, c. 43. TAURISANO, op. cit. 184 sq. On Marino see further EUBEL, *Hierarchia* I 164; *MOPH* XX 69; PTOLEMY, *Hist. eccl.* XXIII 9; *Proc. Neap.* n. 43.

[55] TAURISANO, op. cit. 123. EUBEL, op. cit. I 429.

[56] *Proc. Neap.* n. 76–86. TAURISANO, op. cit. 155–158. SCANDONE, *La vita, la famiglia* 25, 33. *LThK* II 3. MONTI, *Nuovi studi angioini* 63.

[57] *Proc. Neap.* n. 77.

[58] GRABMANN, *Die Werke* 243 sq. BACIC, *Introductio* 56.

⁵⁹ Ibidem 255–260. Ibidem 63–69. VOSTÉ, S. *Thomas Aquinas epistularum S. Pauli interpres* 263.

⁶⁰ GRABMANN, *Die Werke* 263 sq. BACIC, op. cit. 18–20.

⁶¹ Ibidem 305 sq. Ibidem 96–98.

⁶² *I discepoli* 124–126. GRABMANN, *Die Werke* 323 sq. BACIC, op. cit. 114.

⁶³ TOCCO, c. 48.

⁶⁴ MANDONNET, *Le Carême de S. Thomas à Naples* (1273) 195–212. GRABMANN, *Die Werke* 287–289. BACIC, op. cit. 74–78. SCANDONE, op. cit. 28.

⁶⁵ MANDONNET, *Le Carême* 199, 211.

⁶⁶ *Proc. Neap.* n. 58.

⁶⁷ Loc. cit. n. 87.

⁶⁸ Loc. cit. n. 93.

⁶⁹ Loc. cit. n. 88.

⁷⁰ Loc. cit. n. 70. *Expositio salutationis angelicae* (Rossi [Piacenza 1933]). Bull. thom. 9 (1932) [563–584], and *Notes et Comm.* N. 9 (Janv.-Mars 1933) 156 *–167 *.

⁷¹ TOCCO, c. 48.

⁷² Ibidem c. 36.

⁷³ *MOPH* XVI 135 n. 13, 155 n. 37, 161 n. 41, cf. 165 n. 46.

⁷⁴ TOCCO, c. 29, 48.

⁷⁵ Ibidem c. 48.

⁷⁶ Ibidem c. 38.

⁷⁷ Ibidem c. 21.

⁷⁸ Ibidem c. 29.

⁷⁹ Ibidem c. 32.

⁸⁰ Ibidem c. 29.

⁸¹ Ibidem c. 30.

⁸² Ibidem c. 43. On Raymund Étienne see G. GOLUBOVICH, *Biblioteca bio-bibliografica della Terra Santa e dell'Ordine Francescano* III (Quaracchi 1919) 404 sq. R. LOENERTZ, *La Société des Frères Pérégrinants. Étude sur l'Orient Dominicain* I (Rome 1937) 63, 167, 188.

⁸³ TOCCO, c. 29.

⁸⁴ Ibidem c. 36.

⁸⁵ DANTE, *Convivio* IV 30.

⁸⁶ TAURISANO, *I discepoli* 163 sq. GRABMANN, *Mittelalterliches Geistesleben* 354.

⁸⁷ *Proc. Neap.* n. 76.

⁸⁸ TOCCO, c. 55, 29. *Proc. Neap.* n. 70.

⁸⁹ *Proc. Neap.* n. 43, 6, 41.

⁹⁰ Loc. cit. n. 81.

⁹¹ SCANDONE, *La vita, la famiglia* 21 sq., 67 sq. MANDONNET, *Bibliographie thomiste* xi, says that the count died on the 2nd August in the presence of St Thomas.

⁹² SCANDONE, op. cit. 67.

⁹³ *Doc.* 25 (*Fontes* 575). SCANDONE, op. cit. 22. For the situation of friars with reference to wills see *MOPH* III 130.

pp. 154–160]

94 *Doc.* 26 (*Fontes* 576–578). SCANDONE, op. cit. 23 sq.

95 *Doc.* 27 (*Fontes* 578 sq.). SCANDONE, op. cit. 25 sq., 68 sq.

96 SCANDONE, op. cit. 21, 67 sq. PORTANOVA, *Il Castello di S. Severino* 59 sq.

97 SCANDONE, op. cit. 80.

98 Ibidem 81.

99 *Doc.* 29 (*Fontes* 581). SCANDONE, op. cit. 27 sq.

100 *Proc. Neap.* n. 15, 8, 50.

101 *Doc.* 30 (*Fontes* 583). MASETTI, *Monumenta* II 268. Cf. *MOPH* XX 41–42.

102 GUIRAUD, *Régistres de Grégoire X* (Paris 1892) 52 n. 160, 91 n. 220. *AFH* 18 (1925) 169.

103 *Proc. Neap.* n. 19.

104 TOCCO, c. 29.

105 Ps. 70. 9.

106 *Proc. Neap.* n. 83, 42, cf. 15, 19. TOCCO, c. 65.

107 *Proc. Neap.* n. 19, 42, 44.

108 PTOLEMY, *Hist. eccl.* XXIII 16, is better informed on Romano than Tocco. TOCCO, c. 45. GUI, c. 19. GLORIEUX, *Répertoire* I 129. GRAB-MANN, *Mittelalteriches Geistesleben* I 340 sq. At the death of Master Romano every priest in the Order had to offer one Mass for him. *MOPH* III 170.

109 Ps. 47. 9.

110 Cf. R. GARRIGOU-LAGRANGE, *De Deo uno* (Paris 1938) 269–279.

111 TOCCO, c. 34, cf. 52. GUI, c. 23 sq. CALO, c. 18.

112 D'ALENÇON in *Revue Duns Scot* 9 (1911) 76, 89 sq. BALIC in *Bogoslovska Smotra* 23 (1935) 417, *Collectanea franc. slavica* I (Sebenico 1937) 127, and *Wissenschaft und Weisheit* 4 (1937) 185.

113 *Proc. Neap.* n. 79.

114 Loc. cit.

115 TOCCO, c. 47.

116 Ibidem. Cf. *Proc. Neap.* n. 79.

117 TOCCO, c. 54. *Proc. Neap.* n. 87.

118 SCANDONE, *La vita, la famiglia* 30, 57.

119 *Proc. Neap.* n. 79. PORTANOVA, *Il Castello* 85 adds James of Salerno.

120 STHAMER, *Die Hauptstrassen des Königreichs Sizilien* 102. MILLER, *Itineraria* 351, 353, 371.

121 *Proc. Neap.* n. 79.

122 TOCCO, c. 33.

123 *Proc. Neap.* n. 79.

124 *La vita, la famiglia* 30, 57.

FOOTNOTES FOR CHAPTER XI

1 SCANDONE, *La vita, la famiglia* 30, 57, and MANDONNET, *Le carême de S. Thomas à Naples* (1273) 202, maintain that Thomas left Naples during January.

[pp. 160–164

² TOCCO, c. 56. HEFELE-LECLERCQ, *Histoire des Conciles* VI 156, 168. A. WALZ, *L'azione conciliare domenicana pretridentina, Il concilio di Trento* 1 (1942) 45–47. MORTIER, *Histoire des Maîtres Généraux* II 96.

³ *Proc. Neap.* n. 50. Cf. supra p. 144, and note 35 on p. 220.

⁴ EUBEL, *Hierarchia* I 480.

⁵ *Proc. Neap.* n. 78. TOCCO, c. 32, 63.

⁶ MILLER, *Itineraria Romana* 327 sq., 333 sq. SCANDONE, op. cit. 31.

⁷ *Proc. Neap.* n. 8. TOCCO, c. 56.

⁸ *Fontes* 522.

⁹ *Tommaso d'Aquino* 124 sq.

¹⁰ *Die Hauptstrassen des Königreichs Sizilien* 100.

¹¹ GRABMANN, *Die Werke* 326–329. TOSO, *Tommaso d'Aquino* 122–125. LECCISOTTI, *Il Dottore Angelico* 546 sq., 536 (contra Scandone, who regards it as spurious). BACIC, *Introductio* 117. SABA, *Bernardo I Ayglerio* 78 sq., in spite of recent critical studies, considers it to be an original autograph. SCANDONE, *La vita, la famiglia* 31.

¹² *Proc. Neap.* n. 50.

¹³ *Proc. Neap.* n. 8, 15, 19, 50, 80. SCANDONE, ibidem.

¹⁴ *Proc. Neap.* n. 15. In the bull of canonization (*Fontes* 522), the monastery of Fossanova is given as being in the diocese of Terracina. But at that time, as now, the sees of Terracina, Priverno and Sezze had already been united (*Annuario Pontificio* 1944, 289). For the monastery, see M. CASSONI, *La Badia di Fossanova presso Piperno, Rivista Storica Benedittina* 5 (1910) 578 sq., and SERAFINI, *L'Abbazia di Fossanova* &c 223–292.

¹⁵ Enc. Ital. 15 (1932) 773. PTOLEMY, *Hist. eccl.* XXIII 8.

¹⁶ SERAFINI, *L'Abbazia* 224, 249, 253. P. FEDELE, *Fra i monaci di Fossanova che videro morire S. Tommaso, S. Tommaso-Miscellanea* 187 sq.

¹⁷ *Proc. Neap.* n. 8. Fr. Petitot, wishing to determine the nature of this illness, invented a theory which received the following comment, after much discussion, from a kindly reviewer: " Il suffirait, à mon sens, d'ajouter pour avoir une vue compréhensive de la fin du maître: emporté par une maladie inconnue qui l'a terrassé sur le chemin de Naples à Lyon," *Bulletin thomiste* 1 (1925) [17–20] n. 511.

¹⁸ SERAFINI, *L'Abbazia* 225. SCANDONE, *La vita, la famiglia* 33. Cf. E. VALDATA, *Ancora sulla morte di S. Tommaso, L'Italia* 29. 6. 1927. MORTIER, *Histoire des Maîtres Généraux* II 94.

¹⁹ *Proc. Neap.* n. 49–50. SERAFINI, op. cit. 224 sq.

²⁰ TOCCO, c. 56. *Proc. Neap.* n. 50.

²¹ *Proc. Neap.* n. 9, 50. TOCCO, c. 56.

²² *Proc. Neap.* n. 49.

²³ Ibidem. SCANDONE, op. cit. 32: The holy Doctor, after staying about a week at Maenza, wanted to resume his journey.

²⁴ MARTINORI, *Lazio turrito* II 6.

²⁵ *Proc. Neap.* n. 8, 80. *Bulla Can.* (*Fontes* 522). Cf. TOCCO, c. 57. While SCANDONE, op. cit. 32, follows Tocco's account unreservedly, SERAFINI, op. cit. 224, observes that there is nothing impossible in Thomas' idea of being

pp. 164–167]

carried to the abbey. Both writers would, however, have come to more satis-factory conclusions if they had consulted the process of canonization.

[26] *Proc. Neap.* n. 8, cf. n. 80, 49. Thomas rode in the company of the afore-said prior, of the monks, and of his other companions, from the castle of Maenza to the Abbey of Fossanova. TOCCO, c. 62, mentions a mule "upon which he sat."

[27] MARTINORI, *Lazio turrito* I 240 sq.

[28] *Proc. Neap.* n. 8.

[29] Loc. cit. n. 10, cf. n. 8: tempore quadragesimali.

[30] SERAFINI, op. cit. 224 sq.

[31] TOCCO, c. 57. Cf. *Proc. Neap.* n. 49, 15.

[32] *Proc. Neap.* loc. cit.

[33] Ps. 131. 14. *Proc. Neap.* n. 8, 15, 49, 80. TOCCO, c. 57. *Bulla can.* (*Fontes* 522).

[34] *L'Abbazia* 283 n. 1, 225, 223.

[35] *Proc. Neap.* n. 49.

[36] *Proc. Neap.* n. 80: pluribus diebus. TOCCO, c. 52: pluribus diebus gravatus amplius infirmitate. *Proc. Neap.* n. 8: ubi (Fossaenovae) iacuit infirmus per mensem.

[37] *Bulla can.* (*Fontes* 522).

[38] *Proc. Neap.* n. 8.

[39] *Bulla can.* (*Fontes* 523 sq:). *Proc. Neap.* n. 8, 10, 15. TOCCO, c. 57. *XTh* III 180.

[40] *Proc. Neap.* n. 15, 49, 80.

[41] Loc. cit. n. 8. TOCCO, c. 57.

[42] TOCCO, c. 57. GRABMANN, *Die Werke* 244 sq.

[43] TOCCO, c. 63. *Fontes* 521. *Proc. Neap.* n. 49. *XTh* III 51.

[44] TOCCO, c. 58, 59. *Bulla can.* (*Fontes* 523). *XTh* III 180 sq. DE GROOT, *Het leven* 376, is in favour of March 4th. After receiving the sacraments Thomas lived for three days, dying on the third day (*Proc. Neap.* n. 49). According to the old manner of reckoning, it is possible that the first of the three days was the 5th March. It is to be presumed that Thomas' general confession made to Reginald took place before the viaticum. Cf. TOCCO, c. 63, and *Proc. Neap.* n. 58.

[45] TOCCO, c. 58.

[46] *Proc. Neap.* n. 49. *Bulla can.* (*Fontes* 523).

[47] TOCCO, c. 62. EUBEL, *Hierarchia* I 479.

[48] TOCCO, c. 62. Cf. *Proc. Neap.* n. 51.

[49] *Proc. Neap.* n. 10, 80. TOCCO, c. 58.

[50] *Proc. Neap.* n. 80. TOCCO, c. 58.

[51] *Proc. Neap.* n. 49, 27, 80. TOCCO, c. 58. *Bulla can.* (*Fontes* 523).

[52] *Proc. Neap.* n. 49. TOCCO, c. 58: post [unctionem extremam] paululum autem suum spiritum domino reddidit.

[53] TOCCO, c. 65. *Proc. Neap.* n. 10: *nono martii* instead of nonis martii.

[54] From the hymn at Lauds on the feast of St Thomas.

[55] *Proc. Neap.* n. 51. TOCCO, c. 61. SERAFINI, *L'Abbazia* 250.

[56] *Proc. Neap.* n. 75. TOCCO, c. 59, attributes this vision to a Cistercian monk.

[57] *Proc. Neap.* n. 67. SCHEEBEN, *Albert der Grosse* 109, 159.

[58] PTOLEMY, *Hist. eccl.* XXIII 9. TOCCO, c. 60. TAURISANO, *I discepoli* 123 n. 3. MONTI, *Da Carlo I a Roberto d'Angiò* 249.

[59] TOCCO, c. 62. SCANDONE, *La vita, la famiglia* 81. TOCCO, loc. cit. continues: " Quarum cum clamore gemitus cum longius personaret, mulus cui praedictus doctor insederat, de stabulo se, fracto fune, dissolvit et nullo ducente appropinquans ad feretrum, mortuus sine alia infirmitate defecit: ut etiam in animalibus Deus ostenderet, quod magnum lumen ecclesiae defecisset."

[60] TOCCO, c. 62. SCANDONE, op. cit. 81.

[61] *Proc. Neap.* n. 8, 10, 20. *Bulla can.* (*Fontes* 524). After a short time they were moved to St Stephen's chapel. *Proc. Neap.* n. 10.

[62] From the hymn at Lauds on the feast of St Thomas.

[63] TOCCO, c. 63, cf. c. 28. *Proc. Neap.* n. 58. SCHEEBEN, *De Alberti Magni discipulis* 191 sq.

[64] From the hymn at Lauds on the feast of St Thomas.

[65] M. GRABMANN, *Sigieri di Brabante e Dante*, RFNS 32 (1940) 136 sq. VAN STEENBERGHEN, *Siger* II 732. The letter of the philosophers in Paris is to be found in *Doc.* 31 (*Fontes* 583–586).

[66] *Proc. Neap.* n. 83, 6. EUBEL, *Hierarchia* I 359. D. GUTIERREZ, *De B. Iacobi Viterbiensis O.E.S.A. vita, operibus et doctrina theologica* (Rome 1939) 51–57, cf. 14.

[67] *Proc. Neap.* n. 52. TOCCO, c. 61–68, esp. 66.

[68] *Proc. Neap.* n. 80. TOCCO, c. 66.

[69] *Proc. Neap.* n. 8, 10, 16, 29, 52. TOCCO, c. 66. *Bulla can.* (*Fontes* 524).

[70] SERAFINI, *L'Abbazia* 265, cf. 228.

[71] *Proc. Neap.* n. 53–55.

FOOTNOTES FOR CHAPTER XII

[1] TOCCO, c. 38.

[2] *Proc. Neap.* n. 19.

[3] TOCCO, c. 29, 25. *Proc. Neap.* n. 81.

[4] TOCCO, c. 43.

[5] TOCCO, c. 16, 17, 25, 31, 52, 56. *Proc. Neap.* passim.

[6] DE GROOT, *Het leven* 117.

[7] DANTE, *Paradiso* XII 110 sq.: Tomma . . . fu sì cortese; XII 143 sq.: la infiammata cortesia di fra Tommaso.

[8] F. ORESTANO, *Dante e " il buon Frate Tommaso,"* Sophia 9 (1941) 1–19.

[9] *Proc. Neap.* n. 81.

[10] *Summa theol.* II-II 186 6.

[11] *La sainteté de S. Thomas d'Aquin*, La vie spirituelle 42 (1935) 129–140.

[12] *Das Seelenleben des hl. Thomas von Aquin* (Munich 1924) 30–100.

[13] GRABMANN, *La conoscenza scientifica della verità sotto l'aspetto etico secondo S. Tommaso d'Aquino*, RFNS 35 (1943) 139–152. Idem, *Das Ethos*

pp. 172–180]
der wissenschaftlichen Wahrheitserkenntnis nach dem hl. Thomas von Aquin, Jahresbericht der Görres-Gesellschaft 1937 (Cologne 1938) 38–58.

14 3rd ed., Milan 1940, 29–60.

15 GRABMANN, S. *Tommaso*, chap. V. GILSON, *Le Thomisme*, chap. XII, XVII. GAGNEBET, *DThC* art. Thomas d'Aquin.

16 GILSON, *L'esprit de la philosophie médiévale* (Paris 1932) 56, 237. Cf. *Summa contra Gentiles* I 102.

17 TOCCO, c. 17. DE WULF, *Histoire de la Philosophie* II 179: " Il est de tous les scolastiques celui qui explique le maximum d'un problème avec un minimum de notions." A. BACCI, *Il latino di S. Tommaso, L'Osservatore Romano* 4. 3. 1945.

18 J. M. VOSTÉ, *De investigandis fontibus partristicis S. Thomae, Angelicum* 14 (1937) 417–434, esp. 423. Cf. G. PETTERFY in *Theologia* 7 (1940) 64–71, and the article in *DThC* XV col. 642–651 (GARRIGOU-LAGRANGE on Aristotle), 694–738 (SPICQ on Scripture), and 738–761 (GEENEN on patristic Sources).

19 Commentary on II-II 148 4 ad 1.

20 TOCCO, c. 14, 39. GEYER, *Die patrist. u. scholast. Philosophie* 427. DE WULF, *Histoire* II 153, 179. M. TUYAERTS in *Angelicum* 8 (1931) 186.

21 MARITAIN, *Le Docteur Angélique* 24.

22 E. GILSON, *Réflexions sur la controverse S. Thomas-S. Augustin, Mélanges Mandonnet* I 371–383. C. MAZZANTINI, *Platonismo e Aristotelismo nella filosofia dell'Aquinate, Salesianum* 4 (1942) 242–258. A. MASNOVO, S. *Agostino e S. Tommaso*, RFNS 33 (1941) 44–55. Idem, *Il significato storico di S. Tommaso d'Aquino, Acta Pont. Acad. Rom. S. Thomae et Relig. Cath.*, N.S. I (Turin 1934) 9–32. MANSER, *Das Wesen des Thomismus* § 5.

23 *Storia della Teologia Cattolica* 74. GEYER, *Die patrist. u. scholast. Philosophie* 428: " Er hat noch mehr als Albert die Philosophie und in gleicher Weise die Theologie mit durchschlagendem Erfolge zu aristotelisieren verstanden."

FOOTNOTES FOR CHAPTER XIII

1 BACIC, *Introductio* 5–7.

2 Cf. supra pp. 73, 76, 124.

3 GRABMANN, *Die Autographe* 514–537.

4 *Scriptores* I 283 sq.

5 GRABMANN, *Die Werke* 22–52.

6 MANDONNET, *Des Écrits authentiques* 27–44.

7 GRABMANN, *Die Werke* 45–48, 53–57, cf. 75–88.

8 *Siger* II 540–550, 747–750, I 86–99.

9 MANDONNET, *Bibliographie thomiste* xii–xvii. Idem. *Des Écrits* 104–108.

10 GRABMANN, *Die Werke* 241–344. Cf. MANSER, *Das Wesen des Thomismus* 2.

11 Cf. RACKL in *Aus der Geisteswelt des Mittelalters* 1360–1372 (Kydones), and JUGIE in *LThK* IV 381 sq. (Gregorios Scholarios who afterwards became Gennadius II, and died after 1472).

FOOTNOTES FOR CHAPTER XIV

[1] TOCCO, c. 64. MANDONNET, *Thomas d'Aquin novice* 30.

[2] WALZ, *Historia canonizationis* 118–121. F. BOCK, *Studien zum politischen Inquisitionsprozess Johanns XXII, Quellen u. Forschungen aus ital. Archiven u. Bibliotheken* 26 (1935–6) 59 sq. Cf. BOCK, *Kaisertum, Kurie* 171 and passim.

[3] WALZ, *Historia canonizationis* 103–155. P. MANDONNET, *Histoire de la canonisation de S. Thomas d'Aquin, Mélanges Thomistes* (Paris-Le Saulchoir 1923) 1–48. TAURISANO, *Tre documenti inediti su S. Tommaso, S. Tommaso-Miscellanea* 303, 321, 323. SCHEEBEN, *Zur Geschichte der Verehrung des hl. Thomas von Aquin, Angelicum* 15 (1938) 286–294.

[4] WALZ, op. cit. 133–139. *Fontes* 265–407.

[5] WALZ, op. cit. 139–142. *Fontes* 409–510. Cf. *AFP* 11 (1941) 83–84.

[6] WALZ, op. cit. 144. TAURISANO, *Tre documenti inediti* 317, 321, cf. also 141.

[7] WALZ, op. cit. 143–154. *Fontes* 511–518. Cf. *XTh* III 173–188. *Fontes* 519–530.

[8] WALZ, op. cit. 154–156.

[9] WALZ, op. cit. 156 sq. B. H. MOLKENBOER, *St Thomas van Aquino in der Schilderkunst, S. Thomas van Aquino* ed. A. VAN WINKEL and F. VAN GOETHEM (Ghent-Louvain 1927) 143–228 with 131 illustrations.

[10] GRABMANN, *Storia* 136–146. UEBERWEG-GEYER, DE WULF, GILSON &c.

[11] *MOPH* III 169, 204, 235, IV 38 sq., 64, 72 sq., 81, 83.

[12] HOFFMANS, *Les Quodlibets onze et douze de Godefroy de Fontaines, Texte inédit.* (*Les Philosophes Belges*, vol. V, fasc. 1–2, 1932) 100–105.

[13] WALZ, *Historia canonizationis* 160–163.

[14] WALZ, op. cit. 162. Cf. J. KOCH, *Philosophische u. theologische Irrtumslisten von 1270–1329, Mélanges Mandonnet* II 328 n. 2: doctor communis . . . wenigstens seit 1312 nachweisbar.

[15] WALZ, op. cit. 164.

[16] *BOP* V (1733) 155 sq. L. VON PASTOR, *Storia dei Papi* VIII (Rome 1924) 138 sq. BERTHIER, *S. Thomas " Doctor communis "* 97–99.

[17] *Acta Leonis* I (Rome 1881) 255–284. BERTHIER, op. cit. 178–211. J. SCHMIDLIN, *Papstgeschichte der neuesten Zeit* (Munich 1934) II 393–396. A. WALZ, *Il Tomismo tra il 1800 e il 1879, Angelicum* 20 (1943) 323–326.

[18] *Acta Ap. Sedis* 15 (1923) 309–326. Cf. *La. Civiltà Cattolica* 74 (1923) III 209–218. L. LAVAUD, *S. Thomas " Guide des Études "* (Paris 1925). WALZ, *Studi domenicani* 130–147.

[19] *Acta Ap. Sedis* 23 (1931) 241–262, esp. 253.

[20] *Cursus theologicus* ed. Solesm. I (1931) 222.

[21] *Acta Ap. Sedis* 15 (1923) 323. J. M. R. VILLENEUVE, *Ite ad Thomam, Angelicum* 13 (1936) 3–23. *Acta Ap. Sedis* 38 (1946) 384, 388. Cf. M. CORDOVANI, *Da Leone XIII a Pio XII, Angelicum* 16 (1939) 301–304. U. DEGL'INNOCENTI, *Pio XII e S. Tommaso, MD* 57 (1940) 95–100, 130–132. *Acta Ap. Sedis* 31 (1939) 246; 38 (1946) 384, 387; 42 (1950) 573–574, 687–688.

Addendum

The important work of the late Msgr. GRABMANN, so frequently referred to in these notes, *Die Werke des hl. Thomas von Aquin,* was quoted according to the 2nd edition of 1931. A 3rd edition was published in 1949 at Münster. It is desirable to be able to refer to the latest edition, and the following list, supplied by the author, gives the places in the 3rd edition which are referred to in the notes according to the 2nd edition.

chap. 4 note 45: 348–352, 463.
352–353, 463.
note 46: 413.
chap. 5 note 68: 284
note 72: 342–343, 462.
chap. 6 note 46: 329–330, 462.
note 49: 226–228, 462.
note 51: 343–346, 463.
chap. 7 note 25: 257–260, 461.
263–264, 461.
note 27: 264.
note 34: 309–313, 462.
chap. 8 note 33: 261, 461.
note 34: 266–272, 461.
note 35: 254–257, 461.
note 37: 307–309, 462.
note 38: 307.
note 40: 311–313.
note 41: 361–364, 464.
note 46: 261–262, 461.
note 47: 261.
note 55: 313–314, 462.
note 57: 316, 464.
note 58: 322–323, 464.
note 59: 357–358, 462.
note 60: 340, 464.
note 61: 365–367, 464.
note 69: 314–315, 462.
note 70: 324, 464.
note 74: 330–336, 464.
note 75: 336–338, 464.
note 77: 296–301, 462.
note 89: 272–283.
note 90: 278–280, 460.

note 91: 281, 460.
chap. 9 note 14: 329, 463.
note 15: 328, 462.
note 35: 325–328, 464.
note 37: 341, 462.
note 42: 251–253, 461.
note 43: 265–266, 461.
note 44: 302–309, 462.
note 45: 310–312, 462.
note 49: 272–285, 461.
note 50: 284–285, 461.
note 51: 285, 461.
note 53: 327.
note 57: 373–374, 464.
note 60: 338–339, 463.
note 61: 322, 465.
note 82: 476.
note 92: 340, 464.
note 93: 346–347, 463.
note 94: 324, 465.
note 95: 322, 465
note 105: 476, 265, 269.
chap. 10 note 58: 253–254, 461.
note 59: 266–271, 461.
note 60: 276, 461.
note 61: 346, 347–8, 463.
note 62: 372, 464.
note 64: 318–321.
chap. 11 note 11: 377–378, 465.
note 42: 254–255, 461.
chap. 13 note 5: 19–57.
note 7: 58–91.
note 10: 249–395, 461–465.

Bibliography

A. SOURCES

The principal sources for the life of St. Thomas are the following:

1. Decisions and appointments of the chapters of the Order of Preachers (*MOPH* vol. III), and of the Roman province (*MOPH* vol. XX).

2. Papal decrees and university statutes and acts (*Chartularium univ.* Paris, vol. I).

3. The *Vitae Fratrum* of GERARD DE FRACHET, O.P., who collected most valuable facts, 1259–60.

4. THOMAS OF CANTIMPRÉ, a writer often not critical enough, *Bonum universale de apibus*, about 1261–63 (Douai 1597 &c., L'Aia 1902).

5. PTOLEMY OF LUCCA, an accurate historian and an important witness, *Historia ecclesiastica*, about 1312–17 (MURATORI, *Script. Rer. Ital.*, vol. XI; TAURISANO in S. *Tommaso d'Aquino— Miscellanea storico-artistica* 183–185).

6. WILLIAM DA TOCCO, O.P., *Vita* (*Fontes*, fasc. 2), is well-informed, but confuses the dates, and has a weakness for "doublets" in the narrative (the temptation in c. 9 and 10, Marotta— Paris and Rome in c. 44, levitation in c. 33 and 34, perseverance in c. 32 and 63, Isaias in c. 31 and 17, the "bene scripsisti" in c. 34 and 52, &c.). He often clothes his narrative in the style of a legend, and one should heed the warning of SCHEEBEN (*De Alberti Magni discipulis* 192), "ne Guillelmi legenda ad solvendas quaestiones maioris momenti, praecipue chronologicas, ut fundamentum adhibeatur, sed tantum ut confirmatio."

7. The *Processus informativus* of Naples in 1317 leading to the canonization (*Fontes*, fasc. 4), esp. the important evidence of Abbot Nicholas of Fossanova (n. 8), of Peter of Montesangiovanni (n. 49), of William da Tocco (n. 58), of Bartholomew of Capua (n. 76 sqq.), and of others.

8. The *Processus supplementaris* of 1321 at Fossanova, on the miracles (*Fontes*, fasc. 5; cf. AOP 1936, 509–529, 576–631, 632– 639).

9. BERNARD GUI, O.P., an accurate historian but no more than a compiler of available facts, *Vita*, about 1319–21 (*Fontes*, fasc. 3; on Bernard cf. BOCK, *Kaisertum, Kurie* 113–122, 171, 180 sq., 203, and *LThK* II 203).

10. PETER CALO, O.P., a compiler, *Vita* in his *Legendarium*, 1313–1323 (*Fontes*, fasc. 1).

11. The *Bull of Canonization* of Pope John XXII on July 18, 1323 (*Fontes*, fasc. 5).

After the material given by the BOLLANDISTS in the *Acta Sanctorum Martii* (vol. I), Fr. Dominic PRÜMMER, inspired by Fr. Denifle, began a critical edition of the sources for the life of the Angelic Doctor, which began to appear in the appendix to the *Revue thomiste*, and then continued in separate fascicules entitled *Fontes vitae S. Thomae Aquinatis* (Toulouse-S. Maximin 1912–28). In these are presented the biographies of Peter Calo (pp. 17–28), William da Tocco (pp. 65–160), and Bernard Gui (pp. 168–259, 263). The mistake was made of attaching too much importance to Calo's biography, which was placed first. After Fr. Prümmer's death in 1931, Fr. M. Hyacinth LAURENT in 1934 and 1937 provided three more fascicules of the *Fontes*, containing the Process of Naples (pp. 265–407), that of Fossanova (pp. 409–510), an account of the canonization including the bull (pp. 511–532), and various other documents (pp. 532–677).

The value of the various sources has been studied, especially by MANDONNET, PELSTER, JANSSENS, CASTAGNOLI and SCHEEBEN. Bibliographies of the sources are to be found in MANDONNET-DESTREZ, *Bibliographie thomiste* n. 1–16, *XTh* III 157–158, and in the *Bulletin thomiste* 1924 sqq.

B. CRITICAL WORKS

Critical studies of the life have been made by ECHARD, DE RUBEIS, SCANDONE, MANDONNET, GRABMANN, PRÜMMER, PELSTER, SCHEEBEN, CASTAGNOLI, and LECCISOTTI. For work on the cultus, doctrinal influence and iconography, see the notes on chapter XIV. For bibliographies, see MANDONNET-DESTREZ, *Bibliographie thomiste* n. 87–138, the *Bulletin thomiste*, and V. J. BOURKE, *Thomistic Bibliography 1920–1940* (St. Louis, Mo., 1945). For legends see K. BALIC in *Wissenschaft und Weisheit* 4 (1937), 182–201.

C. LIVES

Mention should be made of the following Lives: A. TOURON (Paris 1737 and 1741; translated into Italian and Spanish); K.

WERNER (Regensburg 1858–9); C. A. JOYAU (Poitiers 1886, Lyons 1887 and 1895: translated into Flemish and German); R. B. VAUGHAN (London, 2nd ed., 1890); J. V. DE GROOT (Utrecht 1882, 1907); J. A. ENDRES (Mainz 1910); L. H. PETITOT (Paris 1923: transl. Italian, Spanish and Dutch); A. WALZ (Rome 1927); E. DE BRUYNE (Brussels 1928); A. PUCCETTI (Turin 1928); M. C. D'ARCY (London 1930); R. DIACCINI (Rome 1934); I. TAURISANO (Turin 1941); A. TOSO (Rome 1942); R. M. COFFEY (Milwaukee 1943).

D. STUDIES

The following studies in the life of St. Thomas should be noted: A. PIDAL Y MON (Madrid 1875); M. GRABMANN (Munich 1912: 7th ed. Munich 1946: translated into 7 languages: Eng. tr. V. MICHEL, New York & London 1928); J. MARITAIN (Paris 1929: Eng. tr. J. F. SCANLAN, London 1931); G. K. CHESTERTON (London 1933: transl. French, Spanish, Italian and German); G. VANN (London 1940); L. DE SIMONE (Naples 1944). Also *Anthologies* edited by E. ROLFES (Leipzig 1920); M. C. D'ARCY (London 1939); M. MINDÁN (Madrid 1942); M. MARESCA (Milan 1943). And *Articles* in *The Catholic Encyclopedia* (KENNEDY), *Enciclopedia Univ. Ilustrada Europeo Americana, Enciclopedia Italiana* (PELSTER, GRABMANN), *Lexicon für Theologie und Kirche* (GRABMANN), *Dictionnaire de Théologie Catholique* (WALZ, GAGNEBET, SPICQ, GARRIGOU-LAGRANGE, GILLON). Cf. MANDONNET-DESTREZ, *Bibliographie thomiste* n. 17–86, and the *Bulletin thomiste.*

E. MISCELLANEOUS WORKS

Among other works that are useful to the student are: K. BIHLMAYER, *Kirchengeschichte* (10th-11th ed. Paderborn 1940) §123–136, and works there quoted; P. HUGHES, *History of the Church* (London 1947) vol. III; other Church Histories by DUFOURCQ, POULET, SABA, TODESCO, LLORCA, HAUCK and J. HOLLNSTEINER, *Die Kirche im Ringen um die christliche Gemeinschaft* (Freiburg i. B. 1940); other works such as HEFELE-LECLERCQ, *Histoire des Conciles;* G. SCHNÜRER, *Kirche und Kultur im Mittelalter* vol. II (2nd ed. Paderborn 1929: transl. French and Dutch), *Propyläen-Weltgeschichte* III: Das Zeitalter der Gothik und Renaissance 1250–1500 (Berlin 1932); *The Cambridge Medieval History* vol. VI (1929): Victory of the Papacy, vol. VII (1932): Decline of the Empire and the Papacy; L. HAL-

PHEN, *L'essor de l'Europe* (Paris 1932); G. W. PREVITÉ-OR-
TON, *A History of Europe 1198–1378* (London 1937); GREGO-
ROVIUS, *Storia della città di Roma* (Turin 1925–6); R. MOR-
GHEN, *Il tramonto della potenza Sveva in Italia 1250–1266* (Rome-
Milan 1936); L. SALVATORELLI, *L'Italia comunale dal secolo
XI alla metà del secolo XIV* (Milan 1940); R. CAGGESE, *Il Due-
cento e il Trecento* (Turin 1939); J. WALSH, *The Thirteenth, the
Greatest of Centuries* (New York 1924); R. MORGHEN, *L'unità
monarchica nell'Italia meridionale* and E. DUPRÉ THESEIDER,
Papato e Impero in lotta per la supremazia, both in E. ROTA,
Problemi storici e orientamenti storiografici (Como 1942) pp. 239–
265 and 267–314; A. DEMPF, *Sacrum Imperium* (Italian transl.
C. ANTONI, Messina-Milan 1933); G. TOFFANIN, *Storia
dell'Umanesimo dal XII al XVI secolo* (Rome 1940). Then there
are writers on doctrinal, monastic and academic history, such as
MORTIER, MANDONNET-VICAIRE, D'IRSAY, DENIFLE,
RASHDALL, GRABMANN, DE WULF, UEBERWEG-GEYER
(§15–17, 31–40), VAN STEENBERGHEN, GILSON; publications
like the *Xenia thomistica, Aus der mittelalterlichen Geisteswelt,*
the bibliographies of MANDONNET-DESTREZ, the reviews mentioned in chapter XIII, in particular *Divus Thomas* (Piacenza),
Divus Thomas (Fribourg) with the *Thomistische Literaturschau,*
the Bulletin thomiste, and the bibliography of C. GIACON, *Il
Pensiero cristiano con particolare riguardo alla Scolastica medie-
vale* (Guide bibliografiche II: Filosofia 3, Milan 1943) pp. 114–
146: S. Tommaso.

LIST OF WORKS FREQUENTLY QUOTED AND
OF ABBREVIATIONS USED

AFH–Archivum Franciscanum Historicum, Ad Aquas Claras
        1907 sqq.
AFP–Archivum Fratrum Praedicatorum, Rome 1931 sqq.
ALTANER, B., *Die Briefe Jordans von Sachsen des zweitens Do-
        minikaner-generals (1222–37).* Text u. Untersuchungen.
        Zugleich ein Beitrag zur Geschichte der Frömmigkeit im
        13. Jahrhundert, *QF,* 20, Leipzig 1925.
An. Boll.–Analecta Bollandiana, Brussels 1882 sqq.
Angelicum, Rome 1924 sqq.
AOP–Analecta S. Ord. Praed., Rome 1893 sqq.
BACIC, A., *Introductio compendiosa in opera S. Thomae Aqui-
        natis,* Rome 1925.
BERTHIER, J. J., *Le couvent de S. Sabine à Rome,* Rome 1912.

––––, *S. Thomas Aquinas "Doctor communis" Ecclesiae* I, Rome 1914.

BIERBAUM, M., *Bettelorden u. Weltgeistlichkeit an der Universität Paris,* Texte u. Untersuchungen zum literarischen Armuts- und Exemptionsstreit des 13. Jahrhunderts (1255–1272). *Franzisk. Studien,* Beiheft 2. Münster i. W. 1920.

BIRKENMAJER, A., *Vermischte Untersuchungen zur Geschichte der mittelalterlichen Philosophie,* Münster i. W. 1922.

BOCK, F., *Kaisertum, Kurie u. Nationalstaat im Beginn des 14. Jahrhunderts, Römische Quartalschrift* 44 (1936) 105–122, 169–220.

BÖHMER, F. J., FICKER, J., WINKELMANN, E., *Regesta imperii* V (1198–1272), Innsbruck 1 (1881–2), 2(1892–4), 3 (1901).

BOP—Bullarium Ord. Praed., Rome 1729 sqq.

BOURKE, V. J., *Thomistic Bibliography 1920–1940,* St. Louis, Mo., 1945.

Bulletin thomiste, (Bellevue-) Paris 1924 sqq.

CALO, P., *Vita S. Thomae Aquinatis:* v. s. Sources.

CANTIPRATANUS, T., *Bonum universale de apibus,* Douai 1627.

CASTAGNOLI, P., *Regesta thomistica,* DTP 30 (1927)–32 (1929).

Chartularium: v. s. Denifle.

CLASEN, S., *Der hl. Bonaventura u. das Mendikantentum. Ein Beitrag zur Ideengeschichte der Pariser Mendikantenstreites* (1252–72). *Franzisk. Forschungen* 7, Werl i. W. 1940.

CREYTENS, R., *Pierre de Tarentaise professeur à Paris:* in B. *Innocentius V* (q. v.).

DAVIDSOHN, R., *Geschichte von Florenz* I-II, Berlin 1896–1908.

DE GROOT, J. V., *Het leven van den h. Thomas van Aquino,* 2nd ed. Utrecht 1907.

DENIFLE, H., and CHÂTELAIN, A., *Chartularium universitatis Parisiensis* I, Paris 1889.

DENIFLE, H., *Die Enstehung der Universitäten des Mittelalters,* Berlin 1885.

––––, *Zum Kölner Studienaufenthalt des Aquinaten, Römische Quartalschrift* 34 (1926) 46–58.

DE RUBEIS, I. F. B., *De gestis et scriptis ac doctrina S. Thomae Aquinatis dissertationes criticae et apologeticae,* in S. *Thomae opera omnia* I, Rome 1882.

DE WULF, M., *Histoire de la philosophie médiévale* II: Le treizième siècle, 6th ed. Louvain-Paris 1936 (Engl. tr. E. C. MESSENGER 1938).

DHGE—Dictionnaire d'Histoire et de Géographie ecclésiastique, Paris 1912 sqq.

Doc.—Documenta, Fontes, fasc. 6.
DThC—Dictionnaire de Théologie Catholique, Paris 1909 sqq.
DTF—Divus Thomas, (Vienna-Berlin-) Fribourg (Switz.) 1914 sqq.
DTP—Divus Thomas, Piacenza 1880 sqq.
Enc. Ital.—Enciclopedia Italiana, Milan 1929 sqq.
ENDRES, J. A., *Thomas von Aquin,* Mainz 1910.
EUBEL, C., *Hierarchia catholica medii aevi* I, 2nd. ed. Münster
    1913.
FELDER, I., *Storia degli studi scientifici nell'Ordine francescano,*
    Ital. tr. BERNARD OF BESSA, Siena 1911.
FRACHETO, G. DE, *Vitae Fratrum: MOPH* I.
*Fontes vitae S. Thomae Aquinatis notis historicis et criticis illus-
    trati* curis et labore D. PRÜMMER, fasc. 1–3, Toulouse
    1911 sqq., M. H. LAURENT, fasc. 4–6, S. Maximin 1934–37.
GEYER, G., *Die patristische u. scholastische Philosophie,* 11th ed.
    by F. UEBERWEG: *Grundriss der Geschichte der Philoso-
    phie,* 2. Teil, Berlin 1928.
GIACON, C., *Il pensiero cristiano con particolare riguardo alla
    Scolastica.* Guide bibliografiche. Milan 1943.
GILSON, E., *La philosophie de Saint Bonaventure,* Paris 1924
    (Eng. tr. I. TRETHOWAN and F. J. SHEED, London
    1938).
————, *Le Thomisme,* 3rd ed. Paris 1927 (5th ed. 1945; 6th ed.
    1948) (Eng. tr. *The Philosophy of St. Thomas,* E. BUL-
    LOUGH, Cambridge 1924, incorporating the new elements
    later appearing in the 3rd French edition; 2nd Eng. ed.
    1929).
GLORIEUX, P., *Répertoire des maîtres en théologie de Paris au
    XIII* e *siècle* I, Paris 1933–4.
————, *Les polémiques " Contra Geraldinos,"* RTAM 6 (1934)
    5–41.
————, *" Contra Geraldinos."* L'enchainement des polemiques,
    RTAM 7 (1935) 129–155.
GRABMANN, M., *Die Autographe von Werken des hl. Thomas
    von Aquin, Historiches Jahrbuch* 60 (1940) 514–537.
————, *Die persönlichen Beziehung des hl. Thomas von Aquin,
    Hist. Jahrb.* 57 (1937) 305–322.
————, *Der Einfluss Alberts des Grossen auf das mittelalterliche
    Geistesleben, Mittelalterliches Geistesleben* II 324–412.
————, *Mittelalterliches Geistesleben* I–II, Munich 1926–36.
————, *Das Seelenleben des hl. Thomas von Aquin,* Munich 1924
    (3rd ed. Freiburg i. B., 1949).
————, *Storia della Teologia Cattolica,* 2nd Ital. ed. tr. G. DE

FABIO, Milan 1939: tr. of *Die Geschichte der katholischen Theologie*, Freiburg i. B. 1933.

——, *San Tommaso d'Aquino*, 3rd Ital. ed. tr. G. DI FABIO, Milan 1940: tr. of *Thomas von Aquin, eine Einführung in seine Persönlichkeit u. Gedankenwelt*, 5th ed. Munich 1926 (8th ed. 1949) (Eng. tr. *Thomas Aquinas, his personality and thought*, V. MICHEL, New York & London 1928).

——, *Die Werke des hl. Thomas von Aquin*. Eine literarhistorische Untersuchung u. Einführung, 2nd ed. Münster i. W. 1931 (3rd ed. Münster i. W. 1949).

——, *Guglielmo di Moerbeke, O. P., il traduttore di Aristotile*, Rome 1946.

GREGOROVIUS, F., *Storia della città di Roma nel Medio Evo*, Ital. tr. R. MANZATO, ed. E. PAIS, Turin II 1925, III 1926.

GUI, B., *Vita S. Thomae Aquinatis: s. v. Sources.*

HEFELE-LECLERCQ, *Histoire des Conciles* V 2, Paris 1913–14.

HUMBERTUS DE ROMANIS, (B.), *Opera de vita regulari*, ed. BERTHIER, Rome 1888–89.

INGUANEZ, I., *Cronologia degli abati cassinesi del sec. XIII*, Casinensia, Montecassino 1929.

Innocentius V, (B.), *Petrus de Tarantasia, O.P., Studia et documenta*, Rome 1943.

IRSAY, S. D', *Histoire des Universités françaises et étrangères dès origines à nos jours* I, Paris 1933.

KANTOROWICZ, E., *Kaiser Friedrich II*, Berlin 1927, Ergänzungsband 1931.

KÄPPELI, T., *Una raccolta di prediche attribuite a S. Tommaso d'Aquino*, AFP 13 (1943) 59–94.

KOPERSKA, A., *Die Stellung der religiösen Orden zu den Profanwissenschaften im 12 u. 13. Jahrhundert*, Fribourg (Switz.) 1914.

LAURENT, M. H., v. s. *Fontes.*

——, *Le bx Innocent V*, Città del Vaticano 1947.

LEMMENS, L., *S. Bonaventura, cardinale e dottore della Chiesa*, Ital. tr. G. DI FABIO, Milan 1921.

LECCISOTTI, T., *Il Dottore Angelico a Montecassino*, RFNS 32 (1940) 519–547.

LOE, P. DE, *De vita et scriptis B. Alberti Magni*, An. Boll. 19 (1900), 21 (1902).

LOTTIN, O., *Psychologie et Morale aux XII* e *et XIII* e *siècles*, I: Problèmes de Psychologie, Louvain-Gembloux 1942.

LThK—Lexicon für Theologie und Kirche, Freiburg i. B. 1930 sqq.

MANDONNET, P., *Le carême de S. Thomas à Naples, S. Tommaso d'Aquino, Miscellanea* 194–211.

––––––, *Date de naissance de S. Thomas d'Aquin, RTh* 22 (1914) 652–664.

––––––, *Des écrits authentiques de S. Thomas d'Aquin,* 2nd ed. Fribourg (Switz.) 1910.

––––––, *Thomas d'Aquin novice prêcheur 1244–1246.* Extract from *RTh* 1924–25.

––––––, *Thomas d'Aquin lecteur à la Curie Romaine,* Chronologie du séjour 1259–1268, *XTh* III 9–40.

––––––, *Siger de Brabant et l'Averroisme latin au XIII* e *siècle* I–II, Louvain 1908–11.

––––––, and VICAIRE, M. H., S. *Dominique, L'idée, l'homme et l'oeuvre* I–II, Paris n. d. (Eng. tr. St. *Dominic and his work,* Sister M. B. LARKIN, St. Louis 1945).

MANSER, G. M., *Das Wesen des Thomismus,* 2nd ed. Fribourg (Switz.) 1935 (3rd ed. 1949).

MARTINORI, E., *Lazio turrito,* Rome I 1933, II–III 1934.

MASETTI, P. T., *Monumenta et antiquitates veteris disciplinae Ord. Praed. ab a. 1216 ad a. 1348 praesertim in Romana provincia* I–II, Rome 1864.

MD—Memorie Domenicane, Florence 1884 sqq.

MILLER, K., *Itineraria Romana,* Stuttgart 1916.

Mélanges Mandonnet I–II, Paris, 1930.

Mélanges A. Pelzer, Louvain 1947.

MONTI: s. v. TORRACA.

MOPH—Monumenta Ord. Praed. Historica, Louvain-Rome 1896 sqq.

MORGHEN, R., *Il tramonto della potenza Sveva in Italia 1250–1266,* Rome-Milan 1936.

MORTIER, A., *Histoire des Maîtres Généraux de l'Ordre des Frères Prêcheurs* I sqq, Paris 1903 sqq.

MOTHON, P., *Vie du bienheureux Innocent V,* Rome 1896.

PARÉ, G., BRUNET, A., TREMBLAY, P., *La Renaissance du XII* e *Siècle.* Les Écoles et l'Enseignement, Ottawa 1933.

PELSTER, F., *La famiglia di S. Tommaso.* Studi sulle fonti, *La Civiltà Cattolica* 74 (1923) I 385–400.

––––––, *La giovinezza di S. Tommaso d'Aquino.* Studio critico sulle fonti, *La Civiltà Cattolica* 74 (1923) II 401–410.

––––––, *I parenti prossimi di S. Tommaso d'Aquino, La Civiltà Cattolica* 74 (1923) IV 299–313.

––––––, *Kritische Studien zum Leben u. zu den Schriften Alberts des Grossen,* Freiburg i. B. 1920.

PELZER, A., *Le cours inédit d'Albert le Grand sur la Morale à Nicomaque recueilli et rédigé par saint Thomas d'Aquin.* Extract from the *RNSP*, Aug.–Nov. 1922, Louvain 1922.

PETITOT, L. H., *Saint Thomas d'Aquin*, Paris 1923.

POTTHAST, A., *Regesta pontificum Romanorum inde ab a. 1198 ad a. 1304* I–II, Berlin 1874–75.

Proc. Neap.—v. s. Sources.

PRÜMMER, D., *De chronologia vitae S. Thomae Aquinatis, XTh* III 1–8.

———, v. s. *Fontes.*

PTOLEMY of Lucca, *Tholomeus Lucensis, Historia ecclesiastica,* new ed. by MURATORI, *Rer. Ital. Script.* XI, Milan 1727. Life of St. Thomas ed. TAURISANO in *S. Tommaso d'Aquino, Miscellanea* 183–185: v. s. Sources.

PUCCETTI, A., *S. Alberto Magno* I–II, 2nd ed. Siena 1937.

QUÉTIF, I., and ECHARD, I., *Scriptores Ord. Praed.* I–II, Paris 1719–21.

QF—Quellen und Forschungen zur Geschichte des Dominikanerordens in Deutschland I sqq., Leipzig-Vechta-Cologne 1907 sqq.

RASHDALL, H., *The Universities of Europe in the Middle Ages,* new ed. by F. M. POWICKE and A. B. EMDEN, I–III, Oxford 1936.

RFNS—Rivista di Filosofia neo-scolastica, Milan (-Florence) 1909 sqq.

RHE—Revue d'Histoire ecclésiastique, Louvain 1900 sqq.

RNSP—Revue néoscolastique de Philosophie, Louvain 1904 sqq.

Römische Quartalschrift, Freiburg i. B. 1907 sqq.

RSPT—Revue des Sciences philosophiques et théologiques, (Le Saulchoir-) Paris 1907 sqq.

RTAM—Recherches de Théologie ancienne et médiévale, Louvain 1929 sqq.

RTh—Revue thomiste, (Paris-Toulouse-) S. Maximin 1893 sqq.

RUSSELL, J. C., *Dictionary of Writers of Thirteenth Century England,* London-New York-Toronto 1936.

SABA, A., *Bernardo Ayglerio abate di Montecassino,* Montecassino 1931.

SASSEN, J., *Hugo von St-Cher, seine Tätigkeit als Kardinal,* Bonn 1908.

SCANDONE, F., *La vita, la famiglia e la patria di S. Tommaso,* in *S. Tommaso, Miscellanea* 1–110.

SCHEEBEN, H. D., *Der hl. Dominikus,* Freiburg i. B. 1927.

————, *Albert der Grosse*, Zur Chronologie seines Lebens, QF 27, Vechta-Leipzig 1931.

————, *De Alberti Magni discipulis*, Alberto Magno, Atti della Settimana albertina celebrata in Roma nei giorni 9–14 novembre 1931, pp. 179–212, Rome 1932.

————, *Beiträge zur Geschichte Jordans von Sachsen*, QF 35, Vechta-Leipzig 1938.

Scholastik, Eupen 1926 sqq.

SERAFINI, A., *L'Abbazia di Fossanova e le origini dell'architettura gotica nel Lazio*, in S. Tommaso d'Aquino, Miscellanea 223–292.

SOMMER-SECKENDORFF, E. M. F., *Studies in the life of Robert Kilwardby*, Inst. Hist. FF. Praed., Dissertationes hist. 8, Rome 1937.

STHAMER, E., *Die Hauptstrassen des Königreichs Sizilien im 13. Jahrhundert*, Studi di Storia Napoletana in onore di Michelangelo Schipa, Naples 1926.

SUERMONDT, C. S., *Tabulae schematicae cum introductione de principiis et compositione comparatis Summae Theologiae et Summae contra Gentiles* S. Thomae Aquinatis, Rome 1943.

THOMAE AQUINATIS, S., Doctoris Angelici, *Opera omnia* iussu impensaque Leonis XIII P. M. edita I–XV, Rome 1882–1930.

TAURISANO, I., S. *Tommaso d'Aquino*. I Grandi Italiani, 21, Turin 1941.

TOLOMEO or THOLOMEUS: v. s. PTOLEMY.

TOCCO, WILLIAM DA, *Vita S. Thomae Aquinatis*: v. s. Sources.

Tommaso d'Aquino, S., Miscellanea storico-artistica, Rome 1924.

TORRACA, F., MONTI, G. M., and others, *Storia dell'università di Napoli*, Naples 1924.

TOSO, A., *Tommaso d'Aquino e il suo tempo*, Rome 1941.

TOSTI, L., *Storia della Badia di Montecassino* II, Rome 1889.

UEBERWEG: v. s. GEYER.

VAN STEENBERGHEN, F., *Siger de Brabant d'après les oeuvres inédites* I–II, Louvain 1931–42.

VOSTÉ, I. M., S. *Thomas Aquinas epistularum S. Pauli interpres*, Angelicum 19 (1942) 257–276.

WALZ, A., *Compendium historiae Ordinis Praedicatorum*, Rome 1930, 2nd ed. Rome 1948.

————, *Studi domenicani*, Rome 1939.

————, *I cardinali domenicani*. Note bio-bibliografiche, Florence-Rome 1940.

————, *B. Jordani de Saxonia epistulae*, ed., Rome 1950.

XTh—Xenia thomistica I–II, Rome 1925.

N.B. After this book went to press there appeared M. D. CHENU, *Introduction à l'étude de s. Thomas d'Aquin*, Montreal-Paris 1950.

Indices

I. INDEX OF PERSONS

241

II. INDEX OF PLACES
(M=Map at the end)

III. INDEX OF SUBJECTS

(Usually with reference directly to St. Thomas)

IV. INDEX OF AUTHORS

(Quoted or referred to)

(Contemporary authors are placed in Index I)

A NOTE ON THE TYPE

IN WHICH THIS BOOK WAS SET

This book is set in Caledonia, a Linotype face created in 1939 by W. A. Dwiggins, which is by far one of the best book types created in the last 50 years. It has a simple, hard-working, feet-on-the-ground quality and can be classed as a modern type face with excellent color and good readability. The designer claims Caledonia was created by putting a little of each of Scotch Roman, Bulmer, Baskerville and Bodoni together and producing a lively crisp-like book type. This book was composed and printed by the York Composition Company of York, Pa., and bound by Moore and Company of Baltimore. The typography and design of this book are by Howard N. King.

A CHRONOLOGICAL TABLE OF THE LIFE AND WRITINGS OF SAINT THOMAS

HIS LIFE	COMMENTARIES — on Scripture	COMMENTARIES — philosophical & theological	QUAESTIONES — disputatae	QUAESTIONES — quodlibetales	SUMMAE	OPUSCULA AND DISCOURSES
YOUTH AND EARLY STUDIES 1225 Born at Roccasecca near Aquino, son of Landulf, Lord of Roccasecca, and Theodora, of Naples 1231–39 Oblate at Montecassino 1239 To the University of Naples 1243 Enters the Order of Preachers 1244 Interned in the castles of Montesangiovanni and Roccasecca 1245 Returns to Naples, and then proceeds to Cologne by way of Paris 1248–52 Studies at Cologne under St. Albert the Great, at the priory of Holy Cross						
PARIS 1252–55 Graduates at the *studium generale* in the priory of St. James, and teaches first as *baccalaureus biblicus*, and then as *baccalaureus sententiarius* 1256 Receives the degree of Master (Doctor and Professor) in Theology from the Chancellor; Lectures, disputations, and sermons 1257 His position as Master recognized in the university 1259 He preaches the Lenten sermons. He is on the committee which drew up the *Ratio studiorum* for the Order at the general chapter of Valenciennes	1256–59 In Isaiam In Matthaeum	1253–55 In IV libros sententiarum Petri Lombardi 1257–58 In Boethium De Hebdomadibus In Boethium De Trinitate	1256–59 De veritate			1250–56 De ente et essentia 1252 Principium: Hic est liber mandatorum c.1255 De principiis naturae 1256 Principium: Rigans montes: Contra impugnantes Dei cultum et religionem
ITALY 1259 He leaves Paris, where he is succeeded by William of Alton, and he returns to Italy 1260 He is made a Preachergeneral by the provincial chapter at Naples. As such he attends several provincial chapters of the Roman province 1261–65 At the curia of Pope Urban IV at Orvieto	1259–65 In S. P a u l u m (Rom. & I Cor. 1–10) 1261–64 Catena aurea super Matthaeum	c.1260 In Dionysium De divinis nominibus		1265–67 Quod-	1259 Summa contra Gentiles lib. I 1 2 6 1 – 6 4 Summa contra Gentiles lib. II–IV	1261–64 De rationibus fidei contra Saracenos, Graecos et Armenos Contra errores Graecorum 1261–68 De articulis fidei et ecclesiae sac-